VERSIONS OF THE PAST -
VISIONS OF THE FUTURE

Also by Lars Ole Sauerberg

FACT INTO FICTION: Documentary Realism in the
Contemporary Novel

THE PRACTICE OF LITERARY CRITICISM

SECRET AGENTS IN FICTION: Ian Fleming, John Le Carré
and Len Deighton

Versions of the Past - Visions of the Future

The Canonical in the Criticism of T. S. Eliot, F. R. Leavis, Northrop Frye and Harold Bloom

Lars Ole Sauerberg

First published in Great Britain 1997 by
MACMILLAN PRESS LTD
Houndmills, Basingstoke, Hampshire RG21 6XS and London
Companies and representatives throughout the world

A catalogue record for this book is available from the British Library.

ISBN 0–333–56474–X

First published in the United States of America 1997 by
ST. MARTIN'S PRESS, INC.,
Scholarly and Reference Division,
175 Fifth Avenue, New York, N.Y. 10010

ISBN 0–312–16420–3

Library of Congress Cataloging-in-Publication Data
Sauerberg, Lars Ole, 1950–
Versions of the past —visions of the future : the canonical in the
criticism of T. S. Eliot, F. R. Leavis, Northrop Frye, and Harold
Bloom / Lars Ole Sauerberg.
p.   cm.
Includes bibliographical references and index.
ISBN 0–312–16420–3
1. English literature—History and criticism—Theory, etc.
2. Eliot, T. S. (Thomas Stearns), 1888–1965—Knowledge—Literature.
3. American literature—History and criticism—Theory, etc.
4. Criticism—History—20th century.   5. Leavis, F. R. (Frank
Raymond), 1895–1978.   6. Canon (Literature)   7. Frye, Northrop.
8. Bloom, Harold.   I. Title.
PR21.S28   1996
801'.95'0904—dc20   96–24144
                                                              CIP

This book is printed on paper suitable for recycling and made from fully managed and
sustained forest sources.

10   9   8   7   6   5   4   3   2   1
06   05   04   03   02   01   00   99   98   97

Printed in Great Britain by
The Ipswich Book Company Ltd, Ipswich, Suffolk

Contents

Prefatory Note

This study began to take shape as a book project after a graduate-student seminar on canon formation I ran in the spring term of 1992. There has been no shortage of articles and books on the subject over the past few years, the majority of which have pointed to the need for a more diverse literary canon than the narrow one assumedly in existence until the quite recent past. Using this debate as the sounding board of my study, which relies almost exclusively on primary sources, I have aimed at investigating the function of the canonical for literary criticism at the formation stage, as it were; more precisely, relating to the nature of the interaction between a critic's canonical preferences ('versions of the past') and his desire for improved cultural and/or aesthetic conditions ('visions of the future'). By selecting the criticism of Eliot, Leavis, Frye and Bloom for this purpose I hope to have covered four major critical stances in terms of both literary-critical history and exemplary value.

1
Introduction

Some would perhaps have thought *Versions of the Literary Past* a more suitable title for a book subtitled *The Canonical in the Criticism of T. S. Eliot, F. R. Leavis, Northrop Frye and Harold Bloom*. But the omission of 'literary' in the title is very much deliberate, since canonical issues always seem to widen into renderings of the past which extend beyond the purely literary, renderings which at the same time imply an idealistic or even utopian vision of the future in broadly existential terms.

At its crudest, canonical criticism results in lists of recommended literature. At its more refined, canonical criticism exists as implicit recommendations, requiring carefully analytical efforts to emerge. In all cases, however, the nature of the specific recommendation is decided by the more or less overt and eventually extra-literary purposes of the agency behind the recommendation, whether an individual critic or a government institution.

Words raised to a status beyond the ephemerally spoken, in the forms of inscriptions, manuscripts, printed matter, and recently electronic signals accessible from screen and printer, are automatically endowed with authority, if in some cases only deriving from the relative permanence of the medium rather than from the importance of the document. Literature, in the broadest possible sense of the word, has enjoyed special attention when it comes to exercising authority. There are texts which a community considers the expressions of its essential values, and, following from this, texts which by opposing those very values, are placed on an index of prohibited works. But literature, as an endlessly versatile and therefore potentially endlessly subversive manner of expression able to give voice to direct statement and subtly ironic innuendo alike, is not only, however, the repository of generally accepted norms or the instrument of an attack on them. Literature – perhaps it is its most valuable characteristic – is a sophisticated and context-sensitive medium having a complex relationship, to the point of destruction even, with the authority of which it is the very manifestation.

1

In modern democratic societies the infringement of free speech, and its corollary in the freedom of the printed word, would be considered a blow at the very core of what we understand by democracy. Nonetheless, heated debates on what we ought to and ought not to read recur, especially as one of the tangible aspects of times with shifting values; and they recur now more frequently than in the past, often with several debates going on simultaneously, conducted by various interest groups with different objectives.

The present vogue for a multicultural canon in American literary criticism, which will be discussed in some detail in the following chapter, is a good example of how the rewriting of a literary history is not at all limited to the strictly literary in conventional terms, and how at the same time such rewriting relates to a general cultural-political agenda. In many respects the American canon debate of the 1980s is paradigmatic of any canon debate, as it has in it most of the recurring elements.

The present study was undertaken on the assumption that the canonical is always central to literary criticism and that the canonical implies a version of the past as the model for the future. In English literary history the prominence of canonical concerns is well documented in the neoclassical, Romantic and modernist upheavals. What we have seen in the international critical community since the early 1970s as the foregrounding of canonical issues is not, consequently, a completely new departure, but a repetition of familiar dynamics. This study centres on the work of four critics for whom the canonical is of distinct importance, and I discuss the relation of the canonical both to their other major critical concerns and to their broader existential interests.

A study of the canonical in twentieth-century criticism could have been conducted as an exhaustive mapping of all the relevant work done in this field so as to be able to discern an overall line of development. This would no doubt have resulted in the by now often-told story of an ever-expanding canon, beginning with the make-it-new endeavours of modernism and ending with the multicultural and multi-canonical scene we are facing today. However, I have proceeded according to a different concept, in that I see two main streams in twentieth-century canonical criticism: one concerned with the maintenance of values associated with the idea of a – frequently highly selective – literary canon, another with the idea of literature as a dynamic force for which any notion of a canon is forbidding because of its implication of monopoly, hegemony or downright censorship. I read the critical work of Eliot, Leavis, Frye and Bloom as efforts to salvage a tradition of aesthetic-ethical canon preferences, defining a manner of civilized existence against the threat of what they, each in their time, have seen as an increasing slide of values.

Eliot puts up a defence rooted in religion, Leavis takes the Arnold-inspired and religion-substituting golden-age-civilization angle, Frye constructs a redemptive ethics, based on the possibilities of imaginative power, and Harold Bloom, like his literary and critical heroes, lets go of any rationalistic approach and instead dictates a canon posited by the sheer force of his craving for space.

One critic – Bernard Bergonzi – has suggested that Bloom can be credited with having turned our attention back to the Romantics, after the classical focus of modernist criticism. Whether this justifies us in taking the further step of diagnosing a general revolution from a classically inspired modernism to a Romantically inspired post-modernism is a matter really beyond the scope of this study, but it will be explored tentatively in the concluding chapter.

Canonical criticism is a constant suggestive and critical exploration of issues central to literature and existence. Like literature itself, canonical criticism presents us with the challenge of blurring the line between reason and imagination, and introduces us to the kind of speculation that works as a constructive corrective to actuality, however construed. For this reason the subject of canon always deserves our closest and most open-minded interest, even when we shift our perspective back to those allegedly reactionary critics currently taken to represent a politically incorrect attitude which, it is claimed, must be put right. It may be, then, that we will be able to sit in on a debate which is neither dated, exclusive nor intolerant, but perfectly capable of stimulating current issues in literary criticism, and, ultimately, of safeguarding the free exchange of opinions and feelings which might be thought of as stifled by any effort towards dogmatic canon formation.

2
Canons in the Making

Literary canon formation has been a much – perhaps the most – debated critical issue since the early 1970s, beginning in the USA, but with the international critical community soon catching up. Inspired by new vistas opened up by an increasing scepticism about the premises for and justification of an inherited great-works tradition, critics and literary historians have responded with suggestions for revisions and ramifications, indeed in certain cases, for revolutions. Consequently, most critical contributions to the current canon debate tell stories of expansion and diversification.

Looking back on the epoch-making events in literature and literary criticism in the twentieth century, and in Anglo-American letters especially, the first couple of decades marked a reaction against more than a century's Romantic predilections. The climate of modernism in literature and criticism favoured recourse to a literary tradition beyond what T. E. Hulme called the flights into the 'circumambient gas' of the Romantic imagination (Hulme 1924:120). The preference in literature and criticism since Hulme and Eliot has largely been for the 'classical': a literature and a criticism of rationalistic restraint. Although it is a dubious venture to predict a future swing of the pendulum away from rationalistic modernism to a renewed (postmodernist) Romanticism, there have recently been signs of a breaking-up of the twentieth-century rationalist orthodoxy, as in Bernard Bergonzi's observation on Harold Bloom suggesting that he has

> overturned the map of English poetry outlined by Pound and Eliot and systematized by Leavis; he has restored the Romantics, and Shelley in particular, to a prominence from which they once seemed to have been permanently dislodged (1986:xvi).

The resounding debate on the nature of the canon and the need for expansion and diversification started by Leslie Fiedler, Houston A. Baker, and Paul Lauter in the late sixties and early seventies, and

4

fuelled, in America, by rapidly increasing, and increasingly broad, interest in issues to do with 'political correctness', 'affirmative action', and 'multiculturalism', has tended to give an impression of the literary canon as a formidable enemy in a strongly fortified city having no inclination to parley with the siege troops. The clamour of the self-styled canon-busters has made it difficult to appreciate the fact that throughout the twentieth century the canon has indeed been subject to constant debate and change.

Explicitly or implicitly, a sense of a literary tradition, of a literary canon, is part of all activities to do with literary criticism. The notion of a literary canon is, however, quite alien to literature itself, understood as so many texts written through the ages. A literary canon emerges when the need arises for some of that multitude of texts to appear grouped together for specific purposes. Such purposes may range from an ideal – Arnoldian – pattern of the 'best' to Frank Kermode's suggestion along rather pragmatic lines that the 'canon is mnemonic; it is a device for handling information, a list of what is available; a simple defence against the overwhelming mass of data' (Kermode 1988:258). The sense of a canon is indeed a multi-purpose critical construct, and as such we had always better approach it with an eye on the interests served by the canon in question.

The nature of the literary canon, in the perspective of its English provenance, is such that it is easily affected by even minute changes in the intellectual climate, with its centre in English as a school and academic subject.[1] The work of a single individual may result in the resurrection of an author or authors long since relegated to obscurity. This was the case of H. J. C. Grierson's resuscitation of the Metaphysical Poets in 1921 by his publication of *Metaphysical Lyrics and Poems of the Seventeenth Century*, an effort partly brought about by a radical shift in the cultural climate, partly an event itself contributing significantly to it. Of the same kind is C. S. Lewis's restoration to fame of Edmund Spenser by his ground-breaking *The Allegory of Love* (1936).[2] Such canon-changing efforts, however, are seldom realized until seen in retrospect.

If these instances testify to one individual scholar's serious interest in and concern for a period and its up till then more or less forgotten figures, reputations may be made or unmade for far more fortuitous reasons. No doubt the final volume of *The Oxford History of English Literature* (1963) has contributed considerably to the consolidation in the mid-twentieth-century canonical annals of

Thomas Hardy, Henry James, George Bernard Shaw, Joseph Conrad, Rudyard Kipling, William Butler Yeats, James Joyce and D. H. Lawrence, as the key figures of late-nineteenth- and early-twentieth-century literature in English. The final volume of *The Oxford History of English Literature* was written over a ten-year period by the Oxford don J. I. M. Stewart, third choice after Edmund Wilson and V. S. Pritchett, as Stewart happily confesses in his memoir *Myself and Michael Innes*. Indeed, not only was the choice, with consequences for inevitable personal bias, left somewhat to chance, but Mr Stewart's selection of writers came to depend on a coolly pragmatic approach, as he soberly reveals: 'What I could do was spend the inside of a year with a major author, and then write 35,000 words about him' (Stewart 1987:122).

Indeed, examples of such apparently haphazard canon-making abound. In his biography of Philip Larkin, Andrew Motion has described at length the highly idiosyncratic considerations on the part of the celebrated British poet which led to inclusion in or exclusion from *The Oxford Book of Twentieth Century English Verse* from 1973 (cf. Motion 1993:405–7). The battles fought in the lists of successive Oxford and Faber books of poetry have to a large extent determined the taste of anthology readers over the years, as celebrated anthologies have always seemed to do. Perhaps the best known, and for hosts of British readers the best loved anthology has been *Palgrave's Golden Treasury*, first published in 1861. In Edward Hutton's introduction to the 1906 edition in Everyman's Library, the anthology is described as 'a sort of canon as it were of English poetry within which nothing of doubtful quality or achievement is to be found, a perfect chaplet of beautiful verses' (Palgrave 1861:vii). Anthologizing, for popular use, is perhaps the strongest possible bid for canonization, since the necessarily short pieces and extracts have a way of stamping themselves on the mind of readers with a force like that of proverbs and set phrases.

Despite the fact that in current debates the canon is often considered a rigid and permanent collection of titles, generally approved by some 'authority', it remains true that quite a margin of tolerance actually exists. There is a tremendous difference in the sheer number of titles and writers included in, to take an example from the condensed-textbook market, Ifor Evans's *A Short History of English Literature* from 1940, and comparing it with the densely printed volumes of the *Concise Cambridge Bibliography*, which, in the opinion of one critic, is 'as near an approximation to a fixed and restrictive "canon" of native English writers as we are ever going to get' (Myers 1989:615).

One observer of the debate on postmodernism has suggested that the 'links between the academic world and the world of exhibitions and sale-rooms are much closer' (Connor 1989:104) than the links between contemporary writing and literary institutions, even though 'undoubtedly universities and schools can determine to a very large degree which authors stay in print (especially in a larger market like the US)' (Connor 1989:103). Certainly, in comparison with the cash nexus obtaining in the world of art and design, the literary marketplace presents a far less transparent situation. But this does not mean that efforts are not made to influence sales figures of books ancient and modern – apart from school-and university-curriculum dynamics[3] – thus deliberately modifying the canon.

Affecting the not-so-distant past in the UK, the different promotions of contemporary British literature by the British Council and the independent English book organization Book Trust – formerly the National Book League – must certainly have had an impact on the selection of texts by the reading audience, perhaps especially abroad. There is straight advice to readers in the successive editions of *An English Library* (the sixth (1990) edition compiled and edited by Nigel Farrow, Brian Last and Vernon Pratt, and published by Book Trust in association with Gower). It says unabashedly on the dust jacket that here we have a 'Guide to over 2,500 of the best books in English'. The preface reveals the premise of selection, although probably not all critics will be persuaded by the suavity of the last statement:

> It has been compiled with one objective: to identify the books from the classical and modern heritage that will extend your enjoyment of reading. . . . If a book is listed in these pages it is because it has given an experienced reader real pleasure, not because it fits a particular critical theory of literary excellence (1990:vi).

A thinly disguised British Council promotion of British fiction as literary history, like Allan Massie's *The Novel Today: A Critical Guide to the British Novel 1970 – 1989* (1990), achieves its effect within a largely academic community,[4] whereas the British Council's widely distributed pamphlets cater to a more general readership.[5] An effort like the British Book Marketing Council's less commercially ambiguous 'Best Novels of Our Time' from the mid-1980s is bound to affect canonical consideration, with its panel of distinguished judges. Also the preferences of well-known writers and critics can create quite a canonical stir, or at least cause a few eyebrows to be raised, as happened in connection with the publication of Anthony Burgess's highly idiosyncratic *Ninety-Nine Novels: The Best in English since 1939* in 1984.[6]

In view of the astounding number of literary titles currently published, the need for some guidance is obvious. Reviewers are by tradition canonical stormtroopers, their acceptance of material for review being the first, and perhaps the most important canonical filter of contemporary writing. But publishing lobbies are very active, for instance in the shape of the Book Trust, which exerts considerable canonical influence, not least via its administration of some of the larger literary awards, which have developed into a most significant book-market determinant.[7]

As with contemporary poetry anthologies the system of literary awards in the area of fiction presents a most fascinating topic for canon-in-the-making watchers. And one could go on adding examples of selection mechanisms working their effects on the market, one of the most important of which are the lists of the ubiquitous mail-order book clubs.

Since the mid-1970s issues to do with the concept of a literary canon have had special prominence in the international critical debate. The general dissolution of a mainstream consensus in national literatures, mainly owing to the efforts of literary historians interested in forgotten or neglected figures and groups, has invited discussion about the coming into being and justification of traditional priority lists. In the structuralist and poststructuralist critical climate, with its denunciation of author(ity) in any form, the focusing on critical procedures and principles devised under implicit or explicit assumption of literary hegemonies has proved especially pertinent.

While literary criticism and theory have been quick to reach a level of great sophistication in the field of canon debate, writers of literary histories, compilers of anthologies and teaching staff engaged in the setting up of syllabuses – the practical testers of the viability of theoretical canon revision – have proved less eager to pursue revolutionary goals on short notice. Even literary histories or anthologies marketed vigorously as canon-upsetting often show a surprisingly high degree of canonical conformity. *The Heath Anthology of American Literature*, whose chief editor is iconoclast Paul Lauter (two volumes plus a volume entitled *Instructor's Guide*, 1990) committed to an 'expanded American literature canon' (back-cover blurb, vol. 1), reveals additions to and slight adjustments to rather than radical disturbance of the canon of American literature as it appears in competing but established anthologies such as N. Baym *et al.*, *The Norton Anthology of American Literature* (1989) and G. Perkins *et al.*, *The American Tradition in Literature* (1985).[8]

ACADEMICS ON THE BARRICADES

The critical interest in matters to do with literary canons since the mid-1970s does not mean any absence up till then of canonical debate.[9] But our awareness of the concept of a literary canon has become much acuter with the canonization of the concept of the literary canon itself, the best proof of which is the inclusion of 'canonicity' and 'canon' in the *MLA Bibliography* in 1982 and 1983 respectively. Although historians of the canon debate duly point to Ernst Robert Curtius's *European Literature and the Latin Middle Ages* from 1948 as a pioneer study in the field, it required much more than the publication of a learned book to prepare for the situation of massive interest which has prevailed in the last decades: a total reappreciation of the intellectual climate, in fact.

The paradigm shift in the humanities signalled – often somewhat chaotically – during the 1960s, was, to put the matter briefly, a reaction against political and cultural hegemony, socially in terms of race, class and gender, intellectually in terms of system-building.[10] After the initial phase of iconoclasm, the search for alternatives to oppressive inherited values and priorities started. In literary criticism totalizing systems – no matter how contemporary – like Frye's myth criticism or linguistics-inspired structuralism, were found to retain pernicious remnants of authority, and were replaced by various schools of relativistic approaches, such as deconstruction. The study of texts – 'literature' phased out as too elitist and oppressive[11] – was to focus on previously neglected authors, considered struck off from the canon because of tradition-offensive race, class or gender. Or, if critical work *had* to be done on established authors, to show such authors intrinsically, that is deconstructively, at odds with and alienated from themselves.

The anti-canonical train was put on track in 1971 by Sheila Delany's *Counter-Tradition: A Reader in the Literature of Dissent and Alternatives*. More carriages were soon hooked on, with Louis Kampf's and Paul Lauter's *The Politics of Literature* from 1972, Leslie Fiedler's and Huston Baker's volume of selected papers from the English Institute, 1979, signally subtitled *Opening up the Canon* from 1981, and Paul Lauter's revisionist syllabus handbook *Reconstructing American Literature: Courses, Syllabi, Issues* from 1983 as some of the better-known and college-targeted titles. Since then there has been no shortage of handbooks on alternative and even anti-curricula.

AMERICAN EDUCATORS DEBATING

In a larger and more popular context the call to arms from a group of concerned American citizens came in the form of a paper issued by the National Endowment for the Humanities in 1984 entitled *To Reclaim a Legacy: A Report on the Humanities in Higher Education*, for the final version of which Dr William J. Bennett, later Secretary of Education in the second Reagan administration, was responsible.

Together with 31 'prominent teachers, scholars, administrators, and authorities on higher education' (Bennett 1984:i), Bennett formed a study group to overhaul aims and objectives of the 'condition of learning in the humanities' (i). With more than half of high-school graduates going into some form of post-high-school education, it was felt that the time was ripe for a reassessment of 'whether today's colleges and universities are offering to America's youth an education worthy of our heritage' (ii–iii).

The problem facing Bennett's study group was not one of any lack of high-level learning and education. It requires no documentation that the general capability of the USA in matters scientific and technological is second to none. The cause for worry, however, was an alleged lack of a feeling of national identity, an identity which to some extent is nationally unique but which is in many ways part of the progress of western civilization in general.

The suggested reintroduction of the humanities as the firm foundation for further specialized studies so as to make clear what the shared American cultural heritage really is, first needs a definition of what the humanities are about. Bennett and company decided to expand on Matthew Arnold's touchstone declaration, making it comprise the 'best that has been said, thought, written, and otherwise expressed about the human experience' (3). Students should be made to know intimately a 'common culture rooted in civilization's lasting vision, its highest shared ideals and aspirations, and its heritage' (4).

It hardly requires refined instruments of analysis to spot the tender area in these bouts of rhetoric. Whereas all good Americans can agree that a basic knowledge of the planks of the national cultural platform is, if not indispensable, then at least preferable, an argument is bound to arise over the exact nature of the material supposed to constitute the planks of the platform.

Bennett does not hesitate long before he offers his bid for a possible curriculum based on the proposition that 'some things are more important to know than others' (7). His curriculum, indeed any curriculum, is a declaration of values, and as such there is hardly anything in Bennett's to thwart expectations of an all-American consensus curriculum.[12] What is worthy of note, however, is the feeling of a need to a challenge authoritatively and massively a state of *laissez-faire* and pluralism supposed to have run amok in recent decades: 'The past twenty years have seen a steady erosion in the place of the humanities in the undergraduate curriculum and in the coherence of the curriculum generally' (19). While plurality has always been a key concept in the American collective consciousness, the alleged development into steady erosion justifies the reassertion of a uniform curriculum, and consequently:

> our eagerness to assert the virtues of pluralism should not allow us to sacrifice the principle that formerly lent substance and continuity to the curriculum, namely, that each college and university should recognize and accept its vital role as conveyor of the accumulated wisdom of our civilization (29–30).

With the Bennett study group's report from November 1984 some quick demarcations of position in the fast lane, as it were, had been accomplished.[13] What was needed now was substantial empirically based support of the claim that an erosion had actually been in progress for quite a long time, plus a theoretical framework to complement practical findings. Both of these arrived in book format in 1987, and to prove the fast-lane inclination of what was happening, both soon received bestseller status.

In his report Dr Bennett had mentioned the concept of 'cultural literacy' created by Professor E. D. Hirsch, Jr, at the University of Virginia. Professor Hirsch had been working on questions related to those concerning Bennett and his group since the late 1970s, and had attracted national attention with his article 'Cultural Literacy' in *The American Scholar* in 1983, which is the source of Bennett's reference. In his preface to the book of the same title, published in 1987, Hirsch describes how the warm welcome of his *American Scholar* article from various quarters encouraged him to devote full-time energy to the project, of which the book was the major tangible result.

Unlike Bennett, Hirsch approaches his topic inductively in stating that 'Cultural literacy is represented not by a *prescriptive* list of books but rather by a *descriptive* list of the information actually possessed by literate Americans' (Hirsch 1987: xiv; Hirsch's italics). Somewhat further on, cultural literacy is defined as: 'the network of information that all competent readers possess' (2). 'Literate Americans' and 'competent readers' are synonymous, so the task of Hirsch is twofold: he must delimit his category of 'literate Americans/competent readers' (under the assumption that what they know is universally desirable), and he must find out what they actually know.

Hirsch is not particularly forthcoming regarding the first question. The literate American as the competent reader is characterized by a degree of literacy which

> lies above the every day levels of knowledge that everyone possesses and below the expert level known only to specialists. It is that middle ground of knowledge possessed by the 'common reader.' It includes information that we have traditionally expected our children to receive in school, but which they no longer do (19).

Concerning what is worth knowing, Hirsch offers exemplary lists of the kind of knowledge desired in the introductory interpretations of his findings.[14] The complete list compiled by Hirsch and his assistants consists of more than fifty two-column pages alphabetically arranged.[15]

To represent Hirsch's project as an effort to single out a given number of phenomena that should be known by every educated American is not, however, quite fair. Hirsch was not concerned with any normative aim, but attempted to find a kind of lowest common denominator for the range of areas commonly referred to by educated Americans. Reference knowledge and first-hand knowledge of phenomena – concepts or things – tend to be virtually indistinguishable for communication purposes: the ability to drive a car does not depend on our familiarity with kinds of transmission system. However, a list like the one published by Hirsch, no matter how empirically worked out and aimed, has a tendency to be accepted broadly as normative, and the effort as a whole to have a regulating purpose.

The theoretical counterpart to Hirsch's empirical findings was Professor Allan Bloom's *The Closing of the American Mind*, subtitled in tract-like fashion *How Higher Education Has Failed Democracy and Impoverished the Souls of Today's Students* (1987).[16] Professor Bloom, a hawk in the preservation-of-learning debate, was, unlike Bennett and Hirsch, deliberately elitist in his arguments for the reintroduction of a 'Great Books' programme at introductory college and university level.

Whereas Hirsch's argument, with a somewhat stereotypical metaphor, is that 'cultural literacy is the oxygen of social intercourse' (19), Bloom, himself a philosopher and as such first and foremost concerned with philosophical texts, argues that if the kind of thought represented by the 'great' philosophers and writers is lost from sight, the very concept of democracy is in danger. His ideal is the Platonic symposion, at which ideas and arguments are offered for free and unprejudiced discussion among interlocutors who are willing to listen and contribute fairly. The point of such discussion is not so much to prove that one is right, although that may ultimately be the purpose, but in the process of enlightened argument to turn over every aspect of a case carefully and critically. This is something which can only take place if every participant in the debate has the same kind and amount of general knowledge. Only thus is true democracy saved and continued, but, as some would undoubtedly suggest, by almost forbiddingly exclusive and elitist means.

There are, of course, certain differences between the minimum-requirement Arnoldian touchstone list suggested by Bennett, the comprehensive 'cross-disciplinary' list offered by Hirsch, and the

elegantly phrased apology for philosophy by that archetypal pred-
atory beast of the academic grove, Allan Bloom. But it is more
rewarding to pay heed to the common features of their contributions to the debate in question.

For all three a supposed decrease in fundamental humanistic
learning is of major concern. Hirsch anticipates a severe lack in
social interaction, Bloom fears the withering of democracy, and
Bennett and his study group foresee the crumbling of the national
identity. All recommend that college and university syllabuses be
put together with a greater awareness of national uniformity and
centred on texts agreed on as seminal generally for Western civilization and specifically for the forming of the American culture. By
paradox almost, the grounds for their concern are to be found first
and foremost in the trends set by the long-term-working academics
in the slow lane, who by the time of Bennett's study-group publica-
tions and the subsequent contributions from Professors Hirsch and
Bloom, were in the process of canonizing the erosion and plurality
of values so vehemently reacted against in the fast lanes.[17]

AMERICAN LITERARY HISTORY OVERHAULED

By the mid-eighties the climate in the humanities had more or less
reached a new stable temperature. The upheavals in the sixties had
been slowly transformed from revolution to orthodoxy. Editors of
American prestigious learned journals have been quick to realize
the advisability of endorsing new terms like 'trace', 'gender', 'marginal groups', etc. Perhaps the best illustration of the new orthodoxy, the one considered dangerously corrosive of accepted
American values by Bennett and sympathisers, is the *Columbia
Literary History of the United States*, published in 1988 and intended
as the successor to the *Literary History of the United States* by Spiller
et al. from 1948.

The 1948 Spiller literary history was written as a monument,
celebrating the march of American literature away from its European roots into independence. This objective is made quite clear in
the introductory 'Address to the Reader'. American literature is
seen by the editors to form a pattern such as to make it possible to
'set in order the progress from colonies to republic, from republic
to democracy, from East to West, from sections and regions to a
national unity' (Spiller *et al*. 1948: xxvi). The American experience

as one of revolution and expansion has been reflected in the work of American writers, with the result that American

> contemporary literature, which from comic strip to satiric novel is really the adult education of most Americans, can be rightly understood only by readers who have followed the history of this American tradition (xxii).

Without any doubt, the supporters of the Bennett position will be in sympathy with such a view of a literary history which lends desirable shape to the idea of the American national heritage. The planning and production of the history bears out this view. In the preface to the first edition Spiller *et al.* declare that each generation 'should produce at least one literary history of the United States, for each generation must define the past in its own terms' (vii), but in the prefaces to subsequent editions it is repeated that alterations have not been permitted, apart from bringing the bibliographical volume up to date, and adding a chapter on recent developments.

In the preface to the 1948 edition pains are taken to present the history as the result of a corporate effort rather than a collection of individual essays. The unsigned sections have been ironed into uniformity so as to result in what the editors hope to be a 'coherent narrative' (vii). The preface to the 1953 edition is even more outspoken, in that it characterizes the history as a 'solid whole' designed to tell a 'single and unified story' (ix).

Seen in a larger context, the Spiller literary history of the United States was the product of the generation that rebelled against the European-heritage school of literary historians. The rebellion ensured the success of the Spiller history beyond its own generation, and was not really challenged authoritatively until the work by Professor Emory Elliott *et al.* in the 1980s on a new- concept literary history.

A random glance in the forty-years-younger Elliott history at once reveals a change in atmosphere: the sections are signed by their authors. This is indicative of the basic approach to literary history no longer seen as a unified movement with a purpose, but as something rather more atomized and complex.

In their 'General Introduction' the editors make it clear from the start that although the history is concerned with the emergence, development and nature of the American national literature, the subject itself is extremely complex, and they go on to state as their conceptual basis that

> In order to appreciate the special characteristics of this volume, it is necessary to have a sense of the fundamental transformations in literary criticism that have occurred on the theoretical level over the last twenty-five years (Elliott *et al.* 1988:xv).

The shift from Spiller to Elliott can be described as a shift from deliberately empirical history to deliberately interested history. After having sketched the changes in the intellectual climate from the mid-sixties, Elliott arrives at the conclusion that

> It is no longer necessary or desirable for the critic to argue that one reading is truer than any other, for the aim of historical criticism is to provide the reader with an interesting and feasible approach to the text, informed by a relevant interpretation of historical material. . . . no longer required to sound authoritative and magisterial, the voice of the individual critic can be more distinctive and personal (xviii).

A practical result of this new critical awareness has been the opening up of the canon, to include what has traditionally been considered marginal or sub-literary writers. Also the concepts of the United States, of literature, and of history have come under heavy critical fire.

The Elliott history, despite its explicit editorial intentions, is a new authoritative literary history, whose authority is paradoxically in its aim not to be an 'authoritative proclamation' (xxiii). Like deconstructive analysis, its discourse seeks to 'intersect the lines of tension between the centralizing and unifying forces of our society and those decentralizing powers of individual creative and critical imaginations' (xxiii). The editors have found a suitable image in architecture by comparing their work to the contradictions, paradoxes, and relativism of the postmodernist building, in contrast to the uniform and streamlined modernist style.

The advocates of a return to a Great-Books basis have been busy, we may conclude, uniting to face those who have finally brought the structuralist and poststructuralist rebellion into print and thereby lending it authority. The believers in a Great-Books culture react against an essentially Romantic concept of education which must proceed in harmonious accordance with the needs of the individual. This attitude has only led into looseness and national-identity flabbiness, they claim. The antidote is a rationalistic reintroduction of a properly constructed universe of values, ready to be enjoyed by everybody without any need for the questioning of selective criteria.

In their defence of the Great-Books tradition, those in the arena of day-to-day politics – the rationalists – signal their allegiance to the kind of postmodern tendencies which can be seen as the continuity of the aristocratic and elitist element of high modernism, whereas those in the academic arena, the tenured professors, declare their faith in the heterodox, which is also expressly in the postmodern, although of a certain Romantic inclination. As a witness to this highly serious game one can note that history repeats itself: back at the beginning of the twentieth century modernism succeeded Romanticism; now, towards the end of the century (and definitely not as farce!), modernist and rationalistic postmodernism fight anti-modernist and Romantic postmodernism.

The debate conducted by educators and literary historians outlined above is interesting as a chapter in American cultural history, in which it reflects a major crisis far beyond literary preferences in a nation from its beginnings dedicated to the melting-pot idea. However, the polarization manifest in more general terms – a consensus principle guarded by tradition against an individualist and norm-breaking principle – is found time and again in the canon debate; indeed it occurs so regularly that it seems to constitute the principle of canon formation. But at a late stage in the debate, the very polarization has been made symptomatic of a crisis especially pertinent to the American academy facing the political and social trends of the nation.

LAUTER AND GUILLORY

Lauter's anti-traditionalist energy has been chiefly directed to the change of rather concrete conditions obtaining on the American campus. His collection of essays from 1991, *Canons and Contexts*, places the canon debate in the wider perspective of current trends in college and university administration in the USA. He sees a major threat to the academic freedom needed for any innovation of degree programmes and curricula in the rising professionalization

of college and university government in terms of market orientation and cost efficiency.

Lauter presents a picture of the contemporary American campus
as a vast business concern increasingly susceptible to powers outside academia in the design of programmes and curricula. The
left-winger Paul Lauter being opposed in most respects to the
right-winger Allan Bloom, there is nonetheless a patch of meeting
ground in their shared concern for the target-mindedness of many
American students, who increasingly seem to select their undergraduate college courses according to an exchange rate relative to
attractive professional job opportunities. Bloom in *The Closing of the
American Mind* deplored what he saw as the growing marginaliza-
tion of traditionally central humanistic areas in the liberal-arts
oriented platform of undergraduate studies. By opting for undergraduate subjects designed for easy transference to especially natu-
ral-science and professional graduate programmes, it is possible to
short-circuit a concept of undergraduate studies as providing the
student with a generally and strongly arts and humanities oriented
preparation for advanced studies. This trend, according to Lauter,
is reinforced by university administrations more and more cut off
from what they administrate, only interested in providing the 'products' that the 'consumers' want here and now (Lauter 1991:x).

When it comes to the intrinsic value of the humanities in the
American college and university system, Bloom and Lauter are in
agreement to an extent perhaps surprising to both. When Bloom
recommends a Great-Book programme, based on the Greek classics, he wants to create an opportunity for an informed – the information of course in this case determined by the format of the
Great-Book framework – discussion among persons interested in
weighing points of view against each other, ending up with
answers which can only be rational. Lauter sees the canon debate as
valuable in the very process of the discussion of the premises of the
tradition and the alternatives offered to it. His project is not to do
merely with changing the curriculum in favour of greater diversity
in terms of race, gender and class, but with the upholding of a
democratic way of life. Where Bloom urges an already set curriculum – his version of the essence of Western civilization – as the
platform for enlightening discussion, Lauter, pursuing the same
objective, sees his opportunity rather in the never-ceasing deconstructive analysis of such a tradition by pointing to alternatives as
an essential part of the regular study process.

Ultimately Lauter's argument is political in the sense that he wants to further a decision-making process central to the American tradition, but now, as he sees it, in danger of being swallowed up by Corporate America. His concept of true democracy may not be a realistic mode for political functioning on the national level, but a feasible way of instilling the sense of the democratic 'process in which the maximum number of people participate, discuss, and decide central questions about the direction and configuration of an institution's programs' (1991:xi).

Lauter's approach to the issue of canonicity is an object lesson in the way that the canonical in literature is insolubly tying in with some vaster project, that which I call the broader existential dimension. Lauter's ideal vision of (wo)man is of a person capable of the constructive scepticism which will never tolerate preconceived and inherited ideas unless they can be appropriated by personal avowal which is the outcome of free and unrestricted discussion.

Both Lauter and Bloom are Romantics in the sense that they want to reinstate a kind of democracy which probably never existed, or, if it did, perhaps depended on modes of society which for other reasons would be unacceptable to the modern sensibility. Bloom longs for the rational Greek city-state – with its democracy based on slave labour – and Lauter's Romantic desire is for a kind of democracy which to the extent it has been put into practice has shown tendencies towards anarchy – the Left Bank in Paris in 1968 – or downright state totalitarianism – as in the former communist countries. Behind any canonical issue there is a utopian concept of an ideal social, cultural, political or psychological context in which man can live and work.[18]

Whereas Lauter still sees literature – in the extended sense of the word – as something central to contemporary culture and society for the furthering of desirable developments, John Guillory in his monumental *Cultural Capital: The Problem of Literary Canon Formation* (1993) sees the debate as in itself a symptom of a major and culturally all-inclusive upheaval: 'The canon debate signifies nothing less than a crisis in the form of cultural capital we call "literature" ' (1993:viii).

Guillory focuses on the school as the pivot of the cultural system of which the canonical is a function. The school reproduces social order in accordance with the powers that be. The canon taught in the school is of minor importance compared with the function of the school to provide access to reading and writing, premises for any appropriation of a syllabus. The school provides its pupils with the opportunity to partake of the common language in its culturally approved form and it provides its pupils with the politically and culturally accepted norms of knowledge. In these two forms – linguistic and symbolic – the school administrates a capital accessible to all its pupils.[19] Guillory rejects the idea that the ideological content of the individual works in any canon is important for its collective effect. Rather, he suggests, literary works must be seen as the 'vector of ideological notions which do not inhere in the works themselves but in the context of their institutional presentation, or more simply, in the way in which they are taught' (1993:ix).

Whereas Guillory differs from Lauter in his reluctance to attach special importance to the ideological value of the individual texts in the canon, he shares with him – and remotely with Bloom, odd as it may seem – the suggestion that the rise to power of a new kind of professional life in the contemporary American academy is responsible for the crisis of literature which is making itself felt as the canon debate. The appearance of a 'New Class' or a 'professional-managerial class' as the new power elite has meant the extinction of the old bourgeoisie, the traditional wardens of the cultural capital of literature. Rather than seeing the canon debate as a corrective to a constant named literature, that very debate is symptomatic of the viability of literature as such in the world of the new class. The reason why the canon is now so much the subject of debate has to do with the circumstance that it is increasingly marginalised by a new canon of theory, the mastery of which reflects the new rigour in an academy drawn into the professional-managerial world where the power in present-day America is to be found.[20]

Of course this is a very simplified rendering of Guillory's line of argument, which in itself condenses and generalises a development illustrated by cases from Gray's 'Elegy' to the present.[21] Guillory's analysis of the situation brings into focus what seems an ever-widening gulf between the 'general reader' and academic critics, a development ignored by Lauter but nonetheless needing to be bridged if his project of democratic discussion is to have its way.

BRITISH PRAGMATISM

The massive anti-canonical attack has been an American rather than a European development. A number of explanations for this may be offered; American awareness of the need for constant re-evaluation of the USA's history as one of revolution may perhaps be an essential factor. The English view of the canon is, in comparison, more relaxed.

In Britain there seems to be a high degree of unanimity that there is such a thing as an accepted canon of great works, a tradition which in poetry as well as in fiction is firmly anchored in a realistic approach in the verbal arts, within a canon looking 'harmonious rather than contentious; learned or polite rather than artless or common; national, rather than provincial or sectarian on the one hand, or dispersed and international on the other' (Butler 1987:1349). Of course demands for slanting the perspective of the canon are heard from time to time in contemporary English letters as well, as for instance in the anthology *the new british poetry* (sic) from 1988 (edited by Gillian Allnut, Fred D'Aguiar, Ken Edwards, and Eric Mottram), with its four sections 'Black British Poetry', 'Quote Feminist Unquote Poetry', 'A Treacherous Assault on British Poetry' and 'Some Younger Poets'. The attack expressed by this anthology seems directed at a poetry establishment securely controlled by respectable publishing houses like Faber, the Oxford University Press, and so on. However, a revolt in the grand manner of a *Heath Anthology* seems a distant project. In matters canonical, the British liking is for evolution and compromise rather than revolution, as in this hardly revolutionary contribution to the debate in which a prominent British critic and scholar proposes supplementing the existing canon:

> My proposition is that poets we have installed as canonical look more interesting individually, and far more understandable as groups, when we restore some of their lost peers. . . . I think it will begin to seem more natural to us in the future to replace the old thin line of national heroes with a richer and more credible notion: that writers represent groups and attitudes within the community, and therefore from time to time come dynamically into contention with one another. . . . It helps our modern questioning if we stand ready to readmit to the canon the little sect of dissenters, the awkward squad (Butler 1987:1349, 1359, 1360).

This is a declaration benevolently pacifying any less than radical demand for change, since what is going on is merely the 'annexation of non-canonical works to a hegemonic tradition – a phenomenon of cooptation' (Guillory 1987:483–4). If Sir Frank Kermode can be considered a spokesman for a particularly British view, radical canon-revision is just beside the point. (See the quotation from Kermode on page 5 above.)

Compared with the situation obtaining in the USA, where for the most part the canon debate centres on the presentation of victimised voices from past and present, the significant departure in the UK has been into 'cultural studies.' To a certain extent this has meant a greater inclusiveness of literary texts, but more to the point is the tendency to downplay the literary in favour of the 'textual', and furthermore in the shifting function of the literary – or any – text from an end of aesthetic study to a means of cultural study. Mostly energized by a vaguely neo-marxist methodology – revived in criticism also as 'new historicism' – in the vein of Frederic Jameson and Terry Eagleton, canonical questions seem to be so far a side rather than a central issue.[22]

POSITIONS IN THE CANON DEBATE

There seem, for all practical purposes, to be three main positions in the contemporary canon debate, which are occupied, to borrow terms from Harris (1988), the 'canonical purists,' the 'canonical anarchists' and the 'canonical pluralists'.

Although the purists seem to be the goal of current attacks since the 1970s, orthodox hard-core representatives of the 'assumption that the canon is the doing of old men – a sort of literary House of Lords, or the embodiment of a "great man" theory of literature' (Myers 1989:614) are hard to find. Instead there seems to be a tendency for many purists by pragmatic inclination to subscribe to the somewhat cautious view that

By the general consensus of readers for whom reading is an important part of living, there is an informal canon of books that are worth reading; but, unlike the canon of saints, it isn't prescribed, nor is it changed in the same way – by decree of a council or committee (Morse 1986:148).

Or:

For all the changes through the ages in values and the changes in political arrangements behind them, the literary tradition exhibits a surprising degree of stability. It might be imagined as a large and variegated corpus with a relatively stable center and intermittently shifting borders (Alter 1988:575).

This is quite the kind of argument which is so objectionable to, for instance, gender critics, since it seems to take for granted that whatever is handed down by past authorities suffices for any new reader. One should not, of course, underrate the practical difficulties involved in problematizing the contours of the literary heritage. It involves both the setting up of either an alternative, or at least a complementary aesthetics and a compiling and reading effort which has all the hazards of the pioneer effort.[23]

Radical pluralists trying to squeeze in new names and works tend to find themselves up against the kind of hard wall exemplified by the following argument:

I am making three fundamental claims. First, that Afro-American canon formation regulated by an ideology of pluralism is more an emblem of the prevailing crisis in contemporary humanistic studies than a creative response to it. Second, that this activity – despite its limited positive effects, such as rendering visible Afro-American literary texts of high quality – principally reproduces and reinforces prevailing forms of cultural authority in our professionalized supervision of literary products. Third, that black inclusion into these forms of cultural authority – with black literary critics overseeing a black canon – primarily serves the class interests of Afro-American literary critics (West 1987:198).

This is a kind of argument much harder to handle than the complacent enunciation by Morse cited above. To challenge the anarchists or pluralists with the kinds of argument and the kinds of critical discourse familiar to those preferring alternatives to the purist position is to take the war into the enemy's own camp. Of course West has a point in so far as some approaches to canon criticism result in one hegemony replacing another: we end up with a feminist or a black canon instead of a white-male one. This is probably the reason why so many anti-traditionalist canon critics increasingly tend to avail themselves of a theoretical framework which combines alleged repression of class, gender and race in terms of a more general rationale of execution of power.[24]

The middle-of-the-road-pluralist position is described somewhat defensively by Myers:

> To the revising of canons there is no end. But the canon, the 'old canon,' the 'patriarchal canon', the 'restricted, canonical list,' the 'fixed repertory' – this is a bogey. It has never existed. It has merely changed, from critic to critic and generation to generation; it bears no marks of persistence as well as change. Within the flux of canons the only principle of identity is the name canon. But it is the name for many different selections of many different kinds (Myers 1989:620).

This probably covers the practical understanding of the canon by most educated readers – and critics and literary historians as well. But to speak of such a canon in terms of works alone is to misrepresent the situation, since 'every canon has a ghostly double of commentary, upon which its survival depends' (Kermode 1988:260).[25] Nor should a whole complex of what might be felt to be contingent causes for canon formation be left out of consideration:

> books and authors and other categories of repute possess esteem for many reasons other than endurance or 'literary' value, i.e., reasons of extrinsic value, whether moral, pragmatic, or economic. Some works enjoy high repute less because they are critically respected than because they are historically significant as period, style, or genre exemplars, or because they were regarded as significant by their original audiences. Or works are esteemed for their literary influence upon authors of more 'valued' works, or for their innovations in form, theme, or subject matter. Or because they are valuable social documents, or offer insight into a major writer's personal history or creative process (Rodden 1988:267).

To find examples of 'lists' brought into being by canonical purists may turn out an impossible task, if we ignore the bombastic pronouncements by such canonical populists as William J. Bennett. The nature of literary criticism, the bulk of which is carried out as academic criticism in the college and university community, is such that in so far as research is concerned, there is a strong urge to seek untrodden paths. In the rather cynical perspective of the university careerist with his or her prospect of the publish-or-perish syndrome, it makes best strategic sense to seek out for research and criticism neglected areas, or to focus on new theoretical positions, which make the revision of the otherwise well-illuminated past necessary. In both cases we have to do with a canon-centrifugal or -resisting dynamic. When it comes to the instruction carried out by those same researchers in their capacity of teaching staff, the tendency is the exact opposite. Now some kind of canon is central, not so much, perhaps, for ideological as for pragmatic reasons. Practical considerations such as the stocking of books, the hiring of temporary staff, etc., further a certain inertia or conservatism, although by degrees the research interests of members of a department may be seen to filter through into the syllabus. This state of affairs – the tension between innovative research and conservative teaching – explains somewhat the tendency to hesitate and prevaricate on the issue of the canon in the community of academic critics, as evidenced characteristically in the difficulty of finding hard-core purists in their ranks.

In most critical practice, however, a sense of a literary tradition or canon is both a premise and an objective of any critical activity. As a premise, it is perhaps idiosyncratic and unrealized, though of the utmost importance for critical articulation. As an objective it is the practical manifestation of critical articulation, apparently its end product, but, ultimately (and arguably), also the rationalization of a personal preference, disguised as logical order and system.

INTRODUCING ELIOT, LEAVIS, FRYE AND BLOOM

A study of the factors contributing to the formation of the somewhat shaky concept of the literary canon or tradition cannot be kept within a handy and well-defined purely literary territory. Nor is the territory terminologically clarified. As we have to do with issues arising out of a continued discussion of literary value, authorial intention, and reader approach, educational objective and general *Bildung*, a great number of avenues open themselves to critical demarcation and exploration.

In the USA particularly, as the discussion referred to above shows, the political debate involving canonical issues has been heated, not least because conservatives as well as liberals have been able to muster outstanding academic spokesmen in favour of their respective views. Part of the swing to the right has been a concern for educational priorities, which conservatives feel have been sacrificed by liberal levellers. In this debate national canons will get a central place, as they are the concrete manifestations of values.

Since the general levelling of allegedly elitist assumptions concerning canon and literary tradition from the time of the 'cultural revolutions' in the mid-and late sixties, the critical climate gives the impression of greater tolerance and a more 'democratic' literary Parnassus.[26] Of course this broadening and diversification of tradition and canon is not so much an expression of a genuinely new tolerance as it is a shift of critical focus, with one critical empire arising from the ashes of the old, in Murray Krieger's somewhat wry metaphor (1986).[27]

Canonical readjustments seldom come into being by the *fiat* of a single, individual critic. In order for them to win through, there must have been a climate positively responsive to new ideas or modifications of the old. The not-always-lucid canonical reconsiderations offered by Eliot won through not least because the twenties and thirties were responsive to the break with positivist historicism under the conveniently spacious label of New Criticism, including I. A. Richards, the Southern Fugitives, Czech and Russian Formalism, to name some of the most important origins of exegetical procedures relying on and/or resulting in close reading. Looking back on the achievement of New Criticism as the common label of this broadly conceived critical practice, it is surprising that it has hardly affected the sense of the canon apart from a conveniently closer attention to manageably short and metaphor-saturated texts, typically lyrical works. The same disproportion is true of other critical schools and movements relying to a high extent on formal considerations such as structuralism and deconstruction, whereas more 'content'-oriented critiques such as psychoanalytical and Marxist criticism have tended to create custom-built and theme-oriented canons to prove their efficacy.

It is misguided to believe that up to the 1970s literary criticism worked within a fixed canonical framework and that literary criticism stuck to narrowly aesthetic lines within such a framework. Structuralist and poststructuralist criticism, coinciding with the emergence of the multicultural agenda, has favoured a view of literature as just so many texts. However, it must be borne in mind that in the prestructuralist climate even the *avant garde* modernist drive tended to cultivate a distinction between texts as either literary or sub-literary. In hindsight, the critical efforts of an Eliot or a Leavis may indeed seem restricted by a limited field of vision. But in the contemporary context such revaluation of the literary tradition as did take place in the criticism by them and others represented a no more tradition-complacent attitude than the one with which we are familiar from the multicultural scene. Frye did his work at a time still dominated by this overall distinction between the literary and the sub-literary, but his shifting of the canonical away from individual works to literary structures contributed to paving the way for the great levelling which really came into its own with structuralism's doing away with the authorial subject. Today largely relegated to myth criticism, Frye's systemic poetics, especially in its ethical application, is still a tremendous and awe-inspiring effort to rethink the concept of literary diachronic tradition in terms of synchronic structure. In a current situation characterized by cultural studies taking over from aesthetics, the critical work of Harold Bloom since the 1970s to safeguard an exclusive literary heritage, seems to some an anachronism. In his subjectively qualified insistence on the right to canonical fame of the strong poet only, he has, however, no direct forebear. Even Leavis seems complacent in comparison. But of course, no matter how much Bloom clamours against the various groupings in the School of Resentment, his assumption of a kind and degree of authority and subjectivism readily associated with Nietzsche is surely shared with many of those contemporary critics with whom he disagrees so vehemently. To discard Bloom's criticism as the reactionary retention of a simply old-fashioned position is too facile. Like Eliot, he is an innovator with the freedom of position and choice that only a formidable command of literary history – and of the canon – can yield.

In what follows I offer an exegetical discussion of canon-related issues in the criticism of Eliot, Leavis, Frye and (Harold) Bloom in an attempt to show the interrelatedness of canonical considerations rooted in literature with desires that transcend the purely literary.

3

T. S. Eliot:
The Constant Modification
of Tradition

Between Sidney and Campion in the latter part of the sixteenth century, and Jonson writing towards the end of his life, the greatest period of English poetry is comprehended (Eliot 1932:53).

The history of every branch of intellectual activity provides the same record of the diminution of England from the time of Queen Anne. It is not so much the intellect, but something superior to intellect, which went for a long time into eclipse; and this luminary, by whatever name we may call it, has not yet wholly issued from its secular obnubilation (Eliot 1932: 62).

T. S. Eliot's view of the literary tradition as a flexible order of significant works constantly modified by the arrival of significant new works finds its appropriate illustration in the impact of his own criticism in relation to later generations' sense of literary history.

Perhaps no other figure in twentieth-century literature enjoys Eliot's status as literary and critical paradigm-shifter. Of no other twentieth-century critic is the observation of Tzvetan Todorov on the modern creator-theoreticians more appropriate, to the effect that they 'create works that correspond to their theories at the same time as they impose a canonical interpretation on what they produce, thereby influencing their contemporaries and followers' (Todorov 1993:33). Not that Eliot can be said to have been out there on the barricades waving the revolutionary banner. And not that he was especially clear in his formulations in his keynote essays, compared to, for instance, the pronouncements of T. E. Hulme or Ezra Pound.[1] Most of his fellow writers of the early twentieth century were far more busily – and far less compromisingly – marketing modernism as the antidote to what was widely felt to be a completely exhausted Romanticism with no longer anything to offer to a world under radical change on all fronts.

Like his contemporaries Eliot showed an extraordinarily keen sense of the need for the cooperation of the creative and the critical faculties. In this respect the modernists carried on rather than distanced themselves from a tradition as old as literature itself, dating back to Horace's explication of the principles of poetry in his *Ars Poetica*, and in English letters beginning with Sir Philip Sidney's Platonic defence of 'useless' poetry, and continued in a long line of (by now canonical) poet-critics: Dryden, Pope, Dr Johnson, Wordsworth, Shelley, Keats, Arnold and Lawrence.

The great break in this poetics tradition is, however, to be found in the shift from an apologetics based on justification in terms of compliance with a norm ultimately referred to the classics, to one based on justification in terms of breaking with the norm. In this respect Romanticism is the watershed, in English as well as in Continental–European poetics. The claim in Wordsworth's and Coleridge's 1798 Preface constitutes a break with the past far more radical than that of the modernists' with Romanticism. The Romantic generation of poets replaced a classical heritage presupposing the existence of normative models for the writing of poetry – by implication all literature – with a trust in the individual to construct an artistically adequate response to an existence normless in relation to both (cultural) history and metaphysics. In the distinction suggested aptly by M. H. Abrams, a change from a metaphorics of reflection to one of the source of light.[2]

If the shift in values and outlooks taking place about 1900 meant an explicitly modernistic agenda in the arts, the breakthrough of modernity as something general in the manifestos of Romanticism is, in the perspective of mental history, of far more wide-ranging significance. In this perspective, Eliot and his contemporaries hooked their carriage on to a train already in motion. This state of affairs explains the attempt on the part of several modernists, including Eliot, to introduce measures to regulate the speed, if not the direction of the train, though the direction was determined anyway by the railway line of modernity. Looking at the newly hooked-on carriage from the locomotive, the cry for the return to classical stances must have seemed an impossible, and hence pathetic, attempt to reverse time. Considered in this way, modernism presents an effort directed against the momentum of modernity, a reactionary endeavour to take up arms against an existence threatening in its pointlessness. It is only logical that the retrogressive formal 'innovations' of modernism were accompanied by a longing for metaphysical comfort, an equally retrogressive effort, resulting in Eliot's famous embracing of Conservatism, Anglo-Catholicism, and royalism, and in Pound's equally (in)famous adoption of fascism.

To Eliot the writing of poetry, and later of plays, was the application of an attitude to – some would no doubt say an insight into – the existential conditions of his day, with Eliot the critic attempting to rationalize what Eliot the poet and playwright depended on and believed in for the purposes of poetic creation (cf. Todorov above). The standing out of Eliot's criticism, with its implicit exegetical bearing on his own creative efforts, has led many to draw the narrow conclusion that, in the words of Wordsworth, here indeed was a case of a poet 'creating the taste by which he is to be enjoyed'. Certainly readers of Eliot's poetry and plays profit from familiarity with his criticism, and vice versa. However, since there are so many parallels in the creative work of Eliot's period, and in the critical work as well, and since Eliot, prominent though he was, did not mastermind everything that happened in art in the early decades of the century, it would hardly be justified to limit the importance of his criticism to his own work, but instead to read it as symptomatic of its time.

The criticism is singled out in this study because the aim is not to discuss Eliot's work as a poet, but to engage critically with the principles and premises in the thought which validated so much in the early modernistic version of the literary canon. With the simplification and condensation that time invariably induces, revolution is given priority over evolution in Eliot's critical achievement. However, one should not overlook the circumstance that Eliot's criticism, although usually taken to revolve round a handful of dogmatic pronouncements, is by and large a kind of discursive criticism which is only seldom not derived from a specific text under consideration, and then expressed in a way which always leaves ample room for discussion by an equally capable critic.[3] At the same time there is in his critical work, especially with regard to its implications for the sense of the literary canon, an increasingly central concern for values of a general existential nature. That this is so is perhaps first and foremost in evidence in the development of Eliot's own life, which may be described, with an echo from Søren Kierkegaard, as a three-stage journey from aesthetics, via ethics, into the religious. For the present purpose Eliot's personal development, although providing a handy framework, is of less interest than the way critical observations on the nature of the canon interact with such generally existential validations.

The traditionalism that Eliot, and others with him, reacted against was not so much the essential Romanticism of the preceding century as it was a reaction against the forms in which Romantic literature – and also pre-Romantic literature – were thought of and made available to early twentieth-century readers. The traditionalism was everything but an abstract canon. It was propped up by the vested interests of the emerging mass-market publishing-reading circuits, as described by Hugh Kenner:

> Everyman's, and such rival series as those issued by Oxford and Collins, have this value for our understanding of Eliot, that they pretty well came to define what was meant by 'Tradition': a closed system, terminated decades back. The volumes in those series did stay in print, and that helped with the illusion of stability (1988:173).

With the best intentions of making 'great literature' available to the fast-expanding reading audience created as the result of successive education reforms following in the wake of Forster's Education Act of 1870, Everyman, Oxford and Collins at the same time created very visible monuments of literature. They are easily evoked in the mind as so many shelf yards of modestly, but neatly bound volumes remaining in their chronological place no matter what new volumes are added in the empty space to the right of the most recently published gem. We can imagine Eliot staring at the shelf wondering about what happens to a work when read with the benefit of hindsight, that is, under the impression of other, and later works.

Eliot's synchronic view of tradition presupposes an understanding of the work of art as a verbal construct with its own rationale of being.[4] This may sound only common sense to later generations, but was certainly not so when Eliot published his essay on *Hamlet* in 1919. Writing in a critical climate dominated by A. C. Bradley's *Shakespearean Tragedy* (1904), Eliot reacted against a line of Shakespeare criticism dating back to Goethe and Coleridge, which made Shakespeare's characters into actual persons and discussed them accordingly in psychological terms.[5] Such an approach ignores any essential difference of the verbal work of art from any other verbal account, since both are taken to be representations of reality. Instead Eliot proposed an approach treating the verbal work of art – indeed any work of art – as a unique entity, coming into being by the 'rules' laid down for it: a special use of language, a special genre, in a special medium.

Arguably the most revolutionary step ever taken by Eliot was the suspension of the chronology which was the backbone in pre-twentieth-century criticism and literary history. Introducing the a-chronic view of literature which has become a major angle of critical approach in later literary criticism (New Criticism, myth criticism, and certain types of structuralism and deconstruction), Eliot paved the way for a radically changed phenomenology of reading. It is in this rather than in any concrete proposal for an altered sequence on the bookshelf that Eliot's sense of tradition must be appreciated:

> having read Eliot we no longer read Dante or Webster in quite the same way. We receive them differently because later work has reinterpreted them; and we can see that later work by their light, as if all the works of the canon were one work, like a bible (Kermode 1988:266).

Granted this particular timeless nature of literature, it is easier to allow for the tradition-modifying entrance of the new individual talent and also for Eliot's intriguing doctrine of the artist's impersonality. Although, in Kermode's words, 'this is not mysticism but pragmatism' (1988:266), it is a kind of pragmatism which was new to the early twentieth century. Critics contemporary with Eliot still tended to think in terms of chronology, as, for instance, T. E. Hulme announcing a new classical era.[6]

In Eliot's perspective, time is transformed into values, ultimately based on an ethics which did not emerge as such until he had parted ways with the modernist movement. So when Murray Krieger describes the task of Eliot's essay on Grierson's anthology of the Metaphysical Poets as an attempt to 'persuade readers to take this anthology and these poets seriously, although room had to be made in the canon in order to justify our seeing them as having a place within it' (1986:196), this only goes part of the way to elucidating Eliot's real engagement with tradition as a discovery of existential values through literature.

In what follows my aim is not so much to discuss Eliot as the canonical paradigm-shifter, as to discuss his criticism relating to literary canon as grounded on the notion of the impersonality of art. For his advocacy of impersonality in art Eliot needed the construction of a literary canon to justify empirically an alternative to the personality-centred Romantic tradition of long standing in the verbal arts, and backed by the emerging discipline of academic criticism since the mid-nineteenth century. Central to the canon must be works clearly displaying a dissociation of sensibility with a predominance of objective correlatives as the manifest pivots of his impersonality theory. Eliot found these in what to many readers appears as an esoteric, over-fastidious and studiedly idiosyncratic canon. It is in such perspective that Eliot's canon can be seen to be fundamentally a rationalization of the preference in his own writerly practice for the oblique, indeed often subversive reference or allusion, which in turn is the response to what Eliot sees as the particular characteristic of his time. The foundation for this argument is presented very clearly in his 1921 essay on the Metaphysical Poets, in which he explains the need to respond to a complicated ethos by an equally complicated text, a 'difficult' text, the parallel for which he sees in the Metaphysical favourite figure of the conceit (cf. 1921:65). In the interaction between his own preferred kind of writing and the tradition construed to justify it, the constant modification of the tradition by new works of art as announced in his 'Tradition and the Individual Talent' (1919) is the shaping of a canon in terms of Eliot's artistic preferences.

Eliot's vaguely profiled concept of a literary tradition, dynamically in process of modification, begs the question of the exact nature of this tradition, beyond the banality that the tradition of European literature is one of 'local tradition, the common European tradition, and the influence of the art of one European country upon another' (1948:114). Basically, is it a tradition comprising all literature, or is it a tradition made up of selected works?

If the literary tradition is seen as the sum total of all literary works from all times and climes, Eliot's observation is only the banality that an accumulation is made up of the elements accumulated. Clearly, though, Eliot is after something different, since his perspective is that of the reader modifying his *sense* of tradition under the impression of new works, and since he is concerned with the refinement of literary appreciation.

Although in the Convocation Lecture delivered at the University of Leeds in July 1961, 'To Criticize the Critic', Eliot attempted to situate his early work generally and the various catchphrases just mentioned specifically in a certain context to him no longer applicable, I have chosen to ignore this 'retraction' despite Eliot's irritation when being quoted out of context (1961:14). I believe that what follows demonstrates convincingly that there is a synchronic consistency in Eliot's critical work regarding the canonical, which includes the early as well as the later work. And, despite Eliot's own denial, there is indeed in a historical perspective a coherent development from his theorizing on the nature of the metaphor, through his deliberations on watersheds in English literary history to his pronouncements on culture and religion a quarter of a century later on.[7]

In the first place, the sense of tradition is a distillation of the literature found worthy of contributing to the formation of that sense. It is possible, then, to suggest some parameters of Eliot's literary validations based on his assessment of relative qualities of intellectual and artistic ethoi in consequence of absolute paradigm shift ('dissociation of sensibility'), his theory of metaphor dynamic ('objective correlative' and 'impersonality'), his attempt to establish a distinction between minor and major writers, and his consideration of the status of 'classics'. It may be true of these phrases that to the older Eliot they may have been 'conceptual symbols for emotional preferences' (1961:19) merely and that his general critical opinions are epiphenomenal on writers of his preference (1961:20). However, Eliot would probably be the first to admit to the dependence of emotional preferences on processes of thought and emotions systematised in subtle but eventually rational ways.

DISSOCIATION OF SENSIBILITY: A MATTER OF CANON

In a sense, Eliot in his essay on 'The Metaphysical Poets' from 1921 builds on Schiller's distinction between 'naive und sentimentalische Dichtung' in combination with a psychology not very far removed from Coleridge's three-tier structure of fancy and primary and secondary imaginations, in his splitting up of literary history into a period up to and including unified sensibility and a period following the period of dissociated sensibility.

The conspicuous sign of our period as one of a dissociated sensibility is the tendency towards cultural and religious separation, and the general drift towards specialization in all the areas traditionally covered by the two (1948:26). There is no longer in English – and in Western – civilization any overlap between cultural and religious areas of adjoining functionality, an overlap necessary for a thriving culture to achieve its productive cohesion (1948:24).

Eliot sees in the tradition of English poetry a traditional mainstream broken up, delta-like as it were, during the seventeenth century, with the Glorious Revolution as the point from which the mainstream is no longer visible as such. Donne and Lord Herbert of Cherbury represented a cultural ethos characterized by the integration of thought and feeling, as Eliot puts it: 'A thought to Donne was an experience; it modified his sensibility' (1921:64). The Metaphysical Poets were intellectual poets, prepared by their culture, their civilization, to put no barrier between various kinds of mental activities. Browning and Tennyson, in contrast, invariably compartmentalize their mental activities; they are reflective poets. In Coleridge's terminology, the intellectual poets – more or less identical with Schiller's naive poets – were analytical and synthetic in a seamless process, whereas the reflective poets – the sentimental ones – tended to give priority to the analytic, not because they especially chose to, but because under the impress of their cultural climate, they could not help it.

Eliot situates the occurrence of the dissociated sensibility at the time of the English Civil War in the mid-seventeenth century, with Donne, Crashaw, Vaughan, Herbert, Lord Herbert, Marvell, King, and Cowley (1921:66–7) as the last practitioners of the unified sensibility.[8] It was not the Civil War as a political or a social event which brought the phenomenon of the dissociation about, but forces in the contemporary situation produced political strife as well as artistic upheaval (1947:153). Eliot claims that the difference between poets before and after these times of general unrest is a difference between poets who gave adequate responses to an existential experience requiring their complete attention as human beings, and those poets afterwards, like Milton, Dryden and Pope, who distanced themselves in a concentration on formal conventions.

To Eliot, then, the mid-seventeenth century conditioned poets in such a way as to prepare a new line of development, a line which posterity has wrongly considered the main line, even marginalizing the 'Metaphysical Poets' to the point of extinction.

In his usual cautious fashion Eliot hesitates to point to reasons for this unfortunate shift of tracks. Literary history traditionally marks down these decades as a time of transition between the last stirrings of the Renaissance, bestowing the last rites to a vanishing world picture, and as the preparation for the neo-classical about to occupy the next century of Enlightenment.

No doubt the main factor responsible for the dissociation was to do with the secularization of which the religious fanaticism of the seventeenth century in England can be seen as a symptom. Eliot writes about the religious upheavals in Europe during the sixteenth century as 'schisms' (1948:29), for which there should be accommodation in the Christian Faith.[9] The Glorious Revolution of 1688 was a settlement in favour of pragmatic rationalism regarding faith, as well as a political settlement in favour of a bourgeois national state. If a certain fragmentation set in at the time, this was hardly something the individual poet could choose to accept or reject, but something that gradually became the existential condition. In this perspective it is possible to see Milton, Dryden and Pope as 'victims' of the modern condition, attempting to respond to it in ways to a certain degree preconditioned.

To a modern self-styled royalist, Conservative and Catholic, whose personal problem was one of finding a system of overall intellectual support, the events during the century that witnessed the disappearance of a state of society based on authority at all levels and in its place welcomed scepticism and latitudinarianism, must have appeared as a major spiritual catastrophe.

The downward move indicated by the dissociation of sensibility has nothing to do with any increasing impoverishment of language. On the contrary, Eliot points out, poetic language may be said to have improved in certain respects up through the late seventeenth and the eighteenth centuries. This is, however, a matter of refinement only, and linguistic refinement does not automatically compensate for overall intellectual crudity (1921: 64–5).

To modern readers it may sound curious to exclude Milton, Dryden, Collins, Gray, Johnson and Goldsmith from the mainstream of the tradition of English poetry (1921:64–5). But nonetheless this should be done, according to Eliot. The mainstream is to be identified instead in Donne, Crashaw, Vaughan, Herbert and Lord Herbert, Marvell, King, Cowley ('at his best'), with an occasional glimpse in Wordsworth (1933a:88), and only very intermittently in Shelley and Keats (1921:64–5). Eliot suggests passages in Shelley's *Triumph of Life*, and in Keats's second *Hyperion* (1921:65). Shelley does not pass through the needle's eye, but is accused of subjecting the poetry to dubious metaphysical ideas (1933a:91), and Keats is at his best as a writer of letters (1933a:100). Blake, Scott and Byron are summarily dismissed, Blake because he used poetry only to mediate his visions, the latter two because they tended towards using poetry as social entertainment (1933a:87). Arnold, a practitioner of 'academic poetry in the best sense' (1933b:105), marking a 'period of time, as do Dryden and Johnson before him' (1933b:103), lacks in creative force together with Carlyle, Ruskin, Tennyson and Browning, who 'had not enough wisdom. Their culture was not always well-rounded; their knowledge of the human soul was often partial and shallow' (1933b:104). And later than a few dubious Romantics Eliot does not venture. Eliot's singling out of Kipling, as shown in the rather awkward introduction to a selected-works edition in 1941, seems to rest on an attraction which is only given – and at that rather feeble – support by redeeming the writer according to recognizable Eliot values. Like the Metaphysical Poets his work, 'which studied piecemeal appears to have no unity beyond the haphazard of external circumstances, comes to show a unity of a very complicated kind' (1941:234). But Eliot does have difficulties accommodating Kipling in his canon, as it appears from the fact that he seizes whatever justification is at hand. For instance in this parallel to the implications of the objective correlative: 'the compulsion to find, in every new poem as in his earliest, the right form for feelings over the development of which he has, as a poet, no control' (1941:237). Or when he finds a praiseworthy organic social hierarchy represented in *A Habitation Enforced* opposing modern industrial society (1941:249). But Kipling is really an uneasy exception in a body of literary criticism the scope for which is only reluctantly extended beyond the eighteenth century.

ADEQUATE AND INADEQUATE METAPHORS

The significance of the concept of the objective correlative for a consideration of Eliot's sense of tradition, his canon, is in its relation to period rather than as a general critical category. As an adequate vehicle of communicating an emotionally complex response to impressions, its proper function depends on a state of mind prepared to process it accordingly. This is a state of mind conditioned by the general intellectual climate in which the artist is alive: in concrete historical terms, a climate in existence before the dissociation of sensibility in the mid-seventeenth century, and one which can be reconstructed given the awareness of its necessity, in modern times. The construction of the objective correlative necessitates a consensus culture agreed on the principle that phenomena which to a surface glance may seem disparate can be brought together (be encoded) in a way which a recipient sharing if not the same culture then at least an empathic understanding of it can appreciate (decode).[10] But even if an epoch facilitates the consensus, there is no guarantee that a happy processing into an objective correlative ensues, since in the individual case there may be a discrepancy between the circumstances generally and the specific artistic expressions. Eliot's argument in his 1919 *Hamlet* essay is that whereas there is a balance in *Macbeth* that makes the play a perfect objective correlative, in *Hamlet* this sense of balance is absent so that it does not correlate sufficiently (cf. 1919a:48). Eliot's point is that the emotions dominating the Hamlet figure are more than the circumstances merit. This difference in terms of objective correlative between the two plays illustrates the implicit demand for a certain *kind* of cultural consensus to establish a state of unified sensibility: proportion.

It would be a misunderstanding, however, to think of the objective correlative in too concrete terms as the verbal encoding of a very personal emotional and intellectual experience. The nature of the objective correlative has to do with the kind of experience which separates poetry from other uses of language, and for the proper appreciation of which the reader's response is understanding in terms of enjoyment – the kind of enjoyment proper to poetry. When Eliot suggests that the task of the critic is to point to that in the poem which makes it new to him, he implies novelty within the familiar, and the familiar is that which is already acknowledged as within the tradition. 'The spark which can leap across those 2,500 years' (1956:117) and make the twentieth-century reader understand and enjoy Sappho is not dependent on any specifically Hellenic contextualization, although a general knowledge of antiquity is of course taken for granted (*qua* tradition) and is an essential function of the objective correlative. This is a point borne out in his remarks on the joy derived from Shakespeare's poetry in his discussion of the relative merits of Matthew Arnold as poet and critic. The enjoyment of Shakespeare is not a question of empathizing with Shakespeare's original feelings, but a question of appreciating the poetry in the way that poetry presents itself, uniquely as poetry, for poetic appreciation (1933b:115). Where Arnold would have the reader see the noble sentiment through the poetry, as it were, Eliot suggests that the enjoyment and understanding of poetry, two sides of the same coin, have their origin in the verbal construct of the poem, as objective correlative.

The need for proportion seems to be the ultimate standard in Eliot's critical evaluation of literature. Proportion is what the objective correlative is made to constitute, and critical endeavour aims at distinguishing between more or less proportionate renderings of textual reponses to emotional complexities, thus constituting the necessary standards useful for comparative purposes.

Proportion is the structural aspect of a general desire to create order out of chaos. In Eliot's case, however, chaotic situations obtain before and after the dissociation of sensibility, as situations inviting and resisting objective correlation respectively. In the objective correlative it is possible to accommodate the unfamiliar in terms of the familiar, with the ultimate effect that the felicitous linguistic turn 'enlarges our consciousness or refines our sensibility' (1943:18). The threat to the stability and harmony of pre-dissociation times is to let go of the ratiocinative – the control of the ego – in favour of something unnamed by Eliot, but which is scaring because it appears in ways inviting association with mental unstability – inroads of the id, to complete the Freudian analogy. In connection with the sentimental and Romantic periods, Eliot uses words like 'fits' and 'unbalanced' (1921:65), in contrast to an earlier epoch's cultivation of the 'ratiocinative' and the 'descriptive' (1921:65). In Eliot's creative work and in his aesthetics, the urge and will are always to impose order and control on ever-threatening chaos. When chaos surfaces in poetry, as it often does during the Romantic period, such poetry cannot be admitted to the canon.

MAJOR AND MINOR POETRY

Eliot's distinction between minor and major poetry is the subject of his essay 'What is Minor Poetry?' originally a lecture given in 1944.[11] In his usual hesitation to offer absolute statements about taste or literature Eliot suggests that the term 'minor' is relative to the time it is used and to the individuals using it. Any agreements about lists of minor and major poetry are bound to be disputed, and consequently would give no frame of reference useful for further discussion. Also, Eliot suggests that minor poetry is not a designation of poorer quality or easier accessibility, but a matter of a kind of poetry different from major in terms of certain quantitative elements (1944a:39).

Eliot's distinction between minor and major poetry rests on the degree to which the appreciation of a given poem is improved by the knowledge of other work by the same poet (1944a:48). The test of major poetry is in the reader's desire to know more when he has first hit on a poem he likes. Often a poet's status will be found in the extent to which he invites anthologizing. In the anthology we will typically find highlight pieces – complete poems or extracts. Another common assumption is the length of a given work. Eliot warns against any uncritical acceptance of anthology representation or shortness as indications of minor poetry, but nonetheless seems to be in overall agreement with both criteria as generally indicative of minor poetry.

In structural terms this pointing beyond itself in the case of major poetry – either towards the whole of the long poem or to the rest of the works when it comes to the short text – is a matter of the larger textual scope to add to the appreciation of the extract of the individual short text. In very practical terms this has to do with the balance between unity and variety in the text (1944a:47), this balance in turn demanding 'enough' variety in unity (1944a:48). In other words, major-poetry quality depends on the potential for a kind of contextualization with built-in added value, as it were.[12]

The judge of any presence of added-value potential is the reader. Eliot is quite prepared to accept that not only is there the question of individual taste, but also the dependence of that personal taste on the time of its formation. To such a degree may the difference in individual appreciation be found to exist that a given poem may be considered minor and major by two equally 'competent readers' (1944a:50). But two reader-related elements remain constant: the need for the cultivated taste and the ability to experience pleasure.[13] The potential for pleasure is an obvious function of poetry, indeed, its first general function, as suggested in the earlier essay 'The Social Function of Poetry' (1943:18). But there

Eliot hesitates to go further into the question about the specific nature of this pleasure, offering only the tautology that poetry gives the 'kind of pleasure that poetry gives' (1943:18). The nature of poetry to cause pleasure or enjoyment is correlative to our understanding of
it; there is simply no understanding of poetry without enjoyment, and it is the linking of enjoyment over different poems that shows taste (1956:115). Not that it is impossible to advance further into this, but that the implications would take us too far into general aesthetics. Eliot speaks somewhat vaguely about the ability to 'understand better' (1944a:42–3) English literature when you know Spenser and Wordsworth. Cultivated taste and pleasure are interwoven in that true pleasure derives from cultivation, and cultivation can only come into existence by the desire to experience pleasure.

It is of the first importance to note the interdependence of readerly pleasure and cultivation of taste in competent readers for Eliot's arguments. But pleasure, except for the occasional idiosyncratic weakness in a reader (1944a:42 and 48), is a matter for the educated reader, with the acquired 'disciplined' (1948:30) taste. Eliot keeps as his centre of reference an 'objective ideal of orthodox taste in poetry' (1944a:49), which should not, however, be considered more than a guideline, but still of a kind that ensures a safe journey.

In his 1944 lecture Eliot, then, assumes the existence of a literary tradition, with which a reader is required to familiarize himself to arrive at a state where he can exert taste and enjoy with pleasure. Usually major poetry is found in longer pieces or, in shorter pieces, the enjoyment of which is enhanced by reading further into the poet's work as a whole. But there is room for great vacillation when it comes to the division of poetry into major and minor poems, and the possibility of making the distinction is not really present in poetry contemporary with the reader, although subject to the identical criteria of judgement. The distinction can be made along lines of reader response in terms of greater enjoyment from increasing contextualization, in turn reflecting a poet's ability to accommodate variety within unity. For all practical purposes this is appreciable as the impression on the reader of added value from a whole *oeuvre* or from a long text in comparison with the individual text or the extract.

THE CLASSIC

Also in 1944 Eliot formulated his thoughts about the concept of the 'classic', and in his lecture 'What is a Classic?' Eliot distinguishes between universal classics and what may, for want of better expressions, be called national-literature classics. Of the first kind Virgil is adduced as an example, but the status and nature of the universal classic remains unproblematized in relation to the national-literature classic, which is the primary concern of Eliot's essay, beyond the suggestion that the universal classic relates to several national cultures besides the one of its origin (cf. 1944b:128). For both, however, the *sine qua non* is maturity. There can be no classic unless the civilization in which it is written is fully mature, and the test of that maturity is in the reader's ability to accept it as mature. However, Eliot is wary of defining the kind of maturity he is thinking of, leaving it to the mature reader to recognize maturity when he sees it (1944b:116–17).

Surely, the kind of maturity that concerns Eliot is not a solely intuitive or *a priori* ability to exercise critical distinctions, but an ability acquired by having familiarized oneself with literature. We may assume, then, with reference to the argument presented in connection with the difference between major and minor poetry, that we have to do with a competent reader, whose competence derives from the choice literary diet of those texts already in place as the ones well worth ever-renewed attention. The universal classic would be one of those, presumably.

Eliot indicates that the desired maturity has to do with language. When language has reached a point when it can be said to have achieved its full potential, it has become mature. This is, however, also a question of the language having realized its limitations (1944b:117). The ideal of a literary language is to arrive at a state when the common style reflects a taste brought about by 'order and stability, . . . equilibrium and harmony' (1944b:118–19).

At this point it is possible to see a cause–effect pattern in Eliot's argument. If a given society succeeds in a uniform effort towards the application of generally recognized cultural standards of balance and harmony in all significant aspects of its life, this success will be reflected in its language, which will then exhibit a truly common style. If the balance and harmony of maturity constitutes the premise of a classic period in the life of a society, the opposite, social immaturity, is reflected in a style with great extremes in individual style (1944b:118–19).

It is difficult to see how the realization of this ideal will not lead to mere repetition once the desired state has been reached. If Virgil represents the highest achievement as a verbally mature reflection of the culture of a society – socially mature because of its balance and harmony – there seems to be no room for development. Eliot recognizes this problem, but suggests as its solution that it is only natural for a mature literary culture to relate to the past and to the contemporary with the desire of doing something different from what has already been achieved. But all literary change in the mature society will invariably take place within its boundaries. At this point Eliot provides the metaphor of the harmonious family which will tolerate filial rebellion to the extent that the family characteristics in retrospect will be seen to have developed in accordance with the potentiality of that family but always in response to changed surroundings (1944b:119). The rewriting of the past, but with a difference, can be appreciated in our reading of Milton as both grounded in and departing from Spenser (1944b:120). Although the creative activity of any culture is to be found in the tension between the heed for the past and the urge to renew (1944b:119–20), valuable creativity always takes place under the overall aegis of the tradition.

In this ideal climate of benevolent authority and consent to a tradition Eliot is at ease. But unfortunately it is a state which has never prevailed completely in English literature (1944b:117). An approximation to the desired maturity on all cultural levels was in existence during the Augustan age, with Pope as the prominent figure. Still, something was lacking, and Eliot suggests the lack to be in the restriction of maturity to relatively few elements in society. It was not a common maturity, it lacked in the comprehensiveness required to be a truly classical period.

There is, then, a difference between classic and major poetry in Eliot's view of things. The closest English literature has come to being classic was in the eighteenth century, but its greatest period was in the previous century, before the dissociation of sensibility came about. For attaining to the status of a 'classic' a text needs the characteristics of maturity, in its language as well as in its substance plus comprehensiveness, that is the potential for general appeal. If such a mature text appeals to an audience outside its country of origin, it has achieved universality. In English literature, Pope's work exhibits the characteristics of classic texts, since in him we are able to recognize the kind and degree of maturity required (1944b:121). Otherwise, though, Pope does not range particularly high on Eliot's list of estimation. Together with Milton and Dryden he represents a line of poetic development within English literature which has strayed from the main current (1944b:66–7). Thus the maturity that results in the classic text is not necessarily the element needed for the text gaining Eliot's ultimate approval.

Within the tradition of English literature, which does not include any classics itself, the classic must remain a role model, since the degree of maturity required to bring a literary classic into being is the reflection of an ideal state of affairs, spreading out on all levels in a society. The cultural climate required for the classic, which anyway can always be spotted only in retrospect (1944b:116), seems to be identical with the climate that fosters works characterized by a unified sensibility, the literature of and for the whole man, as the expression of what in another context Eliot describes felicitously as the 'substratum of collective temperament' (1939:18). But if the Augustan age came close to being a classical period, and if the conditions prevailing in an age of unified sensibility are identical with those of the classical period, what prevents Eliot from pronouncing the seventeenth century – the age of the Metaphysical Poets – the great classical age in English literary history? Eliot never answers this question, but perhaps the nature of the society at the time appeared too heterogeneous to satisfy Eliot's stern demands.

Eliot's construction of the classic and its material conditions in a well-balanced and harmonious society is wide open to the kind of critique that sees the concept of an ethos or *Zeitgeist* as just a convenient tag with which to characterize a period in the history of a nation. At the time of Virgil, for instance, did the harmony and balance include the slaves and other underprivileged groups? Was the Latin of Virgil the common style? And so on. But, historically simple, the more severe lack in Eliot's position is surely to do with the vagueness of his critical categories, especially those concerning evaluation. Then again, it must be borne in mind that Eliot never advertised himself as a system-builder, but as a critic always making his point of departure the specific problem originating in the concrete text. The classical is a quality of some texts with an obvious affinity to texts from an era with certain overall characteristics the application of which simply do not make sense in the case of English seventeenth-century poetry.

LITERATURE, EDUCATION AND SOCIETY

Eliot's canonical efforts have as their *terminus a quo* and *terminus ad quem* something vaguely called 'culture'. The existence and nature of this something is taken for granted in Eliot's early criticism as a quality of life shared by the audience addressed by the critic. It is only later, and in close connection with his personally motivated acceptance of authority in matters sacred and profane, that culture is brought into focus for explicit definition and discussion in relation to literary value, and hence to the canonical.

Eliot's extended writings on culture were published within the rough span of a decade from the date of his essays on minor poetry and the classic (both from 1944). From 1939 is *The Idea of a Christian Society*, from 1948 *Notes Towards the Definition of Culture*, and from 1950 'The Aims of Education'. That the topics of the three are insolubly interrelated with the canonical is the argument of the following.

One looks in vain for a central definition of culture in Eliot's writings, just as is the case with 'tradition'. The concept is presented cautiously in a general way. Surely, the list of human activities compiled in a deliberately heterogeneous manner in the first chapter of *Notes Towards the Definition of Culture* – from Derby Day to the music of Elgar (1948:31), elsewhere defined as a 'way of life' (1948:41) – is much too inclusive to provide the basis for the kind of reflections presented in that volume. The list seems to be identical with the totality of life defined as cultures observed by the bacteriologist or the agriculturalist (1948:21), but which Eliot sees as qualitatively different from what is meant by human culture. Also in *Notes* Eliot goes on to imply, in a way associated with the schoolmaster's attitude, that human culture has to do with the *improvement* of the mind and spirit (1948:21), but admittedly in a way given to much debate. Closer to what is in focus in his reflections, Eliot launches the rather facile description of culture as 'that which makes life worth living' (1948:27), which is, if not in contrast to the all-inclusive list, then at least representative of those activities which have only a definite aesthetic dimension. However, it is this definition which has its counterpart in the negative description of religion as that which 'protects the mass of humanity from boredom and despair' (1948:34). Obviously, culture is not something to be listed as a set of activities, but as a deliberately vaguely defined attitude towards existence phenomenologically reflected in a certain aesthetizing of objects and activities.

To Eliot there is no such thing as culture without religion. The two exist in a complementary relationship, the supremacy of either depending on perspective of approach (1948:15), but on the whole with religion as the more important of the two.[14] Complementarity must here be understood in the sense given to it in modern physics (cf. Bohr) as manner of appearance depending on manner of observation. At times culture will appear as religion, if that is the slanting of the angle of observation, and sometimes religion will appear as culture. The precise nature of the interrelationship between the two is perhaps best illustrated in Eliot's suggestion of culture being the *incarnation* (1939:33) of religion, which provides the *framework* (1939:33) of culture. By using these metaphors Eliot attempts to resist descriptions of the interrelationship by terms such as 'relation' or 'identification' (1939:33), which lend a wrong perspective to the mode of co-existence between the two.

Although this emphasis on the significance of religion for culture, and vice versa, is not made explicit until his later writings, opening up his literary criticism to the broader scope of cultural criticism, the interrelationship was latent in the early literary criticism aiming at a narrower field of cultural activity.

A properly unified sensibility cannot exist without religion, and for literature to thrive and criticism to work at its best, there must be an ethical framework different from and of a 'higher' category than both.[15] The time of its incipient dissociation around the time of the Civil War was one of great spiritual turbulence. The troubled Reformation during the reigns of Henry VIII, Edward VI and Mary came to a rest in the Elizabethan settlement, inclining however so much to the Catholic side that the ground was paved for a more permanent schism between a right and a left wing in English church life. Cromwell's political cause lost after the Interregnum and the Restoration; his spiritual crusade in the interest of radical theology found sympathy with the rising trading and industrial middle class, but paradoxically as the social acceptance of mostly secular activities. In other words, the effects of the Reformation in England, as elsewhere but much more prominently in the emerging workshop of the world, meant a bifurcation into the spiritual and the mundane, with the latter proving capable very soon of doing very well on its own. The real catholicity of the early seventeenth-century poets praised by Eliot for their united sensibilities, in spite of professed formal loyalty to the established Church of England as a reformed church, made them, as it were, differ in kind as to cognitive premises from the poets who came after.

On closer examination the critical concept of the objective correlative also gains added significance against a background generally religious, and specifically Catholic-Christian. To suggest a resemblance to the principle of transsubstantion seems somewhat far-fetched, and indeed *is* so as long as we consider the liturgical business of the implications of the celebration of the Lord's Supper. But when we concentrate on the communicational aspect of the process in perspective of the metaphorics involved, there is a striking similarity between the change of the wine and bread into the blood and body of Christ and the change of the metaphor into the original sense experience that prompted the writing of the poem in the first place.[16]

Despite Eliot's turning to religion there is no indication of any Arnoldian substitution of the religious by the literary or cultural.[17] On the contrary, Eliot wished to maintain the complementarity – in terms of incarnation and framework respectively – of the two. When it comes to the organization of the two activities, there is, however, a certain structural similarity in that the proper cultivation of either area of activity calls for the presence of an aristocracy or elite of devotees.

Eliot bases his conviction of the need for a graded society, in which certain groups take care of the well-being of cultural and religious activities, on his analysis of history in this respect. He thus makes it clear that historical experience shows that without the presence of such groupings the production of a higher civilization will be unlikely (1948:49). Eliot's distrust of an egalitarian or democratic society to function optimally in matters cultural and religious is likewise based on his observation and subsequent interpretation of historical evidence.

It follows from this that the guardians of culture and religion will see the need for education to this desired state of affairs to continue [18] – not, however, a kind of education which hands on uncritically received wisdom, which would be empty instruction only. Proper education is the training of pupils to acquire the taste by which they can be relied on to recognize inherited and traditional quality and welcome the new with a properly honed critical awareness. There is thus a nexus between culture and education in the appropriation of culture through canonical texts, first and foremost literary ones.

CULTURE

To Eliot a highly developed culture is a culture in which all cultural activities can be seen in various ways and to various extents to share in a broadly accepted universe of values. This makes Eliot's use of 'culture' something very concrete, with the shrine of worship to be situated firmly in time and place, but at the same time allowing for great variety when it comes to the practices of the culture in question. Eliot centres his thoughts on Western civilization (culture) and Christianity (religion) in general and on English civilization and Anglican Christianity in particular.[19] This focus is not a deprecation of other cultures and religions, but a matter of practical convenience, simply. Nor is it his aim to devise any blueprint for any ideal culture/civilization, but merely to try and define and 'rescue' (1939:17) the word culture from abuse.

Eliot's view of culture at its optimal functioning reflects his view of the interrelationship of culture and religion as a nexus of complementarity. But that nexus, as indicated by the adoption of the metaphors of 'incarnation' and 'framework', is constituted by a relationship of regulations or priorities in terms of a graded society. It would be a mistake, however, to see this system of regulations as a normative system. On the contrary, Eliot is at pains to emphasize the organic growth, the 'hereditary transmission' (1948:15), of a culture or civilization given the presence of thriving local cultures and the framework of religion. A culture comes into being when a great variety of cultural activities, pursued each according to its own generally accepted tradition, can be seen to melt together under a highest common denominator. The impetus must always be from bottom to top, as it were, because culture is never the enforced fulfilling of deliberate aims (1948:19), but a situation felt to be natural by those living in it as the very foundation of our cultural life.[20] Instead of furnishing the reader with a list of cultural goals, the imposition of which would be the very negation of the organic nature of culture, Eliot lists what he considers the necessary elements of any thriving culture or civilization, 'in the absence of which no higher culture can be expected' (1948:19). But at the same time as culture should emerge as naturally as leaves on a tree, by avoiding universalized planning, only ascertaining the limits of the plannable (1948:109), Eliot's terminology betrays the implication of a degree of voluntary awareness in the process of reaching a satisfactory cultural level. In connection with the distinction between the application of 'culture' to the individual, the group and to society as a whole, he writes about *'the conscious aim to achieve culture'* (1948:21; Eliot's italics). When writing about cultural hegemony in the meeting of 'races', Eliot is clearly aware of the possibility of imposing culture deliberately (1948:27). And in connection with reflections on the interrelationship between culture and religion, Eliot notes that neither is something possessed by a group, but something for which they strive (1948:31).

As it would be a mistake to consider Eliot a spokesman for any normative view of culture, it would likewise be a mistake to attribute to him a *laissez-faire* attitude. In terms of political philosophy his platform is that of a liberal Burkeian, with a discreet debt to Lockeian contract-thinking. The organicism which Eliot sees at the very core of any true culture is not a wild and uncontrolled growth in all directions, but a development which constantly pays tribute to tradition. The sense of tradition – not *a* but *the* tradition – is at the very centre of Eliot's conception of culture. Indeed, without it there would be no point of reference, because none of his 'important conditions for culture' (1948:15) – organic structure, segmentability into local cultures, and 'balance of unity and diversity in religion' (1948:15)[21] – can be present without either a deliberately applied programme or some sort of generally recognized guideline. As the former is ruled out as neither possible nor desirable, the alternative remains. For all his cautiously urbane reservations about any normative measures, Eliot comes out a benevolent and gentle but nonetheless unwavering conservative traditionalist, a position which emerges from his detailed discussion of the *sine qua non*s of culture.

The three levels of culture recognised by Eliot as culture on the personal, group and society levels, with the latter level as the dominant (1948:21), exist as so many dynamics leading on to the regulations or practices set up by the next step on the ladder, just as the culture of any time and place is practised with proper adherence to a cultural tradition, and just as that cultural tradition is the 'incarnation' of – or taking place within the 'framework' of – religion. Authority based on tradition hence assumes pride of place, and against this background it is hardly surprising that Eliot considers that a culture functions happily only when it is regulated accordingly.

A good way to illustrate the relationship between the static and the dynamic in Eliot's cultural criticism is to compare with the pre-Enlightenment cosmology described in, for instance, Tillyard's *The Elizabethan World Picture*. The point about such a cosmology is not its stasis as the overall principle, but that the stasis is the appearance of a hierarchy, the individual elements of which function as do sea waves. What seems to be the rolling ashore from a point on the horizon of water brought in from afar is really a repetitive and cyclical movement of minuscule water particles remaining in place despite the impression of forward movement. In the same way, in Eliot's view, the thrust of the cultural 'wave', of any thriving culture depends on the circumscribed dynamic of the single elements, each within its proper sphere.

To combine the static and the dynamic in this way is compatible with the essentially feudal nature of Burke's analysis and defence of the conservative society and with the acceptance of the seemingly paradoxical state of free will in a Christian context, two points of orientation fully commensurable with Eliot's mature position on politics and religion. If it is somewhat difficult to determine the stage in the progress of a culture from the balance of the static and the dynamic, the presence of scepticism is a sure sign of a developed situation (1948:29). Scepticism is the capability of contemplating cultural activities with a view to decision-making. A culture or civilization sceptical of its own doings will prevent itself from making rash decisions. A highly developed culture will be characterized by the routine of reconsideration, and it will audit its cultural accounts so as to remain highly developed.

The status and function of the group are essential for Eliot's analysis of the conditions for a flourishing culture. On the one hand the group is relative to society, from whose cultural traditions and norms it receives a flexible framework within which to pursue its own interests and activities. On the other it is relative to the individuals of which it consists, the level on which concepts of culture are concretized. To Eliot the cultured person is one capable of taking in and giving expression to culture in general, a person educated and affected by a generally cultural environment, in other words a person with a unified sensibility. Of the society of culture the same can be said: such a society exhibits the possession of culture in a non-specialist sense.

Cultural groups are distinct units within society with a certain role, even responsibility, as those who carry on and adapt traditions of culture. The culture of the group will tend towards specialization, with either ossification and/or cultural bifurcation (1948:26) as possible consequences, at the ever-present risk of cultural disintegration.

Eliot suggests that as the consequence of the growing complexity of society 'we may expect the emergence of several cultural levels; in short, the culture of the class or group will present itself' (1948:25). The class and the group, however, are not identical, although they may be. The former is social class in the conventional sense of the term, whereas in Eliot's usage the latter means social formation defined by cultural characteristics, aspirations, and so on.

The organicism which Eliot considers of primary importance as a condition for a higher culture to emerge (1948:15) is a function of the way a given society diversifies into cultural groups, each with a distinct function in relation to the whole (1948:35). It is important to note that the interaction of all these groups, irrespective of relation to class, is necessary for the general culture of the society to thrive.

If the analysis of class can be said to represent a vertical section of society at any time, the analysis of geography represents the corresponding horizontal section, with the concept of the cultural group applicable to both axes. A third axis is provided by the religious dimension.

Whereas Eliot tends towards a certain circumspection in the case of class, very likely because of the political sensitivity of the subject, reflections on geographical grouping lend themselves to a somewhat bolder exposition, since geographical groupings are of a much more consolidated, hence more widely accepted, nature. As in the case of class, the dynamic centre of the regional group is the family, attachment to which commands local loyalty (1948:52). The national culture as a whole consists, in the geographical dimension, of local cultures, each with their own characteristics, yet sufficiently alike to provide the constellation that results in a national unity. The national culture is no more or less than the aggregate of the local cultures, whose constant friction with each other is the organic dynamism.[22] With his introduction of the concept of productive friction in connection with geographical groupings Eliot makes clear the principle latent but never enunciated in his discussion of class, and which counterbalances the situation of absolute stasis otherwise indicated.[23]

Eliot's analysis of the power structure of cultured societies of the past results in the recognition of cultural elites to appear whenever a culture can be said to have reached a certain quality. A cultural elite is a cultural group with an influence greater than all other groups, in fact, recognized as dominant by the rest of society, but on a consensus rather than on an authoritorian basis.

In relation to social class, the cultural elite has always had a particularly close connection with the dominant class, which has supported and preserved (1948:42) the product and activities of the cultural elite, and 'represent[s] a more conscious culture and a greater specialisation of culture' (1948:48). In terms of individuals there has often been a certain overlap between upper social class and cultural elite, but the main distinction between the two is based on their particular functions. As the function of the dominant social class is to provide for social stability and the handing on of values – in a 'healthily *stratified* society' (1948:84; Eliot's italics) they are the political leaders as well – it is the perfect medium for the transmission of culture. As producers of culture, the cultural elite is dependent on the effort of individuals, and the construction of the elite is therefore in principle always a question of individual merit, only the permanent products of which can be made the objects of transmission.

Cultural transmission could be said to be the functional and pragmatic aspect of Eliot's concept of tradition. Approached from that angle it is possible to link the cultivation of the literary tradition with the cultivation of language. Without a living literature readers will soon be alienated from the literature of the past, since language keeps changing constantly and fast. Keeping up with the cultural heritage is a task too special and demanding for the common herd, but is, rather, for 'those few who combine an exceptional sensibility with an exceptional power over words' (1943:21). The task is really twofold, since the cultural elite will have to be able both to decide what in the past is worthy of conservation and to filter whatever seems important enough to deserve special attention in the present. For the purpose of the latter the kind of critical acumen needed is one which is in advance of contemporary fashion, because that which is readily appreciable by all does not fulfil the demand for novelty, which, together with the capacity to please, is the main general purpose of poetry (1943:18). The cultivation of poetry, which means culling the best from past and present by a discerning elite, thus escapes any accusation of ivory-tower activity by implying, as its social function, the ability 'in proportion to its excellence and vigour, [to] affect the speech and sensibility of the whole nation' (1943:22).

As the cultural elite overlaps partially with the dominant class, it also partially overlaps with what Eliot terms the 'Community of Christians' (1939:28 and 35). Whereas we would expect a generally Christian attitude and behaviour on the part of the population as a whole in the culturally mature society of the West, even if such an attitude and behaviour exist only on an unconscious level, there would have to be a high degree of Christian consciousness among those who lead the society. However, even this religious elite would not be a detached or wholly dominant priesthood, but a number of persons with a particularly acute sense of the importance of Christianity,[24] which is, anyhow, ingrained in them if they are the true transmitters of their tradition.

Eliot uses his tentative analysis of the cultural and political situation of the past as argument for the continuation of a similar state of affairs to ensure maximum culture.[25] The past, he suggests, has shown plainly the advisability of retaining a graded society in which there are strong ties between social dominance and cultural elitism. Without gradation, as in a completely egalitarian society, each cultural group would lack a sense of function, since function is essentially to do with finding a place in an already well-functioning organism. In this way Eliot comes round to a definition of true democracy as a form of aristocracy, in which the aristocracy – upper social class and cultural elite – is defined by a special social and cultural function, just as any other grouping in society, but with the burden of the sense of an extra responsibility to compensate for the extraordinary power at its disposal.[26]

Eliot's ideal society, modelled on his analysis of the past, is thus a hierarchical construction, in which social and cultural functions are handed down from one generation to another, with the family as the most expedient unit (1948:43), so that 'each individual would inherit greater or less responsibility towards the commonwealth, according to the position in society which he inherited' (1948:48). An egalitarian society would, in contrast, 'be oppressive for the conscientious and licentious for the rest' (1948:48).

RELIGION

In the compositional structure of *Notes Towards the Definition of Culture* religion is a cultural phenomenon integrated with class and regionalism, the third dimension in a system of cultural values, different in substance from both but like the two others in the way that it may be approached as unity made up of variety, its dynamism growing out of the friction between differing but not mutually exclusive emphases of attitude.

Christianity is central to Eliot's reflections on the interrelationship between culture and religion. This is not only because of his personal familiarity with Christianity, but also because it presents a religious urge sustained for a very long time accompanying the civilization arising out of Graeco-Roman culture and proven as capable of accommodating the variety within unity which Eliot sees as the ideal religious-cultural situation.

The viability of Christianity has been a matter of always striking a balance between central issues and their interpretation and application by various groupings. Christianity has been capable of sticking to a 'core curriculum' while at the same time accommodating fractionality and special emphases. The strength of what Eliot notes as 'the Faith' (1948:29) is exactly this capability of compromising while never letting go of vital points. But for culture and religion to coexist in a mutually beneficent manner is a question of maintaining complementarity and balance. If there is a wide chasm between the two, neither can achieve their potential, and if there is identity between them, inferiority is likewise the outcome (1948:31).

So far there is structural identity between religion, class and region, but clearly Eliot gives a cognitive status to religion which imposes a balance with religion on the one hand and culture, that is cultural groupings within class and region, on the other. And it is clearly stated that in the final analysis, religion is that aspect of existence towards which everything resorts: 'religion, just because it comprehends everything, cannot be compared with anything' (1950:115).

In an anthropological perspective, Eliot distinguishes between stages of poorly and highly developed societies. In the former there is no distinction between the religious and the cultural, and consequently the religious could be said to occupy a place in the unconscious, which makes of it an existential premise taken for granted and which it would make no sense to problematize. In more highly developed societies a distinction between the two makes itself increasingly felt, to the extent that the sign of the high development of a society as a whole is the introduction of a complex of religious scepticism, by which religion and culture may indeed be put in contrast to each other.[27] In the individual human being this phylogenetic development is experienced as a parallel process, ontogenetically as a growth process from child into adult. But in the adult the two stages exist simultaneously, so that the development from lower to higher cannot really be said to be a growing out of one stage and into another but the formation of a complementarity. This is the 'contradictory proposition' with which Eliot approaches religion.

The contradictory nature of the religious coexisting as both unreflected instinct and reflected scepticism is, in Eliot's view, a fact or a premise to be accepted and to be seen as one axis in the system of balances of which a higher culture or civilization consists. Eliot's 'higher religions', although they may seem so, are not really different from the lower, but have absorbed the lower stage.[28] Thus the higher religions by their very definition of being 'high' are more universal than the lower.

Universality could be said to be the hidden agenda in Eliot's reflections on religion, and this is the domain where we begin to see both the qualitative difference between culture as made up of groupings within class, region and religion, and the superiority of the religious over the cultural.

Along with the premise of the lower absorbed into the higher religion goes the proposition that the religions able to stimulate culture optimally are the more universal. Seen against the broad canvas of history the universal religion of Europe, and hence of Western civilization, has been that of the Church of Rome, with the Latin culture as its mirror. In this perspective the Protestant secession of Northern Europe can only be seen as a development of a religious sub-culture, which has set itself up in different varieties as the main religious cultures in individual nation-states. Depending on perspective the Protestant ramification of Anglicanism is a Catholic sub-sub-culture, along with the English free or lower Church, or an English main culture.

Eliot is clearly attracted to the long view of history, on which his whole argument is pivoted. While maintaining the desirability of the 'constant struggle between the centripetal and the centrifugal forces' (1948:82) to avoid either the deliquescence of freedom or the petrification of strict order (1948:81), the intellectual and emotional pull, as is evidenced in many cases of conversion, is 'towards the more Catholic type of worship and doctrine' (1948:80).[29] Just as the shrine of culture is kept and transmitted down the ages by a cultural elite more or less identical with the families of a dominant class, the Mother Church is the best guardian of religious values:

> Not only is it the main religious body which has the more elaborated theology; it is the main religious body which is the least alienated from the best intellectual and artistic activity of its time (1948:80).[30]

Eliot's views on the ideal distribution of responsibility and dominance in a truly cultured civilization could be construed to mean the erection of a theodicy. This, of course, would be to misinterpret the general drift of Eliot's argument, with its emphasis on complementarity, checks and balances. For a culture to be Christian requires the formation of a body politic in sympathy with the main, that is catholic, tenets of the Christian religion, without, however, conforming with any particular Christian sect or cult (1939:12). In modern Western culture there is such catholic foundation (1939:13), although not in any way put to its optimal potential.

EDUCATION

Eliot's views on education, actual and ideal, follow from his analysis of society in terms of culture and religion. Using three categories from a treatise on education by C.E.M. Joad (1948:97 ff. and 1950) as his point of departure, the discussion is conducted within a framework of education seen as vocational, as training towards citizenship in a democracy, and as general personal *Bildung*.

As the term education is presently used, Eliot is of the opinion that it signals a society disintegrated to such a degree that it can only be held together by the belief in the possibility for everyone to be educated to a standard desired as some kind of common denominator (1948:105). Eliot draws the conclusion that this will result in 'education' becoming an abstraction instead of constituting the elements necessary to 'form the good individual in a good society' (1948:105–6). The risk, however, seems to be rather in the automatic lowering of standards to a situation where the current demand for education will always be of the vocational type, that is the education needed at any time for society to function in a short-term perspective.

It comes as no surprise, either, that Eliot is deeply distrustful of the second, for the reason of the inevitably insufficient definition of 'democracy'. His analysis of the necessary conditions for a culture to thrive places the family at the centre of a dynamic centred on a need for the maintaining of stratification and for its undisturbed transmission down the generations. If the family is to remain the culture-transmitting unit, there is no possibility for the 'dogma of equal opportunity' (1948:103) to apply itself, since it would require the complete doing away with all such stratification and transmission. Democracy in the sense of a completely levelled society is the very contradiction of what Eliot sees as the condition *sine qua non* of the culturally vital society. The opposite of a democracy is a totalitarian society. Totalitarianism is not, however, a negative thing *per se*, but because such a thing as a perfect totalitarism is simply unattainable: 'for total rule means that somebody is in control of affairs about some of which he is totally incompetent' (1950:86). The incompetence on the part of rulers in various important aspects makes autonomy within the areas of art and science desirable because necessary. So when Eliot suggests that it is not a 'democracy when a symphony can be deviationist, or a melancholy poem about an unhappy love affair defeatist and decadent, or a biological theory subversive' (1950:86), this is grounded on pragmatism rather than on idealism. One may imagine a totalitarian society happily being governed by a perfectly enlightened despot deserving the name of democracy, and applauded by Eliot.

In order to avoid education as just the 'acquisition of information, technical competence, or superficial culture' (1939:75), there must, in the first place, be a consensus about the 'criteria and values' (1939:75) upon which a society better than the one in existence is to be built. Although Eliot hesitates to present a positive list of such criteria and values, they emerge from his considerations of religion and culture, and can be constructed accordingly.

There would be the need for a foundation in Christianity, and in the Catholic mainstream that forms the backbone of Western civilization, since this is our cultural heritage, like it or not. This does not mean the imposition of any one particular Christian creed on the individual, but would mean for society to 'primarily train people to be able to think in Christian categories' (1939:28), with 'its aims directed by a Christian philosophy of life' (1939:37).

The purpose of education should be to enable the individual to acquire wisdom and knowledge and to treat learning with respect (1948:99). This is a purpose which can be fulfilled only if the conditions for learning allow for their individual pursuit, which is a question of the ways, physical and mental, that we accommodate for education. But Eliot is no advocate of a completely free and unrestrained pursuit of any kind of knowledge. It must always be the kind of knowledge deemed valuable enough to be the cultural tradition of which the learner is part, *in casu* Christian culture, with its assimilation of pre-Christian culture. When Eliot mentions the need for the budding politician to acquaint himself with Greek political history (1948:88), this is not meant as a recommendation from a how-to-do-it manual for the potential politician, but as the urging of those setting out to direct the lives of their fellow human beings to familiarize themselves thoroughly with a tradition of thought and action, the effects of which are still with us as elements of a much larger cultural complex. And this is complemented by the recommendation to retain a central interest in the Greek classics in education (cf. 'Modern Education and the Classics' from 1933), and to focus on the commonsense Greek tradition in philosophy (cf. 'Francis Herbert Bradley' from 1936:60).

Eliot is aware that a certain levelling of society has taken place since the beginning of the twentieth century. Actually, this awareness is what has prompted his considerations. His advice to retain stasis and stratification should be seen against that background. When Eliot states as the goal of education that it 'should help to preserve the class and to select the élite' (1948:100), he compromises with his sense of the necessary cultural values and the realization of a major social upheaval. In the lower-middle-class society of the future there is the material that makes the 'training of an élite of thought, conduct and taste' (1939:77) possible, indeed necessary.[31] The chief principle, however, is for the social classes and cultural groupings to stay in their given places, and for this purpose it is necessary to observe that '[t]oo much education, like too little education, can produce unhappiness' (1948:100). Eliot allows for a degree of upward cultural mobility, as implied in his distinction between social class and cultural elite (cf. above), without prejudicing the need for a conservative holding back when it comes to the main principles for a culture to flourish.

When Eliot observes that a 'nation's system of education is much more important than its system of government' (1939:41) he can do so, because the purpose of education is to equip the individual with the possibilities of availing himself productively of his culture's elements. To go beyond that culture is of course always possible (as Eliot's own loans in his poetry from non-Western cultures testify) but such ventures only make sense when assimilated with the inherited culture.

For the proper kind of education to be possible, that is a liberal education within the framework of a generally recognized cultural tradition correlating with a catholic religion, there must be a study environment from the earliest childhood years up to and including university that, at best, furthers this aim, and, at worst, does not prevent it from actualization. An ideal education is one that takes in all the potential influences on the growing human being, and is not restricted to 'schooling'.[32] It requires a stable consensus culture, agreed on the major principles of the values of its existence, of which schools are restricted to

transmit only a part, and they can transmit this part effectively, if the outside influences, not only of family and environment, but of work and play, of newsprint and spectacles and entertainment and sport, are in harmony with them (1948:106).

It is only natural that the ideal university education should be of a kind by which it is possible to explore the offerings of the common culture in a way whose freedom is defined only by tradition. Universities should not be

institutions for the training of an efficient bureaucracy, or for the equipping of scientists to get the better of foreign scientists; they should stand for the preservation of learning, for the pursuit of truth, and in so far as men are capable of it, the attainment of wisdom (1948:123).

And properly understood, education does not stop at university graduation. It is, in the ideal state, a way of life, a constant inquiry into the essentials of one's culture, so that, 'in the widest sense, education covers the whole of life for the whole of society' (1950:69).

CONTINUITY AND COHERENCE: CANON AND ORGANIZATION OF VALUES

Eliot's thoughts on culture and the need for education were triggered by a repeatedly articulated concern about the contemporary situation of cultural decline (e.g. 1939:19).[33] His reflections on culture in terms of social and ecclesiastical gradation and hierarchy are what have sometimes given a bad name to the later Eliot as arch-conservative. It must be borne in mind, however, that Eliot is not attempting to devise a cultural system in any absolutist way, but is trying to find out what makes a well-functioning culture tick. It is especially important to recognize this avowed goal when considering his thoughts on the need for a culturally – and religiously – graded society led by sufficiently educated elites to provide the continuous conditions for a highly developed culture or civilization.

Eliot's diagnosis of a general cultural decline in England particularly, and in the West generally, is based on his observation of two aspects of modernity separate at one level but identical at another. One is the increasing levelling in the political arena, resulting in the increasing influence of lower-middle-class values everywhere. The other is the tendency for society to become a mass society organized for profit only (1939: 39–40).[34] Eliot is worried about both developments, but to a certain extent fails to grasp the interaction of the two, and at no point does he attempt an analysis of modernity as whole, but confines himself to generalizations like, for instance, 'For one of the things that one can say about the modern mind is that it comprehends every extreme and degree of opinion' (1933c:124).

Put radically, Eliot's collected poetical and critical efforts, all of them bred by modernity, could be said to be the paradoxical setting up of a bulwark against that very modernity. However, Eliot is not reactionary in the sense of advocating a return to the social life and cultural mores of an earlier epoch. On the contrary, he keeps warning against this as a fallacy.[35] Rather, the mobilization of a worthwhile social and cultural set of values is a question of a constant awareness of the long-term development of a congenial culture. In practical terms this means sifting the chaff from the grain in the cultural heritage. And this, in turn, means the presence of a set of values that makes such sifting possible.

The interdependence of a sense of a mainstream cultural tradition and of a set of values producing the tradition is crucial in Eliot's literary and cultural criticism. In terms of literary history the period before the onset of the dissociated sensibility shows how the interdependence works in practice, and by negative deduction it is possible to make it apply to the time after. In terms of literary theory, the concept of the objective correlative could be construed as the metaphor for this interdependence in so far as it is the adequate verbal response to a situation, catching only those implications of the situation that merit transmission in the linguistic 'concrete universal', to borrow W.K. Wimsatt's precise phrase, which is made accessible to the public.

The response to a situation by encoding it into an objective correlative is in no way an innocent choice of a merely decorative phrase, but a kind of positive censorship exerted by the tradition- and value-conscious mind on whatever stimuli the mind in its creative aspect is at work, the choice of which in the first place will of course also have been decided by the mind thus tuned. Therefore the poet is necessarily also a critic capable of analysis, to complement his creative synthesis.

The 'recycling-of-the-past' principle at work in Eliot's poetry is the best possible illustration of how the objective correlative bears on the tradition relating positively to a unified sensibility. It is also the best possible illustration of the need for a common background of knowledge (1939:38), which is not merely the piling up of information data, but common knowledge properly digested and absorbed by the educated individual. There are levels at which this common knowledge can be 'operative', and there must be a 'settled, though not rigid agreement as to what everyone should know to some degree' (1939:40), whereas only a minority can be expected to have the full command of all the implications of the cultural tradition. Concentrated guardianship by a select elite is desirable, indeed mandatory, for maintaining the integrity of the cultural heritage: 'For it is an essential condition of the preservation of the quality of the culture of the minority, that it should continue to be a minority culture' (1948:107). The recognition of the need for a cultural elite can be possible only by general consensus, which would imply a 'positive distinction – however undemocratic it may sound – between the educated and uneducated' (1939:40).

The object of Eliot's fear regarding general education with generally shared standards is that such standards will, in his view,

inevitably be lowered (1948:108). Eliot does not offer specific reasons for this potentially negative development, nor does he imagine the possibilities – or the demands – of a new, postmodernist
civilization existing on radically different conditions. Eliot's vision
of Hell on Earth is indeed the industrialized, *modern* society (whose
positive opposition is God's society (1939:62)), the dystopic renderings of which have become a staple in much modern art since the
triumphant early-modernist embracing of the brave new world of
technology. The contemporary culture invading domains of
ancient cultural history is anticipated with horror if the masses start
taking over and thereby destroy 'our ancient edifices to make ready
the ground upon which the barbarian nomads of the future will
encamp in their mechanised caravans' (1948:108). But it is implied
in Eliot's worrying about lowered standards that he fears the disappearance of disciplines essential to a classics-oriented education,
'our ancient edifices' (1948:108) by which the 'essentials of our
culture – of that part of which it is transmissible by education – are
transmitted' (1948:108). In Eliot's cultural criticism the fear of the
prospect of cultural levelling is axiomatic, since a ' "mass-culture"
will always be a substitute culture' (1948:107).

With the acceptance of cultural – and, on a parallel line, ecclesiastical – guardianship by an elite, with general consent on the advisability of the sufficiency of stratified education, and with a state of
stability in all matters political and economic, there will be that
uniformity of culture which will secure 'continuity and coherence
in literature and the arts' (1939:40).

In the perspective of history, Eliot's criticism in general and the
extent to which it enters on the grounds of the canonical, was an
attempt to cast off the yoke of a Romanticism which had outgrown
itself. As critic and poet he also needed a poetics in terms of which
his own kind of poetry, triggered by the very same reaction to the
poetic climate of the time, could be explained and justified. But
despite his negative attitude to Romanticism, there is in his advocacy of a kind of culture in which all efforts are directed towards a
unified sensibility, a Romantic longing for the experience of whole-
ness. Only Eliot saw this to have happened in English history more
than a hundred years before the beginning of the period to which
we usually attach the tag of Romanticism.

In the perspective of the non-historical, the canonical in Eliot's
criticism cannot be separated from issues of authority. Eliot never
exhorts students of literature to explore new territories by them-

selves. To the degree that such new territories, new literature that is, should be evaluated, it can only be done very tentatively, and only by those who have the proper insight. Novices in literature had better be guided by proven authority, and told to find the values and enjoyment that others have found in literature worth preserving. Now, Eliot never appears as the stern and unrelenting dictator in aesthetic matters. Rather, he is the mild tutor willing to be engaged in controversial discussion – as long as it is certain that his views will prevail generally.

Eliot's canonical stance can be explained by reference both to the cultural circumstances of the time when he made his mark, and to his personal history, which is very much one of explaining the activities of the crucial, creative years with recourse to larger contexts of culture. If authority is the core concept in Eliot's canonical criticism, it is an authority that necessitates common consent and willingness to be led by one's betters – it is Lockian not Hobbesian. But the atmosphere of the tutorial, which Eliot tries to apply to the whole of society, is hardly likely to succeed in the civilization he so expertly portrayed in *The Waste Land*.

4

F. R. Leavis:
Elitist in Pursuit of
Common Values

[W]e want to produce a mind that knows what precision and specialist knowledge are, is aware of the kinds not in its own possession that are necessary, has a maturity of outlook such as the study of history ought to produce but even the general historian by profession doesn't always exhibit, and has been trained in a kind of thinking, a scrupulously sensitive yet enterprising use of intelligence, that is of its nature not specialized but cannot be expected without special training – a mind, energetic and resourceful, that will apply itself to the problems of civilization, and eagerly continue to improve its equipment and explore fresh approaches (Leavis 1943:58-9).

And another critic of importance, Dr. F. R. Leavis, who may be called the Critic as Moralist? (Eliot 1961:13)

The critical-historical tradition usually makes T. S. Eliot the spiritual leader of Anglo-American modernism, with F. R. Leavis his most prominent disciple and missionary, eager, as disciples usually are, to propagate the master's doctrine at its purest, most radical and least compromising.

Leavis, admittedly, did much to pave the way for Eliot's tradition-problematizing poetry and early criticism. Had Eliot not decided to embrace a High Tory tradition in religion and politics in his early middle age, there would perhaps have been no need for Leavis's Arnoldian crusade. As it was, Eliot, in Leavis's view, had failed as Arnold's inheritor and now it was his duty to attempt to set up a bulwark against what he saw as the levelling of values in a God-forsaken modern society increasingly vulgarized and beset by a *kitsch* culture, necessitating in response the sense of a responsible moral heritage in terms of literature; not, however, *any* kind of literature.

But apart from not being able to reconcile himself with what he saw as the master poet-critic's post-1927 apostasy, Leavis from an early date went his own ways in search of general existential values. These he saw reflected most clearly in certain literary works emerging as a canon at one and the same time idiosyncratic and expressive of a widely accepted sense of a central national cultural-literary heritage.

The many parallels in the critical thought of Eliot and Leavis are to be found in a number of shared opinions about concepts and values in literature and society as well as in a particular discursive style presupposing an aesthetic community already tuned in on the same wavelength, transmitting in a language making free use of terms such as 'fine' and 'subtle' as precise analytical descriptions.

Although Leavis's work is saturated with a concern for the cultural environment as a whole from the beginning of his teaching and publishing career with the pamphlet *Mass Civilisation and Minority Culture* (1930), the groundwork for his cultural and educational ideas and pronouncements must be sought in his literary criticism, in his main works *New Bearings in English Poetry* (1932), *Revaluation* (1936), and *The Great Tradition* (1948). The criticism in these works may be said to elaborate on points in the early pamphlet and to foreshadow the cultural criticism on a more general level in *Education and the University* (1943), *The Common Pursuit* (1952), *Two Cultures? The Significance of C. P. Snow* (1962), *English Literature in Our Time and the University* (1967), *Lectures in America* (1969), and *The Living Principle: 'English' as a Discipline of Thought* (1975). Since Leavis's later literary and cultural criticism is very much a repetition and elaboration of what is already present in his early criticism, I shall focus on the three main works from 1932, 1936 and 1948.

There is a certain irony in the fact that Leavis's enormous importance for English as a school and university subject, in England as well as abroad, is founded on relatively exclusive existential valorizations. Leavis had no inclinations towards methodical aesthetic inquiry, but took for granted a set of values and concepts which he claimed to see in the texts under his scrutiny, but which were really *a priori* and integral to a tradition involving the discerning amateur or connoisseur rather than the philosopher or scholar. A sentence like 'I do not think that I have left out much work that is important by any serious standards' (Leavis 1932:10) is quite telling in this respect. The serious standards are ones which are never fully elucidated in any methodological sense in Leavis's work, but which are nonetheless very real, because of their acceptance by a class of readers subscribing to an intuitively perceived code of existential qualities.

Intuition is a key to understanding Leavis's criticism. Leavis himself acknowledged the importance of intuitive readings. After all, the appreciation of poetic value was not to him a matter of abstract argument, but of engaging in the text at hand, without the need for any intermediary element to disturb the assumedly purely textual enjoyment. However, intuition also plays a significant role as a perceptive category by which to grasp the very preconditions of Leavis's readings.

Leavis's particular intuition determining his literary preferences becomes, on closer examination, a general intuition derived from a set of tacit assumptions about an evolutionary culture with a long history, discontinued or overshadowed in periods by revolutionary upsurges. It is a culture which is at heart conservative and rationalistic. Conservative because it preserves values proven by time and hence not subject to questioning. Rationalistic since these values are the result not of metaphysical speculations but of a trial-and-error procedure conducted through generations.

There are passages in Leavis's critical work which, read in isolation, sound as if taken from Romantic manifestos. Shelley's 'Defence of Poetry' comes to mind when reading this declaration about the nature of the poet: 'Poetry matters because of the kind of poet who is more alive than other people, more alive in his own age. He is, as it were, at the most conscious point of the race in his time' (1932:16). Or Wordsworth's and Coleridge's 'Preface' in Leavis's denunciations of the machine age and longing back for 'life rooted in the soil . . . the rhythms, sanctioned by nature and time, of rural culture' (1932:71–2). However, these passages are taken out of a context making it quite clear that Leavis's longings are for a nature not so much in the image of Romanticism's wild outdoors, but instead in neoclassicism's resort to a very much humanized version of nature.

Since to Leavis a sense of value is born out of close personal encounters with texts, there is no better way to approach Leavis's concept of the canon than to begin by looking directly at his manner of reading the literature of his preference.

New Bearings in English Poetry is an apology for Hopkins, Eliot and Pound. A courageous and distinctly minority apology at a time when the reading public, judging by print-runs, would not be likely to have subscribed to Leavis's view of the 'Georgian attempt to regenerate English poetry' as futile (1932:119). What was wrong with the poetry written by those admitted to the volumes of Edward Marsh was, according to Leavis, that these poems did not respond in their verbal texture to the age of which they were the product. They were simply not difficult enough: 'Hopkins is really difficult, and the difficulty is essential' (1932:123). Difficulty, however, phenomenologically speaking, belongs with the experience, the reception of a text, and is a matter of the reader's viewpoint and training. What is perceived as difficulty is the lack of familiarity with a linguistic-cultural code. Leavis here presupposes an in-principle uncomplicated nexus between linguistic referent and referee: the ability of language to represent a non-linguistic entity without interfering with our perception of that entity as such. The existence of this presupposition as a pivot in Leavis's whole approach is clearly seen in a statement like this about Eliot's 'Prufrock': 'We have here, in short, poetry that expresses freely a modern sensibility, the ways of feeling, the modes of experience, of one fully alive in his own age' (1932:61). The possibility of the linguistic rendering of the sensibility, ways of feeling, modes of experience of a person alive in any age is something taken more or less for granted up to the time of Saussurean linguistics, which excuses language of any responsibility for existential contribution. Leavis sees the burden of the difficulty in the condition of the 'one fully alive in his own age'. The reason why the Georgian poets are uacceptable in Leavis's view is their lack of rapport with the climate of their time. Leavis is no sociologist, nor does he even deign to consider the contemporary ethos in the manner of a Tillyard or a Willey. His preference is for the big generalizing sweep, documented time and time again in the seigniorial fashion of his critical readings. The closest we come to a description of the climate impressing the consciousnesses of modern, contemporary poets like Hopkins, Thomas, Eliot and Pound, is a passage indicating very general elements such as 'Urban conditions, a sophisticated civilization, rapid change, and the mingling of cultures' (1932:50). These are, according to Leavis, the social-political-cultural determinants of the age, determinants which in themselves are difficult to grasp and deal with. It is a negative situation, signalling a lack, an emptiness. The new determinants have 'destroyed the old rhythms and habits, and nothing adequate has taken their place' (1932:50). Leavis thus faces a dilemma: on the one hand he longs for the 'old rhythms and habits'; on the other he realizes that even a situation of modern lack and emptiness deserves a response in kind, requiring 'a sense, apparent in the serious literature of the day, that meaning and direction have vanished' (1932:50).

Leavis's dilemma is one that can never be solved. There is no way of bringing back the 'old rhythms and habits', and there is no way to modify the determinants of modernity. But there is a possibility of escaping between the horns. The lack and emptiness can be contained in the literature responding seriously to the situation, and the serious, critical preoccupation with that literature is in itself a redemptive activity.

Leavis's response to literary modernism in terms of an appreciation of the containment of admittedly negative determinants has crucial consequences for his re-creation of a literary tradition, for which the concept of 'impersonality' is the pivot.

THE IMPERSONALITY OF GREAT POETRY

Eliot's subjection of the poet's personality to the particular medium of poetry finds its explanation in the dynamics of a living tradition always available, indeed imposing itself and mingling willy-nilly into the work of any newcomer poet who has done his expected share of reading. The case of Leavis, however, is somewhat different.

The point of departure and the point of arrival in any of Leavis's critical activities, narrowly literary or broadly cultural, is man's situatedness in the contemporary, his being 'fully alive in his own age' (1932:61). Leavis makes this credo clear in *New Bearings in English Poetry*, brings it to bear on Augustan and Romantic poetry in *Revaluation* and transfers it from poetry to fiction in *The Great Tradition*.

In his assessment of contemporary modern poetry in *New Bearings in English Poetry* Leavis introduces a distinction between the (modern) world, the nature of the poet capable of dealing with it, and the poetic artefact.

As observed above, Leavis never troubles himself with systematic attempts to sort out the modern situation, but contents himself with observing that the 'process of standardization, mass-production, and levelling-down goes forward, and civilization is coming to mean a solidarity achieved by the exploration of the most readily released responses' (1932:157). Leavis certainly sympathises less with the modernist futurists praising the mass society of the machine age than with those comparing the world to a heap of broken images. Nonetheless, this heap is the inescapable condition of twentieth-century existence, and as the poet is 'at the most conscious point of the race in his time' (1932:16), it is his bounden duty to use it as his raw material. But with the capable poet as nexus, the transition from negatively-charged world to positively-charged poetry will be possible, as in the case of Eliot's *The Waste Land*, because in it a 'mind fully alive in the age compels a poetic triumph out of the peculiar difficulties facing a poet in the age' (1932:86).

The difference between the frowned-upon raw material presented by the world and the triumphant artefact of the literary work is, then, made possible by the poet's particular capability, yet, according to Leavis, untouched by his personality.

There is ample evidence in *New Bearings in English Poetry* for Leavis's view of the impersonal nature of the successful poem, compare for instance the observation on Pound's 'Hugh Selwyn Mauberley:

> One might, at the risk of impertinence, call it quintessential autobiography, taking care, however, to add that it has the impersonality of great poetry: its technical perfection means a complete detachment and control (1932:105).

The last clause gives a hint at what the impersonality is really about: technical perfection in aid of detachment and control. Ignoring the tautology of explaining impersonality by detachment we are left with technical perfection and control. A closer look at Leavis's positive evaluations of modern poetry for the elucidation of the implications of the terms may lead to a more precise appreciation of this central but generally overlooked element in his criticism. Such a precise appreciation will in turn clarify Leavis's re-creation of a valid tradition in English poetry and prose fiction.

To reach the controlled technical perfection needed for impersonality in literature it is necessary to distil from the 'world' the words adequate to that world as it appears in its essence. As the essence of the modern world is one of fragmentation, of broken images, the objective is a verbal rendering that at one and the same time recognizes and displays this state of being and signals the poet's awareness of his recognition and ability to display. It is this transformation of chaos into order that Leavis praises in Edward Thomas:

> A characteristic poem of his has the air of being a random jotting down of chance impressions and sensations, the record of a moment of relaxed and undirected consciousness. The diction and movement are those of quiet, ruminative speech. But the unobtrusive signs accumulate, and finally one is aware that the outward scene is accessory to an inner theatre (1932:55).

The theatrical metaphor with its distinction between 'outward scene' and 'inner theatre', though without any precise dramaturgical awareness, suggests exactly an ordering principle. But what is hinted at in Leavis's comments on Edward Thomas receives more accurate treatment in his discussions of Pound and Eliot.

In connection with *The Waste Land* read as an 'effort to focus an inclusive human consciousness' (1932:74), Leavis elaborates on the broken-image condition of modern life as the real-life input. Leavis's implicit starting point is here the adverse criticism with which Eliot's poem was received from traditionalist-oriented quarters, whose main point of attack was the alleged incoherence and arcane imagery of the poem. Leavis responds that the

> seeming disjointedness is intimately related to the erudition that has annoyed so many readers and to the wealth of literary borrowings and allusions. These characteristics reflect the present state of civilization. The traditions and cultures have mingled, and the historical imagination makes the past contemporary; no one tradition can digest so great a variety of materials, and the result is a break-down of forms and the irrevocable loss of that sense of absoluteness which seems necessary to a robust culture (1932:70–1).

In this information-saturated passage Leavis both manages to lament the loss of a golden age of a robust culture (whose existence anyway is open to argument and which Leavis does not really seem keen on tracing and upholding), to characterize the ills of the modern age and to prescribe one poetic remedy. If, runs his argument, the present makes impossible an approach in terms of homogeneity, heterogeneity must be contained. What the average person would present as so many loose ends, the erudite mind is capable of bringing together, with the result that some degree of homogeneity as the end poetic product is achieved. The erudition of the poet executes the necessary control, and in becoming a structural device (it fuses incommensurable elements) it turns into a technical tool for handling opposing and fragmentary existential experience.

Erudition may not be recognized as a structural-technical device of a traditional kind, although this is its function in Leavis's redemption of Eliot's poem. We are on more familiar ground with elements of versification, and Leavis is also ready to apply his concept of control here. In his criticism of Eliot's 'Portrait of a Lady' he sees a parallel in the free verse resorted to and modern spoken language: 'The utterances of the lady are in the idiom and cadence of modern speech, and they go perfectly with the movement of the verse, which, for all its freedom and variety, is nevertheless very strict and precise' (1932:62). And in Pound's portrait of Hugh Selwyn Mauberley he suggests that the poet's

> technical skill is now a matter of bringing to precise definition a
> mature and complex sensibility. The rhythms, in their apparent
> looseness and carelessness, are marvels of subtlety: 'out of key
> with his time' is being said everywhere by strict rhythmic means
> . . . The subtlety of movement is associated with subtlety of mood
> and attitude (1932:108).

On the evidence of Leavis's reasons for his positive reception of Eliot's *Waste Land* and Pound's 'Mauberley', it seems that the impersonality and detachment in question must be understood to be the stamp upon reality's raw material of an ordering and very much controlling consciousness. The impersonality and detachment must thus be seen to be situated not only in the specific cast of an individual poetic mind, but as a creative force of an intermittent nature. Leavis admits that reality provided the same kind of raw material to the Pound of the *Cantos* as it did to the poet of 'Mauberley', the difference in outcome being one of poetic 'processing:

> In so far as they [the *Cantos*] have a representative significance it
> is as reflecting the contemporary plight that has already been

discussed – the lack of form, grammar, principle, and direction. To compel significant art out of that plight needed the seriousness, the spiritual and moral intensity, and the resolute intelligence that are behind *The Waste Land*. Mr Pound's kind of seriousness is not enough (1932:117).

But if impersonality and detachment relate to poetic creativity, the nature of the poet's particular powers as the verbal redeemer of his age requires examination.

As will have emerged, we are approaching the familiar terrain of the Romantic concept of the poet: Shelley's man 'more delicately organized than other men' (Shelley 1821:254) and Coleridge's wielder of the 'secondary imagination'. The Romantic idea of the poet-genius is indeed latent in Leavis's appreciation of the modern breaking away from what he elsewhere considers the excesses of Romanticism. Eliot – and Pound in 'Mauberley' – is great because 'he was not a mere individual in isolation: he had a more important kind of originality . . . more aware of the general plight than his contemporaries, and more articulate' (1932:144). Against this background, impersonality and detachment must be reconsidered not as a creative result but as creative process; a process filtering reality in such a way that its broken images are resurrected as verbal aesthetic objects, capable of instilling intellectual satisfaction accompanied by the pleasure that the Romantics never denied as essential to art, but which is so conspicuously evaded by Leavis.

Impersonality and detachment are qualities relating to the poet's control, which in turn is a capability of response at one and the same time faithfully containing the non-verbal characteristics of the time and transforming them into verbal patterns transcending the limitations by making them into meaningful – and pleasing we may take it – verbal statements.

Central, then, to Leavis's positive evaluation of contemporary poetry is the degree to which it is able to display an educated and sensitive person's stock-taking of the world at large by a kind of verbal transformation that reflects structurally and semantically the nature of the non-verbal world. The poet exercises his control by his verbal approximation to the non-verbal reality, and the more successful this approximation, the more the poet will seem to disappear from his text, which will appear a personally unmediated but fully adequate response. This is what Leavis would have us believe. But, paradoxically given the nature of the contemporary world as a heap of broken images, the need for poetic control, indeed the poet's personal control, stands in an inverse proportion to the depersonalized and alienating world. In other words, a personal, but of course not any personal processing is called for. The difference between 'Prufrock' and the *Cantos* is a – indeed *the* – case in point.

In *New Bearings in English Poetry* Leavis attempts to canonize Hopkins, Eliot and parts of Pound. They are the modernist poets *par excellence* responding adequately to a contemporary modern sensibility in discontinuity with any earlier ethos, together representing a 'decisive reordering of the tradition of English poetry' (1932:144).

Leavis is very much aware of the presence of a major general shift of paradigm in his own time, and also of the fact that history can be seen to be a succession of such shifts with stable periods between them. To be a poet in a time of shift requires a critical as well as a poetic ability, as in the case of Eliot, who was

> more aware of the general plight than his contemporaries, and more articulate: he made himself (answering to our account of the important poet) the consciousness of his age, and he did this more effectively in that he was a critic as well as a poet. (A like alliance of creation and criticism is to be found in Wordsworth and Coleridge; indeed we may expect to find them closely associated in any period in which tradition has failed the artist and needs to be radically revised.) (1932:144–5)

According to Leavis here, literary creativity tends to run its own course of inertia, untroubled by any indications of general paradigm shifts in intellectual history. This is why the intellectual, the critic, has to be present to spot such shifts and in turn to assist the creative artist change his course accordingly. The poet-critic thus faces a double task: to create innovatively and to revise the tradition no longer adequate to the purpose.

On the question of the recurrent inadequacy of creative traditions Leavis is not quite clear. When he states that 'decisive reordering of the tradition of English poetry' is called for from time to time and that there are periods when the 'tradition has failed the artist and needs to be radically revised', we may understand it either in the sense that the revision applies to the tradition from now on, so that looking in the rear-view mirror the tradition appears as so many adjustments of the route, or we may understand it in the sense that the tradition has to be reconsidered and remoulded in the light of new needs. As with Eliot, both interpretations seem valid and mutually non-exclusive, but, and again as in Eliot's case, a certain revaluation of (literary) history is actually carried out.

THE TRADITION REVALUED

That Leavis's sense of a valid tradition is tied up closely with his notion of the impersonality and detachment resulting from the approximation of poetry to that of the prevalent real-life mores, shows clearly in his persistent dislike of Milton (cf. Eliot's similar dislike), whose cultivation of a single aspect of the possibilities of language serves a purpose quite opposite to that of approximation:

> I have in mind Milton's habit of exploiting language as a kind of musical medium outside himself, as it were. There is no pressure in his verse of any complex and varying current of feeling and sensation; the words have little substance or muscular quality: Milton is using only a small part of the resources of the English language. ... A man's most vivid and emotional and sensuous experience is inevitably bound up with the language that he actually speaks (1932:64–5).

The approximation to life as lived and its verbal transformation into poetry is here restricted to language, but the principle relating to evaluative distinctions remains identical with the principle obtaining in the case of Hopkins, Eliot and Pound versus the Georgians: that serious poetry distinguishes itself by its ability to be at one with the contemporary sensibility. Milton's deplored capacity for a 'feeling *for* words rather than a capacity for feeling *through* words' (1936:53; Leavis's italics) strikes at the very heart of being, since 'cultivating so complete and systematic a callousness to the intrinsic nature of English, Milton forfeits all possibility of subtle or delicate life in his verse' (1936:56). For all his Grand Style, Milton is out of step with what Leavis sees as the proper English use of the native language, a use that Shakespeare had an ear for: 'the use, in the essential spirit of the language, of its characteristic resources. The words seem to do what they say' (1936:58). In Milton there is no 'pressure behind the words, ... [no] tension of something precise to be defined and fixed, but a concern for mellifluousness – for liquid sequences and a pleasing opening and closing of the vowels' (1936:59). Leavis does not say so expressly, but one might imagine a period in time to which the mellifluousness would indeed have been the adequate poetic response.

Mellifluousness is not in itself the reason for downgrading Milton in comparison with, say, Shakespeare. Leavis is always concerned about the complexity of a given period, its refusal to be put into a formula. For him life is always varied, full of contradictions, and it is the duty of the poet to give expression to the variation and contradictions in his poetry. This is what produces true poetic seriousness, which includes 'among its varied and disparate tones the ludicrous, and demands, as essential to the total effect, an accompanying play of the critical intelligence' (1936:71).

Leavis's stance in *Revaluation*, to which I have turned in this section, is the application to English literary history of the discriminatory principles of *New Bearings in English Poetry*. The reordering of the eighteenth and early nineteenth centuries' poetic tradition undertaken in the later critical book logically leads up to Hopkins, Eliot and Pound, but is also to a large extent a retrospective justification of Leavis's modern preferences, a point borne out already in the earlier work: 'The way in which Hopkins uses the English language . . . contrasts him with Milton and associates him with Shakespeare' (1932:125). Nor is a canonical list missing in the earlier critical work: 'Hopkins belongs with Shakespeare, Donne, Eliot, and the later Yeats as opposed to Spenser, Milton, and Tennyson' (1932:127). It would, however, in Leavis's eyes be a false issue to try and distinguish between a diachronic and a synchronic perspective. In the case of really serious poetry the two merge. Nowhere does this come out more clearly than in Leavis's critical manifesto in the introductory pages of *Revaluation* concerning the business of the critic:

He endeavours to see the poetry of the present as the continuation and development; that is, as the decisive, the most significant, contemporary life of tradition. He endeavours, where the poetry of the past is concerned to realize the full implications of the truism that life is in the present or nowhere; it is alive in so far as it is alive for us. His aim, to offer a third proposition, is to define, and to order in terms of its own implicit organization, a kind of ideal and impersonal living memory (1936:9–10).

When we are in the company of Shakespeare, Donne, Eliot and the later Yeats, we are in the company of the truly civilized community, for which the passing of time is irrelevant, as they live only in any discerning reader's appreciation of them at any time.

A poet, then, to be part of the serious poetic community, must be a person with a particularly developed and keen sense of his time and his surroundings as complex to the point of contradiction even, and he must demonstrate his sense of the complexity in his work, that is by exerting discriminatory and ultimately unifying control. The desired goal is for the poet to lose himself as an individual in the process, so that only the controlled complexity of a given period seems to speak to the reader from the text.

Leavis's revaluation of the 'main lines of development in the English tradition . . . the essential structure' (1936:10) into a canon does not, however, entirely rest on his theory of impersonality, although it is of vital importance for his selective criteria. It is indeed possible to recognize Leavis the critic of Hopkins, Eliot and Pound in his positive comparison of Keats's 'Ode to a Nightingale' to Shelley's 'To a Skylark'. In Keats's poem he sees the 'grasp of the object, the firm sense of actuality, the character and critical intelligence implied . . . in the artist's touch and his related command of total effect' (1936:252), characteristics here described as 'sensuous' in contrast to Shelley's 'spirituality', but nonetheless of the same order as the evaluative concepts of impersonality, detachment and control applied to the more modern poets. But in addition to the element of impersonality, Leavis relies heavily on two other elements, one in the nature of methodological precondition, the other relating to Leavis's special notion of literary development.

From an early point (1932) Leavis has ruled out Spenser, Milton and Tennyson as poets central to his English tradition. The reasons have been glanced at above and can be described briefly as lack of language-and-life interaction. But in *Revaluation* Leavis introduces another reason, which has to do with his overall analytical method. Leavis claims about Tennyson and the Pre-Raphaelites that they

> do not, in fact, lend themselves readily to the critical method of this book; and that it should be so is, I will risk suggesting, a reflection upon them rather than upon the method: their verse doesn't offer, characteristically, any very interesting local life for inspection (1936:13).

Turning Leavis's argument against himself, we may suggest that reflection upon method is certainly involved here. But Leavis's inspectorial method is, of course, well suited for the local life of the poem, 'local life' understood as the poem's own – verbal – universe. We may furthermore assume that the local life is also a qualitative description bearing on the general topicality implied in the impersonality theory. For exactly this reason the tendency in late Romantic poetry, as in much Romantic poetry, is for subjects removed in time and place from the world presenting itself immediately to the poet, but which receive, at best, only mediate attention.

Leavis's reading method is, arguably, the stamp he has left on the world, known broadly as Cambridge English: a method of close reading ignoring by and large any need for philological scaffolding (Oxford English), since the poem is supposed to live in the now of the reader's experience of the text. In *Revaluation* Leavis offers a capsule definition of his reading method, which deserves quoting at length:

> But no treatment of poetry is worth much that does not keep very close to the concrete: there lies the problem of method. The only acceptable solution, it seemed to me, lay in the extension and adaptation of the method appropriate in dealing with individual poets as such. In dealing with individual poets the rule of the critic is, or should (I think) be, to work as much as possible in terms of particular analysis – analysis of poems or passages, and to say nothing that cannot be related immediately to judgements about producible texts. Observing this rule and practising this self-denial the critic limits, of course, his freedom; but there are kinds of freedom he should not aspire to, and the discipline, while not preventing his saying anything that he should in the end find himself needing to say, enables him to say it with a force of relevance and an edged economy not otherwise attainable (1936:10).

However, the method seems to be disinterested and does not *per se* rule out any critical dealings with Tennyson and the Pre-Raphaelites. The contradiction exists only in so far as we accept Leavis's methodological credo at face value. It would, however, be wrong to do so, because Leavis's ruling out of Tennyson and the Pre-Raphaelites for methodological reasons underlines the very interestedness of Leavis's particular practice of close reading. It is a reading method applicable to all kinds of text, but, like the one promoted by the contemporary Agrarian New Critics, specially designed for a definite programme of reading; in the case of the Fugitives, poetry with a heavy dose of complex metaphorics. Poetry answering to Leavis's impersonality theory, in turn means properly controlled dealings with the multi-faceted life-experience of twentieth-century modern man.

Arguably the most important single element in Leavis's canon-selection package has to do with the notion of development: 'we may say that the less important poets bear to tradition an illustrative relation, and the more important bear to it the more interesting kinds of relations: they represent significant development' (1936:11). Admittedly, Leavis here runs the risk of circular argumentation, since at one and the same time he uses 'tradition' on meta and object levels.[1] However, the commonsense drift of the argument seems to be that the poets Leavis considers important are the ones who have been able to see in and extract from the literary tradition the principles of controlled impersonality and detachment, bringing those same principles to bear on any contemporary situation, though, of course, with a difference. In his control the poet shows how he has grasped the essential ethos, but with the change necessitated by the impact of another age.

In his comment on the achievement of Dr Johnson in relation to the Augustans proper, Leavis sees development of the tradition as both continuation of the essentials and radical readjustment, a kind of 'anxiety of influence' syndrome:

> A poet of the later century would, to write successfully in the Augustan tradition, have to have a very strong positive sympathy with it – a sympathy with it as something more than a literary tradition. He would have to be both like enough Pope and, civilization having altered, unlike enough – strongly enough unlike to effect decided positive alterations in that very positive idiom. These qualifications Johnson had (1936:110).

Leavis's tradition of important English poets, then, is one selected on the grounds of accommodating Leavis's particular kind of close reading, of controlled impersonality and detachment, and of a kind of development that respects the latter and makes possible a reading at any time in the light of the former. The poetic tradition emerging is one with an intermittent chronology starting with Ben

Jonson, going on to Donne, Carew, Marvell to Pope, skipping by
and large Romanticism and late Romanticism, and taking up the
thread again in Hopkins, Eliot and Pound. The poetic tradition has
its parallel in an equally fastidious fictional line starting with
Austen, going on to Eliot, James, Conrad, and ending with Lawrence.

THE GREAT TRADITION OF ENGLISH POETRY

Leavis's sense of the viable tradition may have been felt as odd in
the contemporary critical climate, but hardly as controversial as
Eliot's with its predilection for the distinctly off-beat.

The reason for Leavis's preference for the Augustans, and a particular grouping of Augustans at that, as the hub in his tradition or
'essential structure' of English poetry, is the high degree of integration that Leavis sees in the life of the seventeenth and early eighteenth centuries; a kind of life resting on common assumptions
about culture in the broadest sense of the word; a kind of life
qualitatively distinct from the fragmented world impressing itself
on Hopkins, Eliot and Pound, when the control was really built into
the very fabric of contemporary life and did not, as in the case of the
moderns, need special care.

The best poets of the Augustan age were those who were able to
mediate the 'conventional quality of the code – it was "Reason" and
"Nature"' (1936:76) without being aware of it as convention, but as
part and parcel of their everyday life:

> they were in complete accord about fundamentals. Politeness
> was not merely superficial; it was the service of a culture and a
> civilization, and the substance and solid bases were so unde-
> niably there that there was no need to discuss them or to ask what
> was meant by 'Sense' (1936:76).

The Augustan world was a harmonious and self-contained world
evoking in the greatest poets of the age, like Pope, a 'profound
sense of it as dependent on and harmonious with an ultimate and
inclusive order' (1936:82). Leavis's description of the late seventeenth century, the Restoration period, as the age when 'civilization
was virtually inaugurated' (1936:107), is a rough and biased sketch
the validity of which Leavis's own contemporary colleagues in

history were beginning to question. This is Leavis's rather narrow view of the decades after the Civil War:

> As a result of the social and economic changes speeded up by the civil war, a metropolitan fashionable Society, compact and politically in the ascendant, found itself in charge of standards, and extremely convinced that, in the things it cared about, there were standards to be observed, models to be followed: it was anxious to be civilized on the best models. It differed from any conceivable modern fashionable society in being seriously interested in intellectual and literary fashions. Its leaders patronized the Royal Society as well as polite letters and the theatre (1936:107).

Leavis seems to be idealizing the Augustan age, even to the point of misrepresentation. The above is indeed one of the passages where Leavis's urge for some kind of transcendental universal almost spills over into purely Romantic yearnings for absolutes. It is an impression of a historical epoch which reflects the lack of a wish for more than a crude and uncritical understanding of the complexities of the culture of any age. But, then of course, Leavis's approach suffers from his methodological 'short-circuit', that is, the appreciation of whatever non-verbal facts processed into poetry is always and only taking place through that particular poetry. If Leavis sees a certain general Augustan order, it is there not least because the poetics of the age prescribed classical ideas of balance and harmony, but this is how Leavis professedly sees it:

> The development of sensibility represented by the new ideal of poetic refinement illustrates the point: the ease, elegance, and regularity favoured belong, we feel, to the realm of manners; the diction, gesture, and deportment of the verse observe a polite social code; and the address is . . . to the 'outer ear' – to an attention that expects to dwell upon the social surface (1936:107–8).

Leavis's poetic tradition is one that always – like Eliot's – exists in binary opposition to a faulty line. When Shakespeare is praised, Spenser is denounced; when Donne and the Metaphysical Poets are praised, Milton is denounced, when Wordsworth is praised, Shelley suffers, and when Hopkins, Eliot and Pound are given pride of place, Tennyson and the Victorian post-Romantics are blamed in retrospect. The serious tradition made to emerge is one of a controlled poetry of impersonality and detachment, and thus quite in accord with Eliot's unified-sensibility ideal.

Leavis does not cast his glance beyond Shakespeare in time. Perhaps because pre-Shakespearean poets pose linguistic problems which make it hard to read them 'as we read the living'. A more political element may be that Old English and Middle English poetry was felt to be too much within the domain of the detested Oxford English approach to literary studies. Leavis uses Shakespeare as a touchstone with which to detect the validity of the English language employed. The Shakespearian use of English is the 'use, in the essential spirit of the language, of its characteri- stic resources. The words seem to do what they say' (1936:58). Although not very precise, the immediate comparison with the English used by Spenser gives an idea of what Leavis is getting at: 'The consummate art of *Lycidas*, personal as it is, exhibits a use of language in the spirit of Spenser – incantatory, remote from speech' (1936:59). Whereas in Shakespeare there is 'pressure behind the words, . . . tension of something precise to be defined and fixed' (1936:59), the very opposite in the Spenser/Milton vein is an implied lack of feelings ('no pressure behind the words', etc.) resulting in a concern for 'mellifluousness – for liquid sequences and a pleasing opening and closing of the vowels' (1936:59). It is a use – and abuse – of poetic English which is seen especially in the interaction of metre and rhythm, and again here Shakespeare is held up as the prime example of how to do it properly:

> It should be plain, for instance, that subtlety of movement in English verse depends upon the play of the natural sense movement and intonation against the verse structure, and that 'natural,' here, involves a reference, more or less direct, to idiomatic speech. The development in Shakespeare can be studied as a more and more complex and subtle play of speech movement and intonation against the verse (1936:56).

At issue here in the Shakespeare versus Spenser/Milton case is what Leavis elsewhere distinguishes between as tradition versus traditionalism, the former implying tradition-revering change, the latter more or less inane imitation.

Although Leavis credits Shakespeare with the virtues of a later golden age, the great bard is not really the territory of Leavis. It is only with the Augustan age, starting with the Metaphysical Poets, that Leavis comes into his own. With Ben Jonson and Donne as heralds, the true Augustans are Carew, Marvell, and Pope.

The redemption of Ben Jonson into the 'line of wit' of truly serious poetry between Shakespeare and Romanticism is due to the recognition of Jonson partly as the opposite of a classical antiquarian, partly as a pioneer of the 'urbane, mature, and civilized' (1936:25) mode of the Augustans. Jonson managed, runs Leavis's argument, not so much to translate the classics as to resuscitate them into a new environment. Ben Jonson's 'achieved actuality' (1936:25) was possible because Ben Jonson himself was able to read the classics as moderns, with an appeal beyond their own world and time:

> In it the English poet, who remains not the less English and of his own time, enters into an ideal community, conceived of as something with which contemporary life and manners may and should have close relations (1936:25).

Leavis is quite aware that Jonson's intermittent robustness – his 'native good sense' (1936:29) – may not always live up to an ideal of Augustan urbanity, but the 'impersonality and poise that we feel to be the finest fruit of his Latin studies' (1936:29), is what made Ben Jonson into the genius who 'initiated the tradition, the common heritage' (1936:30) of English poetry at its best.

Again in the case of Donne, Leavis renounces critical methodology to burst out in admiration based on the reader's intuition:

> The extraordinary force of originality that made Donne so potent an influence in the seventeenth century makes him now at once for us, without his being the less felt as of his period, contemporary – obviously a living poet in the most important sense. And it is not any eccentricity or defiant audacity that makes the effect so immediate, but rather an irresistible rightness (1936:18).

And there follows an appreciation of the music in Donne's poetry, his ability to pack his verse with a finely attuned verbal reponse to his time and age, a response remarkable for its 'mimetic flexibility' (1936:20), which allows language to move from the highest things to the crudest levity. Donne was a man of his times, a prelate in constant temptation of the secular, at the dawn of the secular modernity in which Leavis sees many faults and unfortunate developments, but which is nonetheless the basis on which modern man must build his response to the world in which he has become the very centre.

Despite Leavis's assertion of the outstanding line of wit with the central figures of Carew, Marvell and Pope, the attention actually given to Carew and Marvell is slight in comparison with the attention devoted to the negative criticism of Milton at the one end of the period and Shelley at the other. The 'urbane grace' (1936:35) of Carew is compared favourably with Waller's 'suave refinement of the polite mode . . . something less fine and sensitive' (1936:35), and Marvell in his 'Dialogue between the Resolved Soul and Created Pleasure' is found to compare equally favourably with Milton's *Comus*, since in Marvell's poem we find that 'his seriousness is the finer wisdom of a ripe civilization' (1936:33).

Alexander Pope, who finishes the line of wit, achieves his prominent status because of his ability to respond in kind to his particular age as a 'complete Augustan, realizing in his poetry the strength of that actual concentrated civilization immediately around him' (1936:37) at the same time as he is able to carry on the best of the previous age achieving a 'strength so closely related to Marvell's' (1936:37). And that strength is a matter of retaining an 'essential element of the Metaphysical' (1936:109). The combination in Pope of the pressures of his own time with the best of the achievement of an earlier age is a lesson in what Leavis means by tradition: a capability to sort out from the past not a particular linguistic turn of phrase but to spot in the forebears the points where they are able to crystallize the essentials of their age. This is what Ben Jonson could see in the classics and was able to retrieve and hand on to his Elizabethan and early Stuart fellow poets, and this is what Pope could take over from them. A constant harvest of the vitality of periods in civilization characterized, according to Leavis, by a very high degree of social and cultural integrity.

That the ideal of Augustan – Roman and English – *civitas* is at the very centre of Leavis's construction of the poetic tradition is seen plainly in his efforts to redeem Dr Johnson and Wordsworth.

The trouble with Johnson is obviously in his attitude of moralizing. In Leavis's perspective explicit moralizing is very much something external to the poetic statement, a message superimposed but not integrated, since really great poetry would have to build the moralizing into its very texture. Johnson found himself living at a time of yet another great social upheaval and accompanying cultural transition. For a poet to carry on the values of the

Augustan tradition – valuable *per se* – he would 'have to have a very strong positive sympathy with it – a sympathy with it as something more than a literary tradition' (1936:110). We are here again at the core of Leavis's sense of tradition as something extra-literary as well as literary (a word, incidentally, which here and elsewhere in Leavis is not meant as a positive epithet). There must be in such a poet the ability to penetrate to the essential response qualities in his predecessors so as to carry on a spirit, not a convention:

> He would have to be both like enough Pope and, civilization having altered, unlike enough – strongly enough unlike to effect decided positive alterations in that very positive idiom. These qualifications Johnson had (1936:110).

Johnson's strength is in this sense the public commitment which was part and parcel of the sentiment of the earlier age, but which must now be explicitly stated. In other words, as the general public of Johnson's time no longer enjoyed common values to the extent of the Augustans, his preaching is justified, because he endeavoured in his epigrammatic style to convey a 'deep moral seriousness' (1936:111).

The interdependence of a certain kind of society and a certain kind of poetry to make up a worthwhile poetic tradition ceased, according to Leavis, with the demise of the Augustan era. What he saw as a common culture of decorum and restraint throughout society was broken up in the new revolution-inclined culture of the successive era. The common cultural emphases had changed away from the conventions which tied men together in a common understanding of the world and themselves as something unified and depersonalized, but at the same time very much concrete. The Romantic emphases had to do with the exact opposite: a highly individualized and abstract view of existence, which, with Shelley as Leavis's favourite *Prügelknabe*, leads to the worst sin of all: 'weak grasp upon the actual' (1936:194).[2] But it is important to understand Leavis's position as one which goes beyond poetry to the society sustaining the poetry. Leavis accepts deploringly that 'Crabbe, however, was hardly at the fine point of consciousness in his time' (1936:122), that a shift had taken place away from an 'order that those who were most alive to the age – who had the most sensitive antennae – had ceased to find sympathetic' (1936:122). So although much could be said against this new order, and much is said by Leavis, there is no lack of ethos, as there is no lack of poetry adhering to that ethos. But the poetry is at fault, because the ethos is at fault: the poetry does not show a firm grasp upon the actual, since the actual has disappeared as a valued entity.

Nowhere else in his critical work is it clearer that Leavis's ultimate point is within the area of cultural criticism, and not restricted to poetry. His treatment of Shelley presents a parallel to his treatment of Milton, with the difference, however, that Milton is misguided, since he had access to the right kind of ethos, whereas Shelley could not help himself, so to speak.

The lamentable path from Pope to Shelley uses Wordsworth as a station. Leavis's appreciation of Wordsworth is overbearing, a kind attitude to a person who has got into trouble unintentionally. Leavis sees in Wordsworth a 'continuous development out of the eighteenth century' (1936:15) in such a way even that the poet 'illustrates a relation between thinking and feeling that invites the critic to revise the limited view of the possibilities that is got from studying the tradition of wit' (1936:15). So the case of Wordsworth is promising, because, like another late semi-Augustan, Dr Johnson, he achieves the desired impersonality ('as an essential characteristic . . . [and] unknown to Shelley' (1936:162), by 'implicit social and moral preoccupations of his self-communings in solitude' (1936:160–1). The redeeming feature in Wordsworth is this striving towards the general, the presence in the poet of the critical sense to direct the creative power (cf. 1936:155). What makes Wordsworth into a Romantic is his religious sense – shared with D. H. Lawrence – a 'mind intent always upon ultimate sanctions, and upon the living connections between man and the extra-human universe' (1936:155).

Wordsworth, then, is an intermediate figure whose attachment to his age – his inevitable closeness to the fine point of consciousness in his time – prevented his continuation of the Augustan ideals. Alas, Wordsworth was unable to appreciate his situation, and the result was accordingly regrettable:

For the sentiments and attitudes of the patriotic and Anglican Wordsworth do not come as the intimately and particularly realized experience of an unusually and finely conscious individual; they are external, general, and conventional; their quality is that of the medium they are proffered in, which is insensitively Miltonic, a medium not felt into from within as something at the nerve-tips, but handled from outside. This is to question, not their sincerity, but their value and interest; their representativeness is not of the important kind (1936:172).

In Wordsworth there is a vestige of value, though, because in his poetry the 'emotion seems to derive from what is presented' (1936:200), whereas Shelley, 'at his best, offers the emotion in itself, unattached, in the void' (1936:201). That this is so, according to Leavis, is due to fact that in Shelley's poetry the intelligence has been, 'as it were, switched off' (1936:197), with the result that 'feeling in Shelley's poetry is divorced from thought' (1936:198). Shelley's mind works in such a way that he tends to forget the tenor that led to the creation of an image as he begins to delight in the vehicle for its own sake (cf. 1936:193–4), an apt gloss on Hulme's thesis of the circumambient gas of Romanticism.

Since the 'assent given to Wordsworth's dictum has commonly been Shelleyan' (1936:196), Romantic poetry is a lost cause in Leavis's system of preferences. Although he admits to genius in Shelley's poetry, it is the strength of his weaknesses that must be recognized as his claim to canonicity. But what Leavis really deplores is what he sees as the characteristic of the age, an invitation to separate thought from feeling – Eliot's dissociated sensibility. Shelley only did his duty to the fine point of consciousness in his time, and he 'achieved memorable things in the modes of experience that were peculiarly congenial to the European mind in that phase of its history and are of permanent interest' (1936:215). Too bad that his times were awry.

It would be to misrepresent Leavis in relation to Romanticism if he is made to seem a complete enemy of all things post-Augustan. As we have seen, his attitude to Wordsworth is ambivalent, and all in all Leavis's objection is to the transcendental nature of the Romantic ethos with its poetic consequences. Apart from passages in Wordsworth, there are occasional Romantic poems which bear out the coordinated activities of the critical and the creative faculties, so that the result is a kind of poetry with a firm grasp upon the actual. This is true, for instance, of Keats's 'To Autumn,' the strength of which in comparison with Shelley's 'To a Skylark' is to be found in the 'grasp of the object, the firm sense of actuality, the character and critical intelligence implied . . . in the artist's touch and his related command of total effect' (1936:252).[3] Leavis's principle for dealing with a period in which he sees a deplorable disintegration of social

and cultural life, and a poetry that follows suit, is to renounce any
collective appreciation and turn to a scrutiny of individual works to
see if there are isolated works or passages that satisfy his ideals.[4]
But such works or passages are the exceptions in a strayed Romantic and post-Romantic tradition, or better, lack of tradition, to
which what Leavis says about Swinburne, who 'depends for his
effects upon a suspension, in the reader, of the critical intelligence'
(1936:223), applies generally.

Leavis's sense of a worthwhile poetic tradition builds on an impression of the values and mores of an age in themselves laudable.
He makes no secret of his admiration for the Augustan period, but
it is a view of a period in history which is never problematized. It
appears as an age of Enlightenment and rationalism, yet allowing
for the full play of educated humanity. What strikes Leavis as ideal
in the social and cultural life of the late seventeenth and most of the
eighteenth centuries is the extent to which there appears to have
been an intellectual consensus combined with a will to live life to
the full and a capacity to respond in kind in poetry, which in this
way retains a firm grasp upon the actual in its full and uninter-
rupted range. This ideal situation no longer obtains when the social
and cultural dimension surrenders consensus and full-range integrity. Leavis sees Romanticism as such a disintegration: intellectual
activity simply losing touch with physical reality. As an existential
approach Romanticism by its very principles is incapable of integration. The poetry written under these circumstances may still
relate faithfully to a Shelleyan sense of intellectual beauty, but
cannot escape inherent invalidity. However, there is another
possible route to failure: poetry may simply miss the point of its
time, although circumstances prove beneficial to valid poetry, since
'if the poetry and the intelligence of the age lose touch with each
other, poetry will cease to matter much, and the age will be lacking
in finer awareness' (1936:17). This was what happened in the case
of Milton. All in all the early Augustan period had the right ethos,
but Milton chose not to, or could not, see that attention to the
prevailing ethos was called for, and continued instead an outworn
tradition. Poetic failure of this kind is to be found only when the
time is right and some poets have seen the light. In the Augustan
period the line of Jonson, Carew, Marvell, Pope runs parallel to the
less serious but still more popularly acclaimed line to Pope via
Waller, Denham and Dryden. When we reach Hopkins, Eliot and
Pound, we face a situation of a shattered civilization, which does

not in itself invite integral poetic expression, but which needs the control of the poet who himself is at the fine point of consciousness of his time. Thus, over a period of more than three hundred years – from the time of Shakespeare to the introduction of modernism in literature – Leavis's tradition of serious poetry performs a cycle beginning in the natural union of a way of life and its poetry (Shakespeare's language), over an Augustan distillation of a particularly close relationship between life and certain writers, followed by the Romantic bifurcation into spiritual/poetic and physical life, back to a happy union between civilization and poetry, though this time not natural but enforced by the distinctly vatic poet.

THE GREAT TRADITION OF THE ENGLISH NOVEL

An advocate of close reading is bound to encounter difficulties when turning to the larger formats of the epic and dramatic genres. The study and appreciation of the kind of detail possible, indeed mandatory, in the smaller lyrical format hardly does justice to works extending over several hundred pages and which, as a rule, use language in a way quantitatively different from that of poetry. Practitioners of New Criticism by and large solved the problem by paying special attention to structural considerations as did Brooks, Warren and Heilman in *Understanding Fiction* and *Understanding Drama*, in an attempt to apply the tension of the metaphor into the larger structural patterns. To Leavis, however, there seems to be no such difficulty. The ideas and categories applied to poetry are carried over to the novel with only one significant change of emphasis.

Leavis's fastidious choice of a valid literary tradition in poetry has its parallel in the brief roll-call of novels making up a tradition worth talking about.[5] Jane Austen, George Eliot, Henry James, Joseph Conrad and D. H. Lawrence make up the great tradition of the English novel.[6] One should be careful here, however, not to understand the designation 'great tradition' in the sense of the greatness of the English novel tradition, but in the much more restricted and precious sense of the 'tradition to which what is great in English fiction belongs' (1948:16). In other words, greatness in the novel corresponds to the seriousness that Leavis attributes to preservation-worthy poetry.

Where Leavis differs most markedly from the criteria on which he constructs the poetic canon is the foregrounding in the novel of morals as an essential greatness-constituting element. But it is a difference in vocabulary rather than in concepts, since what is meant by morals in considerations of the novel is fully covered by 'control' when speaking of Eliot's lyrical force.

It is the presence of a highly cultivated sense of morals in the work of Jane Austen that earns her her place as the first important novelist in the history of English fiction. With her moral sense as the pivot, Austen distinguishes herself from her forerunners and contemporaries:

> The principle of organization, and the principle of development, in her work is an intense moral interest of her own life that is in the first place a preoccupation with certain problems that life compels on her as personal ones. She is intelligent and serious enough to be able to impersonalize her moral tensions as she strives, in her art, to become more fully conscious of them, and to learn what, in the interests of life, she ought to do with them. Without her intense moral preoccupation she wouldn't have been a great novelist (1948:16).[7]

Austen can be seen as the culmination of one of the 'important lines of English literary history' (1948:13), with Richardson and Fanny Burney leading up to her. In comparison with this line Fielding falls short. In *Tom Jones*, for instance, 'we haven't to read a very large proportion . . . in order to discover the limits of the essential interests it has to offer us' (1948:13). The essential interests being here synonymous with the moral interest/preoccupation praised in Austen. It is exactly the same kind of relationship that obtains between George Eliot and Charles Dickens. Against the 'fineness of her psychological and moral insight' (1948:25) Dickens only had the genius of a great entertainer:

> he had for the most part no profounder responsibility as a creative artist than this description suggests. . . . The adult mind doesn't as a rule find in Dickens a challenge to an unusual and sustained seriousness (1948:30).

Also the relationship between, on the one hand, Henry James and Joseph Conrad and, on the other, James Joyce is demarcated by a difference of moral sense. James

creates an ideal civilized sensibility; a humanity capable of communicating by the finest shades of inflexion and implication: a
nuance may engage a whole complex moral economy and the
perceptive response be the index of a major valuation or choice
(1948:27),

and in Conrad

we have a master of the English language, who chose it for its
distinctive qualities and because of the moral tradition associated
with it, and whose concern with art – he being like Jane Austen
and George Eliot and Henry James an innovator in 'form' and
method – is the servant of a profoundly serious interest in life
(1948:28).

Against the moral capability of these two, Joyce is rebuked for his
Ulysses on the grounds that

it seems plain to me that here is no organic principle determining,
informing, and controlling into a vital whole, the elaborate analogical structure, the extraordinary variety of technical devices,
the attempts at an exhaustive rendering of consciousness, for
which *Ulysses* is remarkable, and which got it accepted by the
cosmopolitan literary world as a new start. It is rather, I think, a
dead end (1948:37).

If this sounds familiar, it is because almost the same words were
used by Leavis to describe Pound' s *Cantos* in negative comparison
with the same author's 'Hugh Selwyn Mauberley' and Eliot's work
in general. The shortcomings of Joyce are thrown into further deep
relief in comparison with Lawrence whose credo of ' "One must
speak for life and growth, amid all this mass of destruction and
disintegration" ' (1948:38) is held up in praise by Leavis, and in
whose work we see a perfect counterpart in prose fiction to Eliot's
control of the same destruction and disintegration in *The Waste
Land*.

So the great tradition in the English novel can be established by
recourse to the very conditions that Leavis uses for poetry. The
particular moral aptitude and its verbal transformation by Austen,
Eliot, James, Conrad and Lawrence is a result of being at the fine
point of consciousness of their times, as Leavis says about Conrad:

he is one of those creative geniuses whose distinction is manifested in their being peculiarly alive in their time – peculiarly
alive *to* it; not 'in the vanguard' in the manner of Shaw and Wells
and Aldous Huxley, but sensitive to stresses of the changing
spiritual climate as they begin to be registered by the most conscious (1948:33; Leavis's italics).[8]

But here again, in connection with the history of the English novel,
there is a conspicuous lack of evidence as to the particulars of the
spiritual climate and as to how such evidence may be obtained.
And if we grant a parallel between the favoured Augustan ethos in
the line leading up to and including Jane Austen (Richardson and
Fanny Burney), and a further parallel between James, Conrad and
Lawrence and Eliot and Pound, there is a lacuna with regard to
George Eliot, whose situation in late-Romantic, Victorian Britain is
left unaccounted for, unless of course Leavis prefers to see her as a
belated 'Augustan' like Austen, which the following might just
indicate:

she *was* a great novelist, . . . in her maturest work she handled
with unprecedented subtlety and refinement the personal relations of sophisticated characters exhibiting the 'civilization' of the
'best society', and used, in so doing, an original psychological
notation corresponding to the fineness of her psychological and
moral insight (1948:25; Leavis's italics).

One is left with circumstantial evidence for the passing of sentence
on other, traditionally 'great' novelists of the mid- and late-nine-
teenth century, such as leads to the curt dismissal of Sir Walter
Scott:

Out of Scott a bad tradition came. It spoiled Fenimore Cooper,
who had new and first-hand interests and the making of a distinguished novelist. And with Stevenson it took on 'literary' sophistication and fine writing (1948:14 (note)).

With regard to the dynamics of tradition-making, there are striking parallels in the considerations of the novel and of poetry. As
with the milestones in the poetic tradition, the novel(ist)s that count
are those that relate not to a convention but to the dynamics that
brought in the convention in the first place, that is to something

that actually precedes verbal rendering but relies on it for dissemination. Leavis's fastidious selection of novelists are those who

> count in the same way as the major poets, in the sense that they not only change the possibilities of the art for practitioners and readers, but that they are significant in terms of the human awareness they promote; awareness of the possibilities of life (1948:10).

As in poetry the worthwhile tradition comes into being as the result of writers being at the fine point of consciousness of an age ('awareness') and by being so they are able to make the requisite response, even if to a superficial glance this may seem change. To understand and appreciate Hopkins, Eliot, Pound, James, Conrad and Lawrence is at the same time to tie in with a tradition of which they are the inheritors. That is, inheritors in the sense of being able to empathise with the dynamics of tradition-making, which does not simply mean the carrying on of whatever went before. Putting this in a way that partially anticipates Harold Bloom, Leavis claims:

> What one great original artist learns from another, whose genius and problems are necessarily very different, is the hardest kind of 'influence' to define, even when we see it to have been of the profoundest importance. . . . One of the supreme debts one great writer can owe another is the realization of unlikeness (there is, of course, no significant unlikeness without the common concern – and the common seriousness of concern – with essential human issues) (1948: 18–19).

The common seriousness of concern is at the core of tradition, and consequently at the core of human culture. Jane Austen, according to Leavis, is a textbook example of an original author whose originality is due to her sense of tradition. Being at the fine point of consciousness, that is, responding to contemporary culture with her moral sense, she had to find her way in literature. For that purpose she relied on a view of what was essential in the past (not Fielding but Richardson and Fanny Burney), that is, moral concerns of the certain kind favoured by Leavis, and built her fiction accordingly. In turn she herself became a landmark for later generations:

as we look back beyond her we see what goes before, and see because of her, potentialities and significances brought out in such a way that, for us, she creates the tradition we see leading down to her. Her work, like the work of all great creative writers, gives a meaning to the past (1948:14).

How to disentangle the problems to do with induction and deduction in this kind of chronology Leavis never makes into an issue, but obviously believes in the argumentative power of repetition, as here with regard to Conrad:

Here, then, we have a master of the English language, who chose it for its distinctive qualities and because of the moral tradition associated with it, and whose concern with art – he being like Jane Austen and George Eliot and Henry James an innovator in 'form' and method – is the servant of a profoundly serious interest in life (1948:28).

The impersonality principle, which is so prominent in Leavis's poetry criticism, is played down in his discussion of fiction. Theoretically, there should be no difference between the two genres; one might even believe that it would be easier for the author to hide his personality in the dramatizations of the novel. Nonetheless, impersonality in the novel obviously does not interest Leavis as much as impersonality in poetry. In connection with the introductory remarks on Jane Austen in *The Great Tradition* Leavis credits the novelist with the ability to be able to 'impersonalize her moral tensions as she strives, in her art, to become more fully conscious of them, and to learn what, in the interests of life, she ought to do with them' (1948:16). But this line of argument is closer to his view on art as generally representative of individual experience than to the rather special use to which it is put in connection with his view on poetry.

The great tradition of the English novel, or to be more precise, the tradition of greatness in the novel in English, is a tradition relating to the poetic tradition concerning selection principles. However, in his appreciation of the novel Leavis is concerned first and foremost with the exhibition of moral sense to the relative exclusion of impersonality, whereas with regard to poetry he upgrades the impersonality/detachment principle and seems less concerned with moral sense as such. In both traditions, however, control as a function of insight into tradition as well as contemporary culture, plays a crucial role. Leavis tries hard to conceal the deliberateness of that control, by making it into some sort of end product of a specially sensitive response to tradition and situation. But control is exactly what Leavis is keen to spot and what he himself wants to exert in order to secure for literature an instrumental function in an idealistic vision of improved socio-intellectual relations in a world much fallen from grace.

FROM LITERARY TRADITION TO HUMANE EDUCATION

Like Matthew Arnold's, Leavis's is a project not so much in literary criticism and appreciation as in education – *Bildung* – through literature. From his earliest work, such as the pamphlet *Mass Civilisation and Minority Culture* from 1930 to his reflections on the discipline of English and the idea of the university in the 1970s, there is clear indication that the ultimate goal is the realization of a *humanitas* vision, perfected in the Augustan age and very much in need since. The resuscitation of the wholly cultured man – in organic touch with whatever is most important in his age and able to rely critically and creatively on the tradition in order to respond adequately – is the ever-pressing issue. As Rousseau's Émile must read Defoe's *Robinson Crusoe* as instruction rather than pleasure, so Leavis's students were to benefit from the poet-critics most able to transform a firm grip on life into words capable of self-erasure, as it were, so as to recreate the original, immediate bond.

Leavis does not see the contemporary situation with regard to *avant-garde* modernist literature as an estrangement on the part of the poet/novelist from his or her audience generally, as is the orthodox view of most lay readers and even in some critical circles.[9] On the contrary, to him the great divide is between a cultural elite attuned to modernism – this being the contemporary ethos *par excellence* – on the one hand and those in need of education on the other, from the cultivators of the Georgian taste in poetry to the peddlers of the mass media. To Leavis, culture is ultimately a question of maintaining the highest standards. This is only possible by recourse to a tradition, to which 'traditionalism', that is, the 'academic idea of tradition – . . . the vested interest, for which Scott, Milton, Shelley, Donne and the rest are facts and fixed values (the

fixture constituting "tradition")' (1943:130) is the neg-ative
counterpart. The sense of tradition stands in danger of destruction in the general 'process of levelling-down' (1930:8) in our time
accompanying the 'processes of mass-production and standard-
isation in the form represented by the Press' (1930:7). Contemporary man faces changes

> so catastrophic that the generations find it hard to adjust them-
> selves to each other, and parents are helpless to deal with their
> children . . . [so i]t is a breach in continuity that threatens: what
> has been inadvertently dropped may be irrecoverable or forgot-
> ten (Leavis 1930:6–7).

But it would be a misunderstanding of Leavis to attribute the
present lack of a proper sense of tradition to the present disorder of
things. Not only are his favourite modernist poets and novelists
proof of the opposite, but also his firm belief in the inaccessibility at
any time of any but the most enlightened – the fine points of consciousness – to the true cultural values shows this to be in the
nature of a general principle rather than contingency:

> In any period it is upon a very small minority that the discern-
> ing appreciation of art and literature depends: it is (apart
> from cases of the simple and familiar) only a few who are capable
> of unprompted, first-hand judgment. They are still a small
> minority, though a larger one, who are capable of endorsing
> such first-hand judgment by genuine personal response. The
> accepted valuations are a kind of paper currency based upon a
> very small proportion of gold. To the state of such a currency
> the possibilities of fine living at any time bear a close relation
> (1930:3–4).

A cultural aristocrat and a spokesman for cultural elitism, Leavis
does not, however, simply lock up himself selfrighteously in an
ivory tower, but dutifully takes upon himself the role of the teacher.
It is through teaching that the cultural standards transmitted by
tradition can be maintained. The ideal classroom is the university,
but not any university. And the ideal subject is English literature,
but not any text, nor any method.

Although Leavis's relations with Cambridge were at times
strained, and his position in the academic community often more

than problematic, his idea of the university as the centre for the dissemination of his views and attitudes is very much modelled on the Oxbridge tutorial as the ideal forum for the exchange of educated opinion. The idea of the university represents in itself the continuity of culture in that the universities are

> recognized symbols of cultural tradition – of cultural tradition still conceived as a directing force, representing a wisdom older than modern civilization and having an authority that should check and control the blind drive onward of material and mechanical development, with its human consequences (1943: 16).

In addition, Leavis is enough of a pragmatist to realize the community power of universities: 'The ancient universities are more than symbols; they, at any rate, may fairly be called foci of such a force, capable, by reason of their prestige and their part in the life of the country, of exercising an enormous influence' (1943:16). Once inside the university the aim should be set on studies in pursuit of the humane tradition, an entity which Leavis refrains from describing because of its vagueness. It is

> better to point to English literature, which is unquestionably and producibly 'there,' and to suggest that the 'literary tradition' that this unquestionable existence justifies us in speaking of might also be called a vague concept. And the relation of 'literary tradition' to 'humane tradition' is plainly not the mere external one of a parallel. Here, it may be said in passing, we have a reason for making a scheme of liberal education centre in the study of English literature (Leavis 1943: 17).

A School of English in the university (preferably an ancient one), should have literary criticism as the core discipline, since it is a

> true discipline, only in an English School if anywhere will it be fostered, and it is irreplaceable. It trains, in a way no other discipline can, intelligence and sensibility together, cultivating a sensitiveness and precision of response and a delicate integrity of intelligence – intelligence that integrates as well as analyses and must have pertinacity and staying power as well as delicacy (1943:34).

In classes on practical criticism, with the emphasis on 'practical',[10] discussions will take place in a general mood of tentativeness rather than goal-directedness. The auspices for such spiritual expansiveness are most likely to be found in the ambience of the old universities, 'because they are so much more than educational institutions' (1943: 28) in their favouring of 'informal intercourse – intercourse that brings together intellectual appetites from specialisms of all kinds, and from various academic levels' (1943: 28). The result of such an education would be a human being shaped in the spirit of *humanitas*, with a cultural heritage unmistakably from the period when civilization equalled culture, that is the Augustan age and the ages on which the Augustans modelled themselves and their society:

> we want to produce a mind that knows what precision and specialist knowledge are, is aware of the kinds not in its own possession that are necessary, has a maturity of outlook such as the study of history ought to produce but even the general historian by profession doesn't always exhibit, and has been trained in a kind of thinking, a scrupulously sensitive yet enterprising use of intelligence, that is of its nature not specialized but cannot be expected without special training – a mind, energetic and resourceful, that will apply itself to the problems of civilization, and eagerly continue to improve its equipment and explore fresh approaches (1943: 58–9).

The distance from the close scrutiny of selected texts from English literary history in the seclusion of a Cambridge tutorial to the claim that this activity is the very basis for existential justification may seem overambitiously wide. Yet, Leavis is of course not the first, nor probably the last, cultural critic to have promoted the nexus, and most supporters of a humanities/liberal-arts programme in secondary school, college and university are willing to subscribe in principle to his views. The special place of literature in any culture is denied by very few. So it is not this aspect of Leavis which may give rise to debate. Nor is it his elitism. Such elitism is, after all, part of the game too. Where a critique of Leavis is appropriate, however, is in the subjectivity of his preferences and the way he passes off a tenuously documented and Romanticised view of the past as something universal. But the final irony is that Leavis, having *épaté les bourgeois* so energetically in his time, has been advocating an

English cultural ideal which English culture, personified in the ideal of the gentleman amateur, has really been taking for granted for several hundred years.

5

Northrop Frye: The Grand Vision of a Liberal-Arts Education

To me myth is not simply an effect of a historical process, but a social vision that looks towards a transcending of history, which explains how it is able to hold two periods of history together, the author's and ours, in direct communication (Frye 1990: 60–1).

The encyclopedic range of Northrop Frye's literary horizon suggests that his version of the canon is virtually all-comprehensive. Indeed, criticism has been eager to demonstrate that Frye's archetypal categories are flexible to the point of vagueness in order to include such a universal sweep. But Frye's systematic, or, as he himself prefers it, schematic poetics, is nonetheless one with a discreetly limiting scope.[1] His preference is for works which can be placed in a hierarchy subservient to a distinct cultural vision. My aim in this chapter is to discuss this didactic and canon-validating aspect of Frye's criticism.

The orthodox approach to Frye is to follow the critic's own inductive course beginning chronologically with his study of Blake from 1947 and then to go on to the *Anatomy of Criticism* published exactly ten years later. This is an approach which illuminates Frye's development as a critic systematizing his initial empiricism into mature theory. However, availing oneself of the freedom of perspective exercised with such great pedagogical effect for the argument in 'The Archetypes of Literature' from *Fables of Identity: Studies in Poetic Mythology* from 1963 – a neat capsule version of the *Anatomy* – there is much sense in making *The Great Code: The Bible and Literature* (1982) with its sequel *Words With Power: Being a Second Study of 'The Bible and Literature'* (1990) together with *The Critical Path: An Essay on the Social Context of Literary Criticism* from 1971, the points of departure and of general reference for the present study of Frye as canon-moulder.[2] It is indeed significant that Frye's procedure in expanding the structural scope of the myth and meta-phorics of the Bible to include all literature is exactly like the procedure that took him from Blake to wider contexts of literature in the *Anatomy*.[3] To choose the *Anatomy*, the two studies of the Bible, and the widening out of the aesthetic categories into ethical ones in the systematic and lucid *The Critical Path*[4] is of course to emphasize the texts that suit the concerns chosen for the present study.[5] Frye's critical work on specific texts and authors centres on Shakespeare[6] and Milton,[7] English Romanticism,[8] Canadian lit-erature,[9] and includes a study of T. S. Eliot.[10]

The link between the *Anatomy* and *The Great Code* is the crucial significance of literature as ultimately anagogic. In the earlier study, the appended 'Glossary' explains 'anagogic' as '[r]elating to literature as a total order of words' (1957: 365). In view of the importance of the concept for the understanding of the priorities in Frye's criticism, this definition is on much too general a level. But in the study's second essay – on so-called 'ethical criticism' which coincides with Frye's 'theory of symbols' along a different axis – the full force of the concept for the later work is brought out much more distinctly.

Frye's theory of symbols relies on a spacious definition of the symbol as 'any unit of any literary structure that can be isolated for critical attention' (1957: 71). Such a discernible unit yields meaning, which is then inevitably a kind of symbolic meaning, according to the given context of interpretation, for which Frye chooses the term 'phase' to indicate its dynamic nature. Like the norms in Wellek and Warren's work-of-art ontological construct we have here to do with a system in which the elements make sense according to the angle of reading.

Frye distinguishes between several phases or contexts determin-ing the way the symbol is made to make sense. In the literal or descriptive phases the symbol is a linguistic unit pointing cen-trifugally (in one of Frye's favourite metaphors) as a sign to an external reality – an object or a concept – and at the same time part of a syntagmatic unit as motif relating centripetally to other such symbols. Symbols as signs ordered into motifs yield a kind of meaning which seems like a reflection of the world, in a point-to-point relationship, simultaneously creating a sense derived from the verbal context. Frye is fully aware, though, that what we have to do with is a verbal discourse similar to other descriptive ones, and different from them to the extent that 'literature in its decriptive context is a body of hypothetical verbal structures' (1957: 79).

In the formal phase the symbol appears as an image, that is a unit showing an 'analogy of proportion between the poem and the nature which it imitates' (1957: 84). This is the context or phase where we read formal structures and allegory into the literary text, and where the images systematized into their meaning-forming sequences become illustrative of the ideas they are meant to represent. The creative mind is free to construct its own patterns of images, not held back by anything except by the degree to which literary convention is allowed its rule. As imagination the mind is elevated above the three external compulsions of life in the real world: the compulsions on action, thinking and feeling. In his imagination man is free to move beyond what binds him in the world. In the making up of images there is the 'vision of a decisive act of spiritual freedom, the vision of the recreation of man' (1957: 94).

In the next phase, the mythical one, the symbol appears as an archetype. Whereas symbol as image could be appreciated within the confines of the individual text, symbol as archetype necessitates the comparison and appreciation of analogies between texts. In Frye's system the archetype is the symbol which 'connects one poem with another and thereby helps to unify and integrate our literary experience' (1957: 99). With the archetype we are no longer restricted to the individual text, but move freely between texts. By recourse to symbols read as archetypes literature becomes a system of exchange; it goes public, so to speak. Archetypal criticism focuses on recurrence in literature. Now literature becomes ritual, a repeated structure, attempting to mediate between experience and desire.[11]

In the archetypal phase, imitation is seen to relate to nature not as something static in terms of a system or a structure as in the formal phase, but as something dynamic in which elements are seen in recurrent interaction. Nature as the subject of literary imitation in this phase is seen as a whole. An almost vertiginous perspective offers itself in this phase, in which the literary text takes for its model the interpretation of nature which is civilization, and which, in turn, is energized by the desire to make something of the given elements. In the archetypal phase literature is social, and the critic interested in this phase will look out for whatever in the texts indicates a striving to fulfil the desire for civilization and remove the impediments involved.

Recurrence and desire are what we see in ritual and dream, and together the two form myth when manifesting themselves verbally. In the archetypal phase all of civilization's efforts, that is *work* efforts, are accommodated. In this phase the world in literature appears as so much energy devoted to 'visualize the goals of human work' (1957: 115), which are contained in the urge to make the natural other accessible in terms of human forms.

It is not quite clear at this point in his argument whether Frye considers work a means or an end. There seems, though, to be more than a vestige of the puritan belief in the redemptive power of work. However, the literary text can only be seen as 'useful and functional' (1957: 115) in relation to civilization, in which its role is to present hypothetical scenarios of worthy and unworthy objectives. Here the writer is a contributor to whatever other civilizing activities may be engaged in, at the same time as he holds up a mirror to those same civilizing activities, with literature useful as a prop of society.

In *The Great Code* Frye elaborates on the nature of work, again in the symbolic perspective which literary texts tend to produce. He distinguishes between negative and positive work, the former the kind that a Marxist would recognize as exploitation in its various forms, but also manifest as war-efforts and any kind of idolization. In contrast to these negative outlets of human energy we find the 'genuine work which is founded on the human need for food and shelter and moves into the direction of transforming nature into a world with a human shape, meaning, and function' (1982a: 72). Such work not only raises man above the beast but takes him further 'upwards' in so far as a degree of creative energy is put into the effort to move away from a bare subsistence existence. This is where desire comes in, since the 'world of work is also an expression of desire as well as of need: what man really wants is what the positive and productive work he does shows that he wants' (1982a: 72). The aspect of work which is desire is still, of course, a rationalization of the human-shaped world that Frye sees in the literary text approached as symbol, with its striving beyond merely descriptive reflection. Frye suggests work as a dualism expressed in a literary archetype. In the Bible it is particularly acute in the way that it refuses to freeze into a cosmology but instead insists on a visionary dynamics of upward metamorphosis, of the alienated relation of man to nature transformed into a spontaneous and effortless life – not effortless in the sense of being lazy or passive, but in the sense of being energy without alienation (1982a: 76),

and to that effect quotes Isaiah 11: 6, 9 and Hosea 2: 18. It makes no sense to distinguish between work and play, since the end of positive work is the expending of energy for the sake of a creative activity transcending the requirements of mere sustenance (1982a: 125). On a grander scale, that of the Biblical narrative, it appears in the form of a symbolism constituting the

ideal world . . . which the human creative imagination envisages, which human energy tries to bring into being, and which the Bible presents also as a form of 'revelation': the vision, the model, the blueprint that gives direction and purpose to man's energies (1982a: 139–40).

Frye's attraction to the visionary or the prophetic as a central literary element is latent throughout his critical *oeuvre*, but in *Words with Power* it comes out quite clearly, with the emphasis on Romanticism as the period of the breakthrough (1990: 49 ff).

If the gradual perspectivizing from the symbol as a literal verbal sign to the archetype seems to be in the nature of development by degree, the final shift from the archetype to the monad in the anagogic phase is more in the manner of a shift in kind.

In the anagogic phase literature supposedly 'imitates the total dream of man' (1957: 119). Now the symbol is no longer just a verbal representation of an 'outside' quantity, but the expression of the desire that energizes man's work in the positive aspect described above. It is as if the shift from degree to kind is parallel to the shift in philosophy that takes us from the empiricism of a Locke to the idealism of a Kant. Certainly, the analogy to *Anschauungsformen* in this description is striking:

When we pass into anagogy, nature becomes, not the container, but the thing contained, and the archetypal universal symbols, the city, the garden, the quest, the marriage, are no longer the desirable symbols that man constructs into nature, but are themselves the forms of nature (1957: 119).

With the symbol appearing as monad, that is a 'center of one's total literary experience' (1957: 366),[12] there can be no further manifestation of desire, since desire, in itself without limits, has no alternative channels for expression. In the anagogic phase the symbol stamps reality, and not the other way round. It is proper here to speak of apocalypse, being the 'imaginative conception of the whole of nature as the content of an infinite an eternal living body' (1957: 119). In this reversed state, as it were, of literature impressing itself on existence in order to see existence reflected in identical terms, literature may no longer be thought of as a secondary thing, attempting to approach some extra-literary primary. Here literature comes into its own, 'containing life and reality in a system of verbal relationships' (1957: 122).

The anagogic phase with its monadic symbols is clearly to be seen in texts of cosmological ambitions. Consequently, the Bible presents a particularly interesting case study, both in its own right and as the bridge between mythology proper and its transformations and representations in literature (cf. 1990: xii). With the numinous element intact, the anagogic text is a sacred thing. Having lost this, it becomes a text of considerable imaginative power still, but without 'magical' attributes. As 'literature plus' (1990: xv), the Bible relies on the raw material of myth and metaphor, in total wrought to a degree surpassing most literature (monadic symbols are, however, also to be appreciated in the kind of poetry establishing their own universes, like primary and secondary epics). The literalness of the Bible is known from the imaginative metaphorics of literature (1990: xv).

The imaginative is a special mode beyond the descriptive, conceptual and ideological, a mode that, with a clearly heard echo from Aristotle, distingushes literature from any other verbal discourse, and a mode in which the Bible is firmly lodged:

> An imaginative response is one in which the distinction between the emotional and the intellectual has disappeared, and in which ordinary consciousness is only one of many possible psychic elements, the fantastic and the dreamlike having conventionally an equal status. The criterion of the imaginative is the conceivable, not the real, and it expresses the hypothetical or assumed, not the actual (1990: 22).

Or, to be quite precise, we may say that the actual, as worked on by the imagination, enjoys an epistemological status on a par with the non-actual (the hypothetical or assumed). As literature is the product of an imaginative effort – applied to actuality and non-actuality alike – it is invariably shaped in such a way as to express our instinctive urges, as it were, which, in Frye's vision of existence, always aim at existential improvement, physically and spiritually.

RESONANCE

Even though the erudition of Frye sometimes threatens to make the reader lose his bearings in the mass of literary and critical observations in his works, Frye is basically, as he points out in his introduction to *The Great Code*, a teacher (cf. 1982a: xiv–xv). And as teacher, he is fond of the pedagogically helpful, for which simplification is the classic expedient. In *Anatomy of Criticism* he describes his exploratory and explanatory procedure by justifying the regular reliance on literary works which, by most conventional standards, are not considered worth serious critical work:

> If throughout this book I refer to popular fiction as frequently as to the greatest novels and epics, it is for the same reason that a musician attempting to explain the rudimentary facts about counterpoint would be more likely, at least at first, to illustrate from 'Three Blind Mice' than from a complex Bach fugue (1957: 104).

It is this pedagogical stance that has led many to consider Frye the great critical egalitarian: no need to distinguish in terms of quality, since the point is to deal with categories with a potential for literature. Although Frye, on the whole, is reluctant to pass definitive value judgment on specific texts, it would be misleading to take this as evidence of indifference to literary value. In the passage just quoted one would, in this respect, be well advised to pay attention to the expression 'greatest novels and epics'. To a superficial reading it would seem that there is an absolute contrast between greatness and popularity. But in Frye's system the two should be seen as two different manifestations of the same principles. Consequently, the standard for canonical measurement must be looked for elsewhere. In order to arrive at an appreciation of Frye's canon-making efforts it is necessary to look into what Frye has chosen to call (using a metaphorically evocative word) 'resonance'.

Explaining 'resonance', Frye again resorts to the pedagogically effective – comparison and simplification – although the appeal is to the intuitive rather than to the rational faculty. Frye suggests that there is a difference between listening to music 'on the level of say, Schumann or Tchaikovsky' (1982a:216) and listening to compositions like certain masses and requiems by Bach and Mozart respectively. The difference is one of the degree to which the music can be said to liberate itself from being specifically 'Schumann' or 'Tchaikovsky' and felt to be 'absolute' music, rendering the quintessence of the musical.

The difference, Frye suggests, between just competently composed music and the greatest music, is the difference between the subjectivity of the two Romantic composers and, by implication, the objectivity of Bach or Mozart, that is, a 'sense of listening to the voice of music itself' (1982a:216–17). Obviously by proceeding from Schumann to Bach we have transcended the qualitative threshold into the anagogic phase with the works of the two composers as musical monads: 'This, we feel, is the kind of thing music is all about, the kind of thing it exists to say. The work we hear now is coming to us from within its contexts, which is the totality of musical experience;' (1982a:217). No doubt the validity of Frye's point is highly questionable: the fondness in the West for counterpoint and harmony goes a long way to making us think of the works mentioned as the epitome of the 'principle' of music, disregarding the historical element. Furthermore, in the light of Frye's arguments about literature, the sacred nature of the compositions certainly play a role in their suggested uniqueness. Be that as it may, the example illustrates very well the nature of the point Frye sets out to make. Thus pedagogically sweetened, Frye is ready to transfer the point to literature.

Just as Bach's *B Minor Mass* and Mozart's *Requiem* are both individual pieces of music and carriers of the musical essence, as it were, the same can be seen to apply to literary texts: 'It is the voice of drama itself that we hear in Shakespeare or Sophocles, and the sense of a totality of dramatic experience, of what drama exists to set forth, looms closely behind them' (1982a:217). When the voice of drama – or of certain musical genres – emerges from the individual work, it is a phenomenon to be traced to the point where the archetypal turns into the anagogic, or in other words, where the recurrent literary units (symbols) no longer serve to respond to an external 'reality' but turn into the very condition of being able to take in that reality. According to Frye, this capacity of certain works to transcend themselves is a capacity to be seen especially in the 'classics' (1982a:217; Frye's quotation marks).

Frye's argument is best understood upside-down, as it were: his theory does not come first, requiring the singling out of works fitting the theory, but the works have already been singled out as valuable because the 'poets whom we consider the most serious and worthy of exhaustive study are invariably those who have explicitly used the kind of imagery studied here [i.e. in connection with the Bible]' (1990: xxii). At this stage in the argument Frye relies on the 'classics' as ready-made, a reservoir of generally accredited literary texts already in existence, but, as we shall see, there is more to the making of a true classic in the sense of a great literary work than just an accepted inheritance. What Frye is after here is something that we may term 'general wisdom'. It is a quality readily appreciated in works by, for instance, Shakespeare and Dickens in English literature, when characters or utterances step out of the page and become existential household concepts, 'equipped with a relevance to hundreds of situations in addition to their original one' (1982a: 217). But that this is hardly the same thing as literary essence nor the same thing as literary value is apparent to Frye, as it appears from his admission that 'quotability' is a quality which indeed is characteristic of the 'classics', but is certainly very often found in works outside the classic mainstream, such as in, for instance, *Alice in Wonderland*, which is extremely rich in potential quotations. That the quality of general wisdom in terms of quotes is not synonymous with literary value Frye himself makes quite plain in his suggestion that 'this quality of being quotable in a variety of situations is unpredictable . . . and it correlates with no system of value' (1982a: 217).

Literary value, then, does not depend on the degree to which a work – 'classic' or not – can offer existential advice in the form of apt quotes. Nor does it depend on the degree to which the different modes and phases laid bare by Frye stand out in the work. If that was the case, popular literature – its popularity ensured by this very circumstance – would be at the very top of the quality ranking. But Frye cannot quite leave the idea contained in quotability. Not very surprising either, since the metaphor of the literary-existential echo is so central to his thought.

The bridge-making effort is made in the concept of 'resonance': 'Through resonance a particular statement in a particular context acquires a universal significance' (1982a: 117). By way of example Frye adduces Greece and Israel, which have 'imposed themselves on our consciousness until they have become part of the map of our own imaginative world, whether we have seen these countries or not' (1982a: 218).[13] The Bible in particular has a tremendous potential of this kind. Held together by what Frye terms its 'imaginative unity', which he sees first and foremost in the system of metaphorical figuration relating the Old and the New Testaments, this collection of a vast number of texts of different origins and authorships has the quality of resonance, being impossible 'without, first, an original context, and, second, a power of expanding away from that context' (1982a: 218). That power is one that makes the text more than just text, and also more than just mere quotability in a household context. It is something that involves the notion of 'seriousness', but in a sense different from Matthew Arnold's.

When we start to connect seriousness with resonance, the connecting element, according to Frye, is to be found in the *care of literary craftsmanship* (1982a: 220; Frye's italics). And this is exactly where the problem of the quality of popular literature comes into the picture.

Resonance involves the principle of 'polysemous' meaning, which is the potential in a text to be suggestive of new meanings triggered by new angles of approach.[14] This is not, however, the same thing as the capacity of a text to be interpreted differently by different interpretive communities according to, for instance, shifting ideological outlooks; that is, as a gross – perhaps superimposed – change of overall sense. The text remains itself, and whatever new understandings it may give occasion to, they are still at one with the text, existing as a 'single process growing in subtlety and comprehensiveness, [as] different intensities or wider contexts of a continuous sense, unfolding like a plant out of a seed' (1982a: 221). Whatever the problematic implications of the simile, the point is that the polysemous meaning of a text is always potentially there, in its original verbal structure.

When a text has been made 'carefully', it has a polysemous meaning potential that makes possible the transcending of its own finite design. The careful artistic handling of a given subject, if of the first rate, is characterized by the use of verbal units (symbols) in such a way as to form a satisfactory design at the same time securing the polysemous meaning potential. It goes without saying that this latter is hardly something that the artist can set out to do. Actually it would be a contradiction in terms to do so, as only time shows if the artist has been successful in this respect.

Popular literature, though pedagogically useful to the critic as a training ground, usually fails when it comes to polysemous meaning potential. Frye again here resorts to the detective story, whose meaning is exhausted when we know the identity of the culprit. Popular genre fiction (such as the detective story) is not serious, because it lacks the polysemous meaning potential residing in the degree of structural complication:

> Once we see a joke we do not want to hear it again; or, if we read a detective story only to see who the murderer is, we do not normally want to reread the story until we have forgotten his identity. But with the *Divine Comedy* or *King Lear*, the seeing of the total structure is something that there could never be any question of completing (1990: 70).

So far in his argument Frye is able to pronounce on polysemous meaning as a dominant 'feature of all deeply serious writing [with] the Bible . . . the model for serious writing' (1982a: 221), because of its extremely high degree of polysemism deriving from a tradition of figural readings.

Frye seems to find the essence of the literary in the particular passages in the text that, like a lighthouse, as it were, guide the reader in his or her search for representations of primary concerns, the concerns which find their verbal expressions in a 'mythical language of hope, desire, belief, anxiety, polemic, fantasy and construction' (1971a: 57), in contrast to the 'logical language of fact, reason, description and verification' (1971a: 57) characteristic of the logical language of fact, representing truths of correspondence rather than truths of concern. The more saturated the text is by such 'oracular' passages, the more the reader's 'contact expands from the oracular flash into the possession of or identification with the narrative' (1990: 114). Needless to add, the Bible is particularly saturated in this respect. Now, saving the risk of Frye falling prey to the joke about the theatre spectator who found *Hamlet* too full of quotations, his argument is of course based on the reverse

assumption of certain texts being more polysemous, hence resonant, than others, and by such difference making for the distinction
between significant and insignificant texts. This line of argument
also serves to explain why Frye is not really interested in the
'revisions of value-judgments' (1990: 113) constituting much critical history, if only as a symptom of the way that critics of certain
periods may nourish a wish for cultivating the oracular quality of
texts. This can be said to have been the case when the critical vogue
left authors of continuity, such as Tennyson, Goethe, Hugo, in
favour of authors such as Hopkins, Hölderlin, or Rimbaud (cf. 1990:
113). Frye seems to suggest that the modernist breakthrough was a
reorientation in terms of reader didactics rather than a decisive
shift of cultural paradigm.

Implied in Frye's dogma of resonance is the assumption of a
literary-value distinction based on the difference between a Pla-
tonic-Aristotelean reliance on a poetics of mimesis and a Longinian
poetics of what we, for lack of a better phrase, may call 'transportation'. The history of literature, according to Frye, is the history of
the dialectics of mimesis and transportation. In the names singled
out by Frye above, the mimetic aspect is very much in evidence in
the work of Tennyson, Goethe and Hugo, in the reading of which
the reader must sift for her- or himself the particularly resonant
passages, whereas in texts by authors like Hopkins, Hölderlin or
Rimbaud the work is done to a greater extent by the authors themselves, because their way of writing tends much more towards the
oracular. To Frye, despite his claims to the opposite, there is certainly literary value judgement at stake in trying to sort out passages, texts and authors in which the urge to go beyond the purely
mimetic in search of the oracular is strong. It explains why authors
and critics like T. E. Hulme and the early Eliot and Pound are seen
as short-term apologists for a limited secondary-concern ideology.

Great literature is kerygmatic, as Frye prefers to term the oracular
element in its literary manifestation. The kerygmatic is what takes
literature out of itself and into the ultimate existential testing
ground. The kerygmatic is not confined to the literary or sacred
text, but has a secular counterpart in political manifestos. The concerns of political manifestos are invariably time-serving and short-
term, since

> political kerygma lacks a mythology of traditional stories and
> archetypal allusions, and the sense of a shared cultural tradition

that only such a mythology can give. A kerygma without the full support of a mythology soon becomes a rhetorical vacuum, and a vacuum is something that consciousness, like nature, abhors (1990: 117).

The kerygmatic inheres in the traditional sacred texts of given societies, in the form of the Bible, the Koran, the Buddhist or Hindu Scriptures, texts which do not lend themselves to conventional lit.-crit. evaluation. But they share with literature the reliance on a 'mythical and metaphorical . . .basis' (1990: 116), and in that sharing it becomes clear that what they share are central existential concerns mediated in traditional configurations of myth and metaphor interwoven to such a degree that 'it seems to be language that uses man rather than man that uses language' (1990: 116), which is Frye's touchstone regarding the kerygmatic.

In the first part of the sentence quoted just above, Frye suggests that the anteriority of language in relation to man is the proper sequence recognized 'surprisingly often in contemporary writing' (1990: 116) without, however, naming names. In order to get this line of writers into focus it is quite telling to look at the way that Frye redeems the Hulme-inspired follies of the early Eliot and Pound: 'But Eliot later spoke of wanting to go beyond poetry in the *Quartets*, and Pound expanded – exploded would perhaps be a better word – into even broader dimensions' (1990: 115). The central place of the imagination with its reliance on myth and metaphor for the exercise of the kerygmatic ensures the literary as the most efficacious outlet, second in importance only to a society's traditionally sacred texts.

It is tempting to suggest that by now we are in possession of an outline for the principle of evaluation on which Frye's canon builds. This principle could be boiled down to the requirement that a text is particularly successful as a resonant monad, which, in turn, means a high degree of seriousness brought about by a potential for polysemous meaning of the organic kind suggested by Frye's plant metaphor. But Frye himself is wary of drawing this conclusion:

A value judgment is a possible, though not inevitable, inference from our experience of the fact of continuing response, and of the feeling that the work itself keeps growing in reality along with our comprehension of it (1982a: 221).

But it had better not be so, since the 'hierarchy created by value judgments is a mirage based on what we think we already know, an illusory form of the upward path of discovery that we are embarked on' (1982a: 221–2). The last few words refer to the context of the argument in *The Great Code*, but also have a significance beyond this particular work.

In the passages just quoted, the effect of which is to warn the reader of hasty conclusions to do with literary evaluation, two phrases seem to invite further speculation: 'growing in reality' and 'upward path of discovery'. In combination with the pronouncement on the Bible as the 'model for serious writing', a tentative idea of Frye's canonical implications may be arrived at if we concern ourselves with the particular status of the Bible as this model, always remembering Frye's assumption that the Bible is not intended as a work of literature, but that for all practical purposes its literal meaning inheres in myth and metaphor.

EVALUATION AND CANON

Frye seldom offers opinions on the literary quality of a text. The reason, he suggests, is that 'I realized early in my critical life that evaluation was a minor and subordinate function of the critical process, at best an incidental by-product, which should never be allowed to take priority over scholarship' (1982a: xvi). The theoretical foundation of this non-evaluation position is made quite clear earlier, for instance in Frye's conclusion to the *Literary History of Canada* from 1965. There Frye seems to be somewhat on the defensive in his suggestion that for the study of that particular national literature any notion of a canonical list of classics, on which evaluative criticism builds, is best forgotten: 'Canada has produced no author who is a classic in the sense of possessing a vision greater in kind than that of his best readers' (1965c: 213). Canadian literature still lacks works with the quality of drawing the reader towards the very essence of the literary experience in the sense explained above, for the illustration of which Frye refers to the sacred music of a Bach or a Mozart. Instead of being centripetal by furnishing us with examples of unique literary feats, Canadian literature never gets quite out of the contexts to which the individual works relate, so that 'Even when it is literature in its orthodox genres of poetry and fiction, it is more significantly studied as a part of Canadian life than as part of an autonomous world of literature' (1965c: 214). For the proper study of Canadian literature, then, it is necessary to 'outgrow the view that evaluation is the end of criticism, instead of its incidental by-product' (1965c: 213). But this very principle, which seems a convenient way out of a situation embarrassing for its lack of truly classic works, is elsewhere one of the key positions for his overall critical argument, such as in *The Critical Path*, in which Frye suggests various principles to do with the verbal expression of myths of concern.[15]

One is the proposition that there is a difference between the teacher of the myth of concern and its verbal perpetrator, the poet, from whom we expect adequate verbal treatment, but whose personality or general behaviour is of no importance for the achieved verbal product. A second is that the reader always aims at possessing the poet's vision. A third is that it is meaningless to distinguish between positive and negative literary visions of the myths of concern. All contribute to 'man's body of vision, and no *index expurgatorius* or literary hell . . . exists on any basis acceptable to a student of literature' (1971a:127). It should always be remembered that literature in itself is not a myth of concern but the potentially verbal medium of such myths. A myth of concern is finite, we may add pedagogically, as a literary work is finite, but literature is, like the alphabet, the carrier of infinite permutations of such myths, capable of 'indicating the horizons beyond all formulations of belief, in pointing to an infinite total concern that can never be expressed, but only indicated in the variety of arts themselves' (1971a:128). If there can be such distinction within literature as a total order of words, it follows that criticism has to consider it in this perspective, which excludes evaluation, concentrating instead on the scholarly and critical procedures of description, categorization and interpretation.

If criticism begins to concern itself with evaluation, the critic commits a categorical mistake, since evaluation 'always means that the critic wants to get into the concern game himself, choosing a canon out of literature and so making literature a single gigantic allegory of his own anxieties' (1971a:127). We have seen above that the potential for repeated study is what gives resonance to a given text. On the same account 'uniqueness' as an often asserted literary, hence canon-qualifying quality is discarded. Apart from the fact that a poor literary text may be held to be just as unique as a good text, uniqueness is not in the text as verbal structure but in the eye of the beholder, since

> criticism is a structure of knowledge, and the unique as such is unknowable; uniqueness is a quality of experience, not of knowledge, and of precisely the aspect of experience which cannot form part of a structure of knowledge (1971a:27).

The structure which is subject to critical study is nonetheless a structure of experience, but in contrast to the kind of experience that finds expression in purely impressionistic descriptions like uniqueness, the sensible experience is one of coherent structure (1971a:29). Frye may be somewhat vague about the phenomenological leap from the 'wrong' kind of experience to the 'right' one, from the one building on presumably random impressionistic observation to the one that forms a system by recognizing the 'organizing patterns of convention, genre and archetype' (1971a:29), but the distinction is useful. It enables him to draw a demarcation line, separating off the 'evaluating hierarchy that limits us to the evaluator's reading list' (1971a:29), providing instead the possibility of archetype-hunting in all kinds of texts, the disinterested activity and justification of the criticism practised by the 'real reader' who 'knows better' (1971a:29) than to subject himself to mere, unsystematic impressionism. In literature, considered as the body of all verbal constructs referred to that category, there can be no works subsuming other works just because they are considered great or unique. The study of Shakespeare does not make the study of Massinger superfluous (1971a:29). Scholarship and value judgement are things apart, value judgement at best having an initial, heuristic function, furnishing the scholar with a tentative working hypothesis or a short-cut to texts proved by experience to be well worth continued scholarly investment. Frye points to Shakespeare as the obvious case.

Frye, as indicated in the quotation above, does not deny the possibility of practising evaluation, but considers it an ancillary critical function, the preoccupation with which blocks from view the really important critical work that has to do with the extent to which a text can be said to be rewarding for critical study. The reward consists in the way a text can be made to open itself to yet more expanding contexts, always being contexts of words, not however confined to the traditional literary domain, but going beyond it into our verbally conditioned civilization. Evaluation terminates with literature and prevents us from taking the step into wider contexts. As the Bible would hardly be subject to literary evaluation of the traditional kinds, but nonetheless remains a work – several works edited together – of literature, the distinction between evaluative and scholarly efforts is accentuated.

The objection to Frye's line of reasoning here is pivoted on the narrowness of his implied definition of 'literary evaluation'. Frye assumes that value judgement is 'at best an incidental by-product', (1982a:xvi), that is, something that can be separated from the scholarly activity which should be allowed dominance. Still, as we have seen, there are works which merit more attention than others because of their resonance quality, and since it is especially rewarding to work critically on them, they assemble to form a canon of 'rewarding works'. And if we carry this further into the context where Frye wants to end up, in civilization as the grand total order of words, we shall have a sum of literary texts standing out on two accounts: the degree to which they hypostatize the structures of narrative and the degree to which this hypostatis relates symbolically to what may, for want of a more precise wording, be called human experience. In practice this means looking for and appreciating variations on the theme of which the Bible – from Genesis to Apocalypse – is the epitome.

Frye may consider value judgement or evaluation irrelevant for the purpose of coming to terms with resonant texts, for which purpose the application of the critical operations of scholarship (Frye's own terms, cf. 1982a:xvi) is a quantitatively (cf. 'a minor and subordinate function of the critical process' (1982a:xvi)) and qualitatively different venture. But still a canon of a sort, and actually of a very distinct and not very controversial sort, emerges.

The putting together of Frye's canon must proceed by fits and starts rather than by relying on the existence of an explicit and consistent argument. Frye has pointed to the advisability of using relatively simple and homogeneous texts for demonstrative purposes. In Frye's canonical hierarchy detective stories and nursery rhymes have significant heuristic values, but their very perspicuity makes them fail to engage the critic beyond this. Therefore generic fiction and the like do not merit a place in Frye's canon, however much he preoccupies himself for pedagogical reasons with such literature. The Bible is there because of its unique hypostasis of the deliverance or redemption pattern. Shakespearian tragedy and comedy are there, because in them we witness the very essence of the genres, but in a form much more rewarding, that is complicated, than in most other instances of the same genres. The established primary and secondary epics, Western and Oriental, are there for the same reasons. Novels and poetry with strongly accentuated patterns signifying deliverance, or at any rate, its potential, such as *Moby Dick* and 'The Rime of the Ancient Mariner' are there, again for exactly the same reason.

There is nothing arcane or over-studied about Frye's sense of literary value or critical mission. His line of reasoning is simple and to the point: man makes sense of his existential concerns in a symbolic way, the most widespread of which is language. By linguistic differentiation basic myths responding to such existential concerns are glossed over, and to get down to mythological basics critical efforts are indeed needed.

The relation of criticism to its object is that of one cultural tradition to another, since Frye defines criticism as the 'conscious organizing of a cultural tradition' (1982a:xviii), in which the implicit difference seems to be the absence – in mythologically derived texts – of conscious organizing in contrast to the presence – in criticism – of consciousness. Frye never elaborates this parallel between 'art' and 'craft', which invites a third instrument removed twice from myth and literature and once from criticism in a manner cultivated by post-structuralists and deconstructionists, or the deliberately Talmudic/Kabbalistic position of a Harold Bloom. But it gives to the critics the role of the master pedagogue keeping humans alert to basic existential concerns.

Frye's belief in the value of resonant literature is grounded upon the observation that whereas man is 'conditioned by nature and finds his conception of necessity in it, so the first thing he finds in the community of the word is the charter of his freedom' (1982a:22). In what Frye calls first-phase language, metaphor is still undetached from the speaker's or writer's general relating to his universe. It is in this first-phase metaphorical use that language attains its liberating power by re-establishing that very point of difference between nature and culture (that is language) where the contact is at one and the same time at its closest, with virtually nothing to separate naturally given from cultural metaphor. However, that 'virtually nothing', which is the metaphor vibrating between magical and poetic use, is enough to create a principle of linguistic possibility against which nature can place no barriers.

Whereas the magic spell is language as metaphor designed to control nature, poetry, of all linguistic uses the most metaphorical, shifts from the intended control of nature to the intended control of human minds reading and listening.

THE BIBLE, MYTH AND LITERARY CANON

In a temporal perspective myth anticipates literature, and in a formal perspective myth shares with literature basic patterns. In a functional perspective, myth is 'concerned knowledge, what it is important for a society to know' (1982a:47). In most respects, this functional aspect has developed into non-mythical, hence non-literary, kinds of discourse. In myth and in literature, however, it persists as a concern taken beyond the world of the limited possibility in the actual and into the verbal world of actually unlimited possibility, in which it expresses not so much the given, on which it of course builds, but the exhortatory or the wished-for.[16]

The mythical element in literature is clearly discernible in the combination of the actual, or reality, and the imaginative, verbal response, which may seek to explain, alleviate or counter the limitations imposed by the actual. The Bible does this to an eminent degree, since it seeks both to rationalize the given (the two creation myths, for instance) and to compensate for a feeling of human insufficiency (redemption and revelation).

Frye's attitude to the Bible hinges on the insights and attitudes of modern critical theology working towards its fragmentation and secularisation but at the same time with a clearly expressed wish to retain its status as a unity of a special kind. If the Bible has a special place in Frye's literary cosmology, bordering in places on a certain numinous attraction, it is surely in the possibility of establishing that unique unity:

> The Bible does not, for all its miscellaneous content, present the appearance of having come into existence through an improbable series of accidents; and, while it is certainly the end product of a long and complex editorial process, the end product needs to be examined in its own right (1982a:xvii).

Countering critical, historical and anthropological theology with a practice of literary criticism which short-circuits one kind of

rationality by another, Frye quietly brings back the Bible to a syn-
chronicity or timelessness which the Higher Criticism of the last
few centuries has attempted to bring into a diachronic dimension.
Needless to say, Frye's de-historicizing of the Bible has nothing
whatever to do with the lack of temporal perspective that the age of
the church fathers, lacking such perspective, necessarily had to
deploy. Frye's synchronization is matter of considering the heterogeneous texts of the Bible manifestations of a few recurrent patterns as the verbal reponses to existential needs, or what Frye in
1990 prefers to term 'primary concerns' in contradistinction to the
'secondary concerns' typical of ideological discourse. In Frye's
view, the Bible is a collocation of texts as a whole and in its parts
expressing a basic teleological desire on the shared latent premise
that the literal sense of the Bible as an order of words is identical
with the poetic sense.

The Bible is partly within, partly outside literature, according to
Frye. It makes use of literary elements, and its literal meaning is its
poetic meaning (cf. 1982a:62).[17] Yet the Bible cannot be exhausted
by the kind of critical analysis normally applied to literature, which
has to do with the function of the text. Put somewhat differently:
critical analysis may be used to open up the Bible. The results of the
analysis will not be ends in themselves, however, but instrumental
for the attempt to wring the uniquely Biblical meaning out of the
many texts of the two testaments. But it needs to be pointed out that
in this process of transcending the purely literary Frye does not
accept faith as the resolving factor, since he suggests that 'With the
Bible we are involved in a more complex theory of meaning and
truth than we are with other books' (1982a:62). The complexity is
what Frye is at pains to point out in his two Bible studies, but we
may observe here that the complexity in question is in terms of
quantitative elaboration rather than of a qualitative leap. Perhaps
this is most clearly seen in Frye's distinction between basic pagan
and Biblical myth structures: 'Paganism, . . . seems to be dominated
by the vision of cyclical recurrence. . . . Biblical myth, in contrast,
stresses a total beginning and end of time and space' (1982a:71).
This is a distinction of radical importance to the existential visions
involved, but in relation to the mythical 'explanations' offered they
are on an equal footing. On the whole, as a 'simultaneous metaphor
cluster' (1982a:76), the Bible offers a 'cosmology as a vision of
upward metamorphosis' (1982a:76), of which the point is that there
is 'energy without alienation' (1982a:76).

If the study of the Bible has a purpose in Frye's arguments, it is surely to do with the way that the Bible, by its unique status in combination with its literary characteristics, can be said to stand as the ideal of literature, formally and functionally.

Frye points out (1982a:51f.) that in a historical perspective, in which myth came before science, there has been a tendency towards increasing differentiation regarding branches of knowledge. Frye imagines an initial situation when myth was all-embracing, gradually surrendering more and more to science, with occasional atavistic leaps into totalitarian ideologies, the point of which is exactly to provide the individual with one universal frame of reference. On the whole, however, myth and mythologies have been allotted a more and more marginal place, as the curious remnants of old and backward cultures, made superfluous by the centrifugal advances of science and other kinds of learning. Both science and myth, however, show social concern, though pursued by different routes, at the same time as they find it necessary to consolidate their self-awareness, as it were. In whatever activity which has a bearing on the actual and is presented as text, there is a built-in dialectic between the centrifugal and the centripetal. In the case of science, the overall tendency is to give priority to the centrifugal over the centripetal: new insights have a definite bearing on the self-awareness of science. In the case of literature, one should have thought that the ratio was the opposite, with the pattern always trying to impress itself on the malleable actuality. But, as Frye argues,

> It may be more difficult for some to see that the writer or artist also may owe a loyalty to his own discipline, and may have to defend that discipline against the concerns of society, but the same principles hold there (1982a:51).

In other words, there is a disciplinary purity about the literary work, which should be safeguarded against an actuality all too likely to sacrifice literature in the name of social concern. Frye realizes the problem of the centrifugality of social concern tending to take precedence over the centripetality of disciplinary principles. Facing the Platonic dilemma, Frye sides with Aristotle, as did Shelley in the identical situation, and proposes a solution by which there is a balance between inner and outer necessity, the 'simultaneous sense of both the social relevance and the inner integrity of all the elements of human culture' (1982a:52). Myth, manifest as the mythical elements in literature, with its emphasis on primary concerns, overrides the secondary concerns of historical records (cf. 1990:61).

A critic of a Marxist-oriented persuasion would probably object that Frye holds out visionary or prophetic literature as the opium for the masses, and counter that the historical record is the best we have, but that its application to the future requires the proper dialectic-materialistic sanitation. To Frye, however, such an argument would be beside the point, since the synchronic perspeetive of myth is the only way of lending hope: 'it is only the myth in the present tense, not the event in the past, that has the power to give all the other poor wretches who have been victims of brutal injustice a place in the center of human vision' (1990:61).

It seems that Frye has been shifting tracks imperceptibly in his argument, in that he started with a discussion of the falling away from the shared core of knowledge and belief provided by myth until our own pluralistic times but ended up with observations on the identically constituted 'elements of human culture', all relying on social relevance as well as inner integrity. The message of the God of the Bible, Frye suggests, is a 'concern for the continuation of human life in time that goes far beyond the purely imaginative, together with a view of the human situation that goes equally far beyond the purely historical' (1982a:52). The original track is here found again with the suggestion of reestablishing the text – the Bible – as the ultimate testimony of this possibility. But Frye is really progressing along a double set of tracks, or rather one track set above the other as conductor rail in an object–meta relationship. The literary is the way towards redemption by force of its potential for imaginative liberation. At the same time literature furnishes us with an instrument for calibrating the proper proportion of the centrifugal opposite the centripetal.

Formulated somewhat differently, we may say that what Frye offers is a credo in a culture that favours a balanced view of society and humans, with enough intellectual integrity to be able to regulate any tendency towards excesses and agreed on the same values without which it would make no sense to talk about excesses. Frye somewhat diffidently uses the term democracy, as the opposite of totalitarian regimes (which include religious bodies), to describe the attractive kind of communal life:

For us democracy, as a source of loyalty, does not only mean the machinery of elections or a greater tolerance of religion and art or a greater relaxation of leisure, privacy, or freedom of movement, but to what all these things point to: the sense of an individuality that grows out of a society but is infinitely more than a social function (1982a:100).

The ideal existential state for the human being is one in which there is no longer any difference between work and play, in which energy is expended for its own pleasurable sake, and in which the

real form of wisdom in human life as the *philosophia* or *love* of wisdom that is creative and not simply erudite ... using past experience as a balancing pole for walking the tightrope of life, finally grows, though incessant discipline and practice, into the final freedom of movement where, in Yeats's phrase, we can no longer tell the dancer from the dance (1982a:125).

There will be no need to believe in the Bible in any fundamentalist way, but there needs to be consensus that the Bible – and other works of strong resonance – offer instruction in the way that individuals and societies articulate their existential concerns. Faith is here an irrelevant concept. The ultimate goal is vision, and

perhaps it is only through the study of works of human imagination that we can make any real contact with the level of vision beyond faith. For such vision is, among other things, the quality in all serious religions that enables them to be associated with human products of culture and imagination, where the limit is the conceivable and not the actual (1982a:232).

The real strength of the Bible is in opening up our eyes to this instead of slave-binding us in predisposed attitudes.

VISION, MYTH AND *BILDUNG*

Frye's poetics are wonderfully teachable: they justify in a very sophisticated manner literature as the truly civilizing force; they furnish the teacher with a 'syllabus', admittedly as a heuristic instrument, of a closed list of basic myths and an inventory of critical concepts all in accordance with the bulk of state-of-the-art manuals of critical concepts and terminology; they provide the teacher with a didactic procedure ready-made for classroom purposes, assuming the unity of the work of art as the 'practical working assumption that every act of criticism must begin with' (1990:101). And they give to literature a role sharing with sacred texts a perspective that takes the reader out of everyday reality into an alternative provisional reality based on a wished-for probability rather than the given actuality: 'So literature, with its sense of "anything is possible" and its convention of suspending disbelief even in the most fantastic assumptions, is a mode of language with a particular relation to hope' (1990:130). The Bible – and the best literature with it – holds up to the reader not an insight into a better world to come, but an insight into the way that human beings have tried to give a form to their hopes and fears, its validity tested by the survival of the texts through a very long time as a small inventory of structures, displaced according to contextual needs.

In the kind of literary criticism attempting to comprise all literature, either in its historical aspect or a specific verbal mode 'in the present tense as a total form of verbal imagination' (1971a:98), there is very often a note of apologetics, as even the titles of Sir Philip Sidney's and Shelley's famous essays testify. Sometimes this note takes the shape of an explanation of why literature has strayed from whatever a given society accepts as its central values, assuming that to begin with there was no such division and heralding a time when that will no longer be the case. Such an approach naturally leads to a view of literary history as something cyclical. Frye finds a place in this tradition of apologetics with his favourite Vico and his relations in spirit, Sidney and Shelley. In Frye's view the golden age vanished with the introduction of a writing culture. When writing became a means of communication rather than a ritualistic end, the uses of writing not serving the purposes of day-to-day business became of secondary importance, luxury activity, and consequently assigned to the private rather than the public sphere. In response to the growing neglect of conventions, the stamp of the public on art, literature develops into so many individual, private texts. This roughly, is the development of literature from primitive societies to the industrialized period of Romanticism. In Marxist terminology, the poet has become alienated, singing, in Shelley's words, to sweeten his own solitude. The state of artistic alienation perseveres until our own times, when an 'important and significant writer may be reactionary or superstitious: the one thing apparently that he cannot be is a spokesman of ordinary social values' (1971a:81). With the emergence of the age of science and technology the rift between the social scene formed by their language of truth of correspondence and the social concern which is the domain of literature are as far apart from each other as can be imagined.[18] Against a background of contemporary society literature seems to be either a relic or simply beside the point. Beside the point because it cannot integrate advanced truths of correspondence and so tends to go into directions different from those that sustain society. A relic because what it concerns itself with belongs to an age in which this integration was possible since scholars, artists and scientists agreed on metaphysical principles – an age of unified sensibility. Literature in this view is helplessly anachronistic, since it

> attempts to unite the physical environment to man through the most archaic of categories, the categories of analogy and identity, simile and metaphor, which the poet shares with the lunatic and the lover, and which are essentially the categories of magic (1971a:84).

The rift, however, is one based on a categorical misunderstanding, since the concern channelled by metaphors and archetypes as literature is one that accompanies man up through the times, as an essential part of his humanity. This of course places literature and its existential points in another light altogether, and the contours of its importance become visible.

It is essential to note that in Frye's view literature is the realization of shared experiences rendered in recurrent structures. Literature is part of the public sphere, and there is nothing in literature which cuts it off from the public, not even what is usually thought of as private imagery (1971a:22). The structures of literature have come into existence in response to basic existential needs, and these structures have proved useful through the ages for accommodating new experience, but on the principle of variations on a theme, so that we are not facing innumerable repetitions but recognizing an identity in what we read. Therefore Frye can approach the literary text at one and the same time as tying it in with the historical period which saw its emergence and raised it above the temporal, since the text, by necessarily assuming its shape through archetypal mediation, enters into a system of purely literary coherence, which is timeless.

The literary text as something existing out of time, subject to public ownership, and through its archetypes patterned to render an idea or a vision of something more in tune with presenting our fears and wishes as integral wholes in contrast to the multiple loose ends of actuality, assumes a central role as a truly civilizing force. It follows from this that education, in the widest possible sense of the word, is a key concept in Frye's critical thought, together with considerations on the kind of society that allows the optimal conditions for such an education to be practised.

At heart an Aristotelian relying on literature as the structured representation of men and women in action according to imagined probabilities rather than actual possibilities, Frye pleads for literary experience rooted in what he calls myths of concern. But counteracting the implications of the myth of concern there is a myth of freedom. The proportional relationship between the two basic myths is constantly changing according to the actual situation. Although Frye himself never uses the parallel, it is tempting to compare the myth of freedom with Freud's id and the myth of concern with the policing function of the super-ego.[19] The energy that forms society is given expression in the complex of myths and mythically-based practices which degenerates into an all-powerful conservative drift if not regulated by the myth of freedom, which 'constitutes the "liberal" element in society' (1971b:45).[20] The two myths exist in a relationship of checks and balances. The two myths – the dialectic of a sense of the given and a sense of the ideal – give rise, Hegel-wise, to a 'third order of experience, . . . of a world that may not exist but completes existence, the world of the definitive experience that poetry urges us to have but which we never quite get' (1971a:170–1). At this point Frye is on the verge of formulating an erotics of literary criticism, substituting for Aristotelian structuralism and analogous mimetics a Platonic phenomenology involving longing for a metaphysical Other, which has the status of the highest attainable. Platonic, because the kind of experiential phenomenon is not confined to any one category of experience, but fuses all categories of insight, working by analogy:

A direct experience or apprehension of such a world would be a microcosmic experience, an intelligence or imagination finding itself at the centre of an intelligible or imaginable totality, and so experiencing, for however brief an instant, without any residue of alienation (1971a:32).

We long to recover this identity, but 'Most of us, at least, never reach it directly in experience at all, but only through one of the articulated analogies, of which literature is a central one' (1971a:32). Frye applies his idea in more concrete terms to the Canadian destiny in his Whidden Lectures, in which he takes as his theme the centenary of the confederation of Canada:

> In a year bound to be full of discussions of our identity, I should like to suggest that our identity, like the real identity of all nations, is the one that we have failed to achieve. It is expressed in our culture, but not attained in our life, just as Blake's new Jerusalem to be built in England's green and pleasant land is no less a genuine ideal for not having been built there (1967a:123).

Life never attains what literature puts forth as desirable and which is always experienced with joy.[21] If that was the case, literature would have ceased to matter as the ethical corrective presented aesthetically which it is in Frye's 'system'. Education, which should be based on literary experience, is the holding up of models to the person being educated, models which the person may like or dislike, may find repulsive or attractive, but which by their very nature complete the gap which is found to exist between the world as we know it and the world as we would like to see it, whether through the lenses of irony, satire and tragedy or the lenses of pastoral, romance or comedy.

There seem to be two requirements for making this optimal literary experience possible. One is a society that has matured into a state in which the myths of concern do not fetter the myths of freedom. This rules out societies held in the sway of ideologies, as examples of which Frye keeps referring to communist and theocratic societies. On the other hand, a certain amount of shared existential values is required so that the myths of concern do not yield completely to myths of freedom. The balance between the two is always precarious, but literature must be presumed to contribute to an awareness of the precariousness by essentially implying this very balance in its deployment of timeless archetype in timely subject matter. In this very balance are both the *terminus a quo* and the *terminus ad quem* of literature in relation to the interests of a civilized society: 'The basis of all tolerance in society, the condition in which a plurality of concerns can co-exist, is the tension between concern and freedom' (1971a:108). To be truly educated means to be able at one and the same time to hold a belief and to question it critically, as Frye puts it: 'there is nothing that is not the concern of concern, and similarly there is nothing that can be excluded from free enquiry and the truth of correspondence' (1971a:109).

In his quest for an ethics through an aesthetics Frye arrives at a vision of an ideal but unattainable state in which there is full identity between our wishes and reality. However, in the world we live in, there is the possibility of an approximation to this state of existential bliss via the literary imagination, which receives and produces literature. Through the application of the literary imagination the texts of religion will turn out to make sense as poetic language. Those who have been educated to appreciate the difference and the interdependence of concern and freedom, and for whom the university with its tradition for critical inquiry is the *alma mater* in a broader sense than the usual, will bring their understanding to society, which, if receptive, will react with a cor-responding balance in public and private life, in a 'liberal or "open" mythology, of the sort appropriate to a democracy' (1967a:115).[22] The very idea of a canon as a list of approved works is anathema to this desired state of society, since it inevitably contributes to closing the myth(s) of which it is the function. Hence Frye is in a position to conclude that 'an open society has no canon' (1967a:118). In a truly democratic society there are no guardians of faith to act as thought-police, no general elite to regulate public life: 'in a democracy everybody belongs to some kind of élite, which derives from its social function a particular knowledge or skill that no other group has' (1967a:118). To a certain extent this kind of society is already in existence, or rather the conditions for it, in Europe and in North America. Frye is hardly a revolutionary preacher but a spokesman for the existential values held by liberals all over the world.

At the centre of Frye's blueprint for a proper education into civilization is the central position given to the study of literature and, within literature, to the foregrounding of poetry as the centre of literature in contrast to much contemporary educational practice centring on literature as communication hence giving priority to prose, literary and utilitarian (cf. 1971b:144). It is the study of poetry as the essential verbal manifestations of our anxieties and

hopes that must form the hub of the liberal education needed to
form the ideal citizen. The study of poetry, and of literature generally, instils a sense at the same time of a need for myths of concerns
and their counterparts, the myths of freedom. The privilege of
poetic language is its untired service for the verbal expression of
what we fear and hope. We learn at one and the same time about
the concerns and their destruction. But as it is equally dangerous to
be swallowed up uncritically in a myth of concern, and to lose
one's bearings completely in myths of freedom, the essential importance of poetry is in its invitation to dialectical movement between certainty and uncertainty. To argue in favour of closing
the canon is to embrace a closed myth of concern; and to do the
opposite, to argue in favour of total pluralism, is to lose orientation
completely. The only way, the proper critical path, is to read on and
sort out with a sceptical mind equally aware of the need for a sense
of tradition and the accompanying need for its constant questioning, for the 'free authority' as Frye calls it. This is the legacy of
the universities with their commitment under the educational contract to the application of the myths of freedom to the myths of
concern, which is the environment best suited to the furtherance
of humanity's hopes and needs.[23]

For all practical purposes, Frye's transformation of a canon of
texts into a canon of reading is a charter for a truly liberal education, that is, one that imaginitively sets us free.

6

Harold Bloom: Swerving into Ever-Renewed Strength

Whatever the Western Canon is, it is not a program for social salvation (1994:29).

For why do men write poems? To rally everything that remains, and not to sanctify nor propound (1973:22).

[T]he covert subject of most poetry for the last three centuries has been the anxiety of influence, each poet's fear that no proper work remains for him to perform (1973:148).

To Harold Bloom canon formation is 'ultimately a society's choices of texts for perpetuation and study' (1975a:200), and in this there seems to be no basis for quarrel between Bloom and the great majority of canon defenders. But with Bloom's principle of agonistic misreading there are certainly differences in the premises that lead us to this conclusion, since the canon is also an *'achieved anxiety'* (1994:526; Bloom's italics). The literary tradition in Bloom's perspective is not a handing down of similarities and friendly borrowing from past masters. On the contrary, it is brought about as the result of fierce fights for self-assertion on the part of younger writers in relation to their forebears. In Bloom's critical universe the stakes are ruggedly existential in a Darwinian struggle for survival, and the tradition-making struggle is no more merciful and humane than the rest of creation in a Darwinian world: 'Out of the strong comes forth strength, even if not sweetness, and when strength has imposed itself long enough, then we learn to call it tradition, whether we like it or not' (1975a:200).[1]

Bloom, unlike the other three critics studied in this book, does not find in the setting up of the canon a process or a result with wide-ranging and positive significance for something vaguely known as society, culture or mankind. When writers gain for themselves a place in the canon – which anyway it takes at least two generations to determine (1994:522) – it is a very private and selfish showdown with a beloved but also paradoxically hated precursor. To the reader the only ethical value of the canon is its constant reminding of the imposition of limits (1994:35), forcing the reader ultimately to face the final limit of death (1994:32 and 200). This is one reason why Bloom calls himself an 'elegiac' critic in *The Western Canon* (1994), the other, the rather more readily appreciable one, that he sees himself as the last agonist against a production and consumption of literature serving ends different from the aesthetic.

Bloom, however, shares with less radical canon theorists a concept of the valid literary tradition as an extremely fastidious selection in terms of a process which is dialectical within an overall logic of spiral circularity. Bloom is metonymical in terms of ever oblique contiguity, whereas Eliot is metaphorical with intertextual substitution as the principle of his own writings (both explicit and implicit reference and allusion). Eliot strives to define a tradition of objectively defined textuality – a classical tradition – purified of personal elements, whereas Bloom arrives at a Romantic tradition characterized exactly by the presence of productive personalities strong enough to assert themselves by their violent and patricidal individualism. So, according to Bloom's own dogma, by his very opposition to Eliot, he is his true heir.[2]

The number of poets to have merited the sustained critical interest of Bloom makes up an exclusive canonical list. Compared with the astounding scope of Frye's literary frame of reference, Bloom's steady and narrow focusing most recently on Shakespeare and previously on the Romantics proper – Blake and Shelley having both been given book-length attention – and two Romantic modernists – Yeats and Stevens, also treated at considerable length – appears to ignore many of the standard major as well as almost all the standard minor writers who go into conventional literary history.

Bloom's literary history is a history consisting of unique individuals and unique texts related paradoxically to each other by their intertextual tensions, producing in effect an inevitable sadness or melancholy, an anxiety deriving, in the examplary case of Thomas Mann in relation to Goethe, from the knowledge that 'one cannot write a novel without remembering another novel' (1973:55). Artistic creation thus contains an enormous negative charge gathered together by the artist's terrible anxiety of being smothered by his forebears, and his equally terrible urge to destroy them. One is entitled to query where the pleasure traditionally associated with art is in this negative and gloomy approach to literary art. Only very sporadically does Bloom admit to joy or pleasure in connection with poetry, and then as a corollary of defence in the Freudian sense of the term: 'the beautiful necessity of defense' (1975b:82). In his description of the dynamics of poetic response, Bloom sees the encounter of a poet with the precursor poem as a process which 'takes the poet back beyond the pleasure principle to the decisive initial encounter and response that began him' (1975a:18). The 'high unpleasure' or the 'more difficult pleasure' (1994:30) characteristic of the canonical text is derived for the investment into it of its author's 'cognitive acuity, linguistic energy, and power of invention' (1994:46) which 'fuse in an ontological passion that is a capacity for joy' (1994:46). As the final, difficult and authentic pleasure (1994:443) it gives to the idea of literary pleasure another dimension than the mere appreciation of harmonious sound pattern or even the Coleridgean unity-in-variety condition. The nature of pleasure or joy in connection with literature is hence something that Bloom never really considers to be a subject of its own, but always integral to the very canonicity of a given work. The object of pleasure, poetic beauty, appears as the presence of the structural order emerging from the application of an assumed interpretative pattern. In the early criticism, the appreciation of Blake's apocalyptic endeavour gives to Blake's works such beauty (cf. 1963:9); later on, beauty is seen to depend on the extent to which the principle of strength applies.

Bloom's focus is almost invariably on the semantic side of the poetic text to the exclusion of its formal aspects. Poetry, to Bloom, is constituted by what a more conventional poetics would call the content or substance aspect.[3] In the early work he follows Emerson – who in this respect is in agreement with Shelley, Wordsworth and Coleridge – in suggesting that the poetic is a question of the nature of the idea seeking expression. Bloom quotes Emerson to the effect that

it is not meters, but a meter-making argument that makes a poem, – a thought so passionate and alive that like the spirit of a plant or an animal it has an architecture of its own, and adorns nature with a new thing. The thought and the form are equal in the order of time, but in the order of genesis the thought is prior to the form (Emerson quoted in 1975a:20).

And the example adduced is a sweeping interpretation of what in Hardy constitutes this metre-making argument, that is, a 'skeptical lament for the hopeless incongruity of ends and means in all human acts . . . the truest name for the human condition is simply that it is loss' (1975a:20). Bloom, despite his insistence on the 'idea-ness' of the poem, never really engages with the problem of the phenomenology of poetic constructs. The closest he comes is in the Peirce-inspired rejection of New Criticism, supposedly favouring an approach to poems as monads, whereas a triad concept, with reference to Peirce's suggestion of a sign relation termed 'third-ness', being a relational mediation between a 'sign, its object, and the interpreting thought' (Peirce quoted in 1975b:56), is much more appropriate, since to Bloom a poem is a 'mediating process be-tween itself and a previous poem' (1975b:57), a 'relational event' (1975b:106), which is interpretation itself.[4] Bloom's view of the mode of existence as a literary work of art is, then, if we consider Wellek and Warren's Ingarden-derived structure of norms, the distillation of New Criticism poetics, different in so far as the work of art can never be made to stand still for the observation of a specific norm level. The poem is a troped rendering of an idea, the trope, however, being the rhetorical abstraction of a poetic image (1975b:65).[5] As soon as the image is taken in by the reading con-sciousness, in the act of interpretation that the act of reading necess-arily is, the image-realized-as-trope changes into a psychic defence. In *The Western Canon* the image, in the light of the strong focus on Shakespeare, appears in the *Gestalt* of the character, since accord-ing to Bloom the achievement of originality is most difficult and therefore most important in 'everything that matters most: repre-sentations of human beings, the role of the memory in cogni-tion, the range of metaphor in suggesting new possibilities for language' (1994:10). However, Bloom has not succumbed to any A. C. Bradleyan approach to literature, but his critical attention has been directed to the lodging of the image potential in character, which is different from reading literature (drama) as the verbal transcription of human action.[6]

Recognition of an image as a reaction to an earlier image in the act of reading – the poet's and the reader's – constitutes the mo-ment of truth, the moment when the poem comes into its own. That moment is not to be considered any 'right' reading of a text, since there are no such right readings of texts, only strong and weak readings, but a reading imposing itself by its immediate strength, setting a whole system of texts in motion, as it were.

It follows that any discussion about influence must ignore not only issues that have to do with 'verbal resemblances between one poet and another' (1975a:19) but also the traditional tracing of motifs and themes that academic comparative criticism specializes in. The critic must dive down into what Bloom somewhat vaguely calls the 'depths' (1975a:21) which are, supposedly, more or less the subconscious – the Freudian id – where primal-scene love-and-hate battles are fought.[7]

It goes without saying that such an approach to literary history relies on a mediating critical consciousness different from the one able to make out the textual and conceptual similarities on which conventional literary history is based. The mediating critical consciousness in Bloomian literary history is one able to make out textual traces of resistance and opposition to other texts. This requires will to interpretation in terms of a scheme designed to bring out not only differences rather than similarities, but also of a nature that naturalizes such interpretation in a framework larger than literature itself, a framework within which literature can be read as a symptom of an ongoing, never-ending struggle for dominance and power. Such a framework Bloom has devised by a combination of psychoanalytic and kabbalistic concepts and terminology. It is therefore necessary first to take a look at Bloom's interpretative system to see how it validates his critical interpretation and then to move on to its application to his chosen canon.

THE DYNAMICS OF AN AGONISTIC CANON

Although perhaps not his best book, *The Anxiety of Influence: A Theory of Poetry* from 1973 is Bloom's articulation of his central poetics, standing in the same kind of relation to both his theoretical and practical work as Frye's *The Great Code* does to his. Bloom's work prior to *The Anxiety of Influence* – the studies of Shelley (1959), Blake (1963 and Erdman 1965) and Yeats (1970) – points forward to it for a theoretical resolution, and it forms the matrix for what has followed, regarding his elaboration of the hermetic framework, in *A Map of Misreading* (1975) and *Kabbalah and Criticism* (1975),[8] and of his practical, interpretative criticism, of which *Wallace Stevens: The Poems of Our Climate* (1977) stands out as a singular triumphant critical achievement of a deliberately strong critic. With *The Western Canon* (1994) the focus is somewhat changed, but the lens remains the same. In this bid for 26 canonical writers, with Shakespeare as the central figure with whom all later writers have to struggle and by whom all previous writers are judged, Bloom makes clearer some of his main issues, and delimits his ground against what he loosely and wryly terms the School of Resentment, which includes most structuralist and poststructuralist criticism.

Bloom's central distinction between weak and strong poets rests on an ability to decide the manner in which a poet has managed his anxiety of influence as 'creative misunderstanding' (1975b:62). In a poet like Oscar Wilde, this anxiety is all too visible as the poet's consciousness of having absorbed and recycled the poetic past, and in the process lost his own personality, the net result, despite a show of idealization, being a sense of loss, of dilution (1973:5–7). Strong poets – and they are the ones who make poetic history (1973:5) – overcome their anxiety of influence by reacting against those supposed to be capable of exerting influence in order to free themselves of any fetters whatsoever.[9] The main objective for strong poets is to create 'imaginative space' (1973:5) for themselves, and this involves deliberate or instinctive evasion of influence, usually appreciable not as evasion but as opposition. By this logic, the study of poetic influence, which has to do with 'imaginative priority' (1973:72), that is, the (strong) poet's will to creation, with due attention paid to the kind or degree of anxiety of influence, turns into the study of poetic misprision (1973:7), involving the study of the 'life-cycle of the poet-as-poet' (1973:7).[10]

That this complex argument is not without difficulties, even contradictions, I shall return to below, but first the term 'misprision' deserves attention, since it is one of Bloom's key terms and in itself a demonstration of a strong person's appropriation of a word away from its usual line of derivative influence for his own idiosyncratic purposes.

'Misprision', according to the *OED*, is an Old French word ('*mesprison*') meaning mistake or error, whence it has entered English legal language in the sense of judicial misdemeanour, a failure of duty on the part of a public official. In the special sense related to treason or felony, 'misprision of treason' came to mean the concealment of a person's knowledge of treasonable actions. In popular parlance the term took on the more general meaning of 'mistake' or 'misunderstanding'. An obsolete sense of the term is 'malformation of nature'. The *OED* lists as another, and archaic, sense of the term, derived from a slightly different French root (*'mespris'*), 'contempt, scorn', or 'failure to appreciate or recognize as valuable'. No doubt all these overtones appeal to a critic keen on tracing influence as anxious anti-influence in terms of evasion and opposition, in other words as treason – contemptuous or not – against a well-protected sense of literary history as a process of imitation and adaptation.

Although Bloom is attracted by Nietzsche's appropriation of the antithetical and by Freud's theory of defence as analogous supports for the revisionary ratios on which his elaboration on intra-poetic relations rely, there is nonetheless a need for modification.[11] It is true that in the development of his theory of poetic misprision in terms of radical revisionism, Bloom approaches the stance of Shelley – the subject of his first and in retrospect tentative major study – attributing to poets – Shelley's *vates* or *hierophants* – and to poetry more power than conceded by Nietzsche or Freud. But at the same time Bloom considers the power of the imagination or phantasmagoria exaggerated in their teachings. The reason is that Bloom finds Nietzsche somewhat wide of the chosen mark by his idealism, for which he wishes to substitute the literal, and in his preference for the rational, which must yield place to divination. Indeed, even though Shelley is more than just a hovering shadow in this situatedness of poets and poetry as strong literalists with intuitive access to what in *The Anxiety of Influence* is still only vaguely hinted at, there is no embracing of the Romantic poet's neo-Platonic burning fountain as the *ne plus ultra*. So Bloom's invocation of Nietzsche and Freud, with a view to the antithetical and mechanisms of defence respectively, only brings him to the point of highly tentative analogues, as he readily admits (1973:8) to the dynamics of the six revisionary ratios[12] – clinamen, tessera, kenosis, daemonization, askesis, apophrades[13] – instrumental for the understanding of intra-poetic relationships as influential anxiety. Bloom himself provides a capsule definition of the first five in the following manner: 'For *clinamen* and *tessera* strive to correct or complete the dead, and *kenosis* and *daemonization* work to repress memory of the dead, but *askesis* is the contest proper, the match-to-the-death with the dead' (1973:122). The sixth ratio, *apophrades*, is then the return of the dead in the poetry of the living, to such an extent even that it appears as if the precursor imitates the later poet. In *A Map of Misreading* the six ratios are correlated within a dialectic of revisionism in which the antithesis of 'limitation' and 'substitution' receive their synthesis in 'representation', a dialectical operation covering the relation between every successive pair of two ratios. To the six ratios correspond six Freudian psychic defences. Between on the one side the revisionary ratios and their corresponding psychic defences and on the other the three dialectic pairs, we find the textual categories in which these are manifested, both described by the proper rhetorical trope – irony, synecdoche, metonymy, hyperbole/litotes, metaphor and metalepsis – and by the kind of imagery to which the tropes apply. 'What I have called "revisionary ratios" are tropes and psychic defenses, both and either, and are manifested in poetic imagery' (1975a:89). It should be added that to complete Bloom's strong appropriation of Freud we need to take into account that the process of poetic misprision is considered (almost) identical with the sublimation on the part of writers and readers of aggressive instincts.

Misprision in literary history is, however, a phenomenon with a double edge. On the part of the poet, misprision, the necessary revolt against the precursor, is experienced as a sin, as the rejection of an earlier authority (1973:78). No wonder that the 'ephebe' or the newcomer feels at a loss at what must be felt as betrayal of one most dear to him. But at the same time, looking beyond the personal situation of the individual poet, the commitment of misprision is a sign of health. In a kind of antithetical Darwinian process, the survival of the fittest poet is a matter not of adaptability but of the exact opposite: poetic survival is granted to the poet most able to stand out.

In Bloom's view, Freud is not a sufficiently strong 'poet' since it is the very nature of his notion of defence mechanisms that they provide a 'second chance'. Defence mechanisms are essentially remedial, taking the pressure out of primordial urges, thus always aiming at the restoration of a balance as a secondary stage. This goes right against Bloom's axiom that '[p]oets as poets cannot accept substitutions, and fight to the end to have their initial chance alone' (1973:8). Strong poets show their strength exactly in their intuitive bull's-eye hit. They do not need, indeed they scorn any attempt at rationalistic or trial-and-error workings-out of trajectories. Only the power of divination will suffice to provide the necessary condition for the strong poet to produce his literal 're'-creation.

Caught in an all-too-human propensity for defence reaction (Freud) and the intuitively realized need for refusing to let go into defence, the strong poet instinctively opposes (Nietzsche's antithesis) to subliminally defend his own being, thereby creating the necessary space. The ultimate point of opposition is death, in Hartman's phrase quoted by Bloom (1973:9), a natural priority opposed to spiritual authority.

In Bloom's view, the motive force in every new poet's effort is the rebellion against the necessity – the priority – of death, 'a poem is written to escape dying' (1975a:19), later on modified into the 'final antagonist, which is not death but time and time's "it was"' (1977:11).[14] This realized, the fight is foredoomed, since death will assert itself indiscriminately of poetic endeavour. The grandeur of Wordsworth's 'Immortality Ode' rests exactly on the persistence of its antithesis to death, and its comparative failure is in its assumption of the defence mechanism of successful sublimation, a characteristic it shares with its stronger precursor poem, Milton's 'Lycidas'.

Bloom's main tenet, then, is the assumption that a poet will inevitably try to rebel against the fact of death, the basic natural priority. This he will do by forcing the natural into the poetic. The success of the poet – his strength – is in his relative success of offering opposition to the existentially unavoidable without it petering out into sublimation – mere verse.

In mapping out the theoretical foundations, Bloom offers for illumination a capsule literary history, which, relying on an implicit cyclical perspective, again reminds the reader strongly of Shelley.

It is hardly surprising that Bloom turns to Romantic poetry for this theory. On the one hand it provides him with a poetics – the distillation of which is in Shelley's 'Defence of Poetry' more than anywhere else[15] – which celebrates the intuitive leap of the specially gifted seer. On the other it forms the conceptual background to the theorizing of both Nietzsche and Freud, in Bloom's shape of things comparatively weak Romantic latecomers, but useful for heuristic purposes. But one should not be led into the error of categorizing Bloom as a mere idolator of Romanticism. Rather, Romanticism is to be seen as an especially pedagogical example of the strong poets' rebellion, first and last against death.[16] The greatness of Wordsworth's 'Intimations of Immortality' ode is to be found in its high aim of attempting to negate what Hartman terms nature's priority by the imposition of cultural authority. This is an impossible venture, doomed to failure, but marks will be given for trying hard. In Wordsworth's case the desperation stemming from the realization of the ultimate impossibility of merging nature with culture is added to by the circumstance that the ode not only attempts to evade death but also attempts to overcome the anxiety of influence from Milton's 'Lycidas', a poem which, according to Bloom, refuses even harder not to succumb to that arbiter between natural necessity and cultural possibility, sublimation.

The gist of Bloom's anxiety theory then, is to be found in a view of poetry as always more or less attempting to deny death, and not just in the trivial sense of a poem becoming 'immortal' by entering the literary canon. A degree of defence, as sublimation, is always present, because this is culture reacting against nature; and poetry, except for the very first poem ever written, reacts both in relation to the poet's awareness of death and in relation to earlier attempts at containing death, hence the anxiety of influence.

It is not Romanticism as a period which is attractive to Bloom, but the rebellion against and the denial of the natural by insisting on its cultural transformation into an ideal merger – Hulme's derogatory 'circumambient gas' – which Romanticism espouses. The greatness, the strength, is in the insistence and the ultimately ensuing tragedy of vast and irrevocable failure. Romanticism, in this sense of an existential attitude, not an epoch, is to be found throughout literary history, but with the progress of time as an increasingly diluted version of the essential struggle against nature since the poet's reaction in terms of anxiety of influence will lead further and further away from the real thing. When Bloom deplores the weakening of English poetry (1973:10) since the Renaissance up through the Enlightenment, Romanticism, modernism and postmodernism, he finds that weakening a regrettable but inevitable fact in view of culture's, that is, poetry's, accumulating and repeatedly anxious evasion of nature. So poetry is bound to diminish in existential importance with time because increasingly weighed down by its past strength. In Bloom's view, then, the project of Romanticism, as trendy modern critics would call it, was bound to fail, because the burden of the past cannot be shed but keeps on growing. The favourite Romantic image of Prometheus, the giver of fire to mankind, must yield his place to blinded Oedipus, ignorant of the Sphinx as his muse (1973:10).

This defeatist view of cultural history with, presumably, the Renaissance and antiquity as the golden ages of poetry, would presumably lead to a necessarily decreasing critical interest in poets since Shakespeare.[17] But Bloom's analytical tool of the six revisionary ratios applicable to individual poets at any time redeems certain poets by the degree to which they can be shown to fight against their anxiety and thus to enter into the tradition – the canon – of great strugglers which makes up Bloom's Parnassus. For that purpose the blindness and the ignorance of Oedipus may be turned into an asset. Again here, the solution is the intuitive leap of 'Romantic' man. Oedipus, Bloom asserts, 'was on the path to oracular godhood' (1973:10), and by the same oracular short-circuit 'strong poets have followed him by transforming their blindness towards their precursors into the revisionary insights of their own work' (1973:10).

THE ROLE AND ACTIVITY OF CRITICISM

The validity of Bloom's literary theory and its consequences for practical critical work depend first on the degree to which his argument is felt to provide readers with new interpretative positions. In the conventional view of critical history, Bloom's 'method' is the rationalization of impressionism in terms of tropes related to psychoanalysis and a rather customized view of literary history. The centrality of tropes in Bloom's poetics is to be found in their status as approximations to divine creation via the 'sefirot' of the Zohar of the Kabbalah (being 'ten complex images for God in His process of creation' (1975b:27)) in that the sefirot are 'complex figurations for God, tropes or turns of language that *substitute* for God' (1975b:25; Bloom's italics). In this way Kabbalah is made to serve both as methodology and as theory:[18] the latter by constituting a conceptual model – the 'classic paradigm upon which Western revisionism in all areas was to model itself ever since' (1975b:33–4) – for the study of tradition and influence applicable to literature. The Kabbalah serves as a methodology by instituting misprision as both a descriptive and an operational element for practical criticism working on a post-Enlightenment tradition analogous to an inherited religious tradition 'already so rich and coherent that it allows very little room for fresh revelations or even speculations' (1975b:33). Indeed, Bloom admits to working in a way identical to the poet ridden by anxiety of influence. Helped along by the work of Angus Fletcher, Geoffrey Hartman and Paul de Man, he has been made to see the 'impasse of formalism', the 'barren moralizing' of archetypal criticism, and the 'dreariness of all those developments in European[19] criticism that have yet to demonstrate that they can aid in reading any one poem by any poet whatsoever' (1973:12–13).[20] Although Bloom would hardly count himself a deconstructionist, both the description of the state of modern criticism – including the arrogant dismissal of contemporary European work – as an *aporia* situation and his almost violent effort to get away from it by nothing but individual willpower, are certainly recognizable to those familiar with Derrida.[21] Having dismissed established critical approaches and endorsed deconstructive departures, Bloom is ready to embrace the critical muse of free play, presenting his theory of poetry 'as a severe poem' (1973:13) and his readings of poems as 'antithetical practical criticism' (1973:13).

Bloom works as a literary historian, in so far as he is first and foremost concerned with the situatedness of the poem in a tradition and as a pronouncement of a poet responding to previously written poems making up the tradition. But here the resemblance between the conventional literary historian and Bloom ceases. In his rejection of 'understanding' as a viable approach to poetry (1973:43) – thus gibing at the accredited pedagogy of New Criticism[22] – he suggests that we give up reading poems as entities, replacing this reading practice by always reading beyond the individual poem on to its precursor poem or poems. This poem or these poems can only be reached by the route of misprision. The redeeming virtue of this method of critical appreciation, which requires a singular empathy with Bloom's mental activity, supposedly saves the power of the poem, since the anxiety or the poet's sense of loss will remain not only intact, but will indeed be highlighted (1973:43). Modern literary history, according to Bloom, consists of the 'accurate recording of these revisionary swerves' (1973:44), an expression which to the non-initiate may sound to some extent as a *contradictio in adjecto*, and we are not helped much more by the declaration of the antithetical critic's task half-way into *The Anxiety of Influence*. After having objected against both tautological and reductive criticism, the first apparently associated with formal criticism and the latter with historical criticism of various kinds, Bloom asserts that only another poem can be the meaning of a given poem, and certainly not in the sense of conventional theories of influence, which deploy the concept in the sense of the 'passing-on of images and ideas from earlier to later poets' (1975a:3).[23] The idea is to hunt for 'any central poem by an indubitable precursor' (1973:70), and the poet's familiarity with the text is irrelevant. Great responsibility is here placed on the critic. For it is left to him to assess the indubitability of the precursor, and when found, the exact text which is the central one. Bloom's habit of not deigning to explain in any detail exactly how the precursor poem is found except by an intuitive leap is exemplified by the taking for granted for instance, of Shelley's daemonized – in the revisionary-ratio sense – rewriting of Wordsworth's 'Intimations of Immortality' ode as the 'Hymn to Intellectual Beauty' (1973:108).[24] One suspects that the reason for considering these two together is to be found in the obvious parallels in the two poems, first in the shared idealism but also in the tone and atmosphere; in other words, in a conventionally influential relationship between the two. A central series of misprision as influence can be traced in Wordsworth's 'Intimations', Shelley's 'West Wind', Keats's 'Ode to Psyche' and Tennyson's 'Ulysses' (1975a: 144 ff.). That a more conventional idea of 'influence' is at work at least at a certain stage in the antithetical process of misprision emerges in Bloom's direction on how to find the poet who will turn out at a later stage in his personal development as a really strong poet. The relationship between ephebe and precursor is a presence in the ephebe's early writing of a kind of distillation of the precursor's voice, a repetition of something, but at a high level of intensity, which makes the swerving away from it all the more obvious (1975a:17).[25] However, this kind of observation is not really called for except in the cases when we know – and we need the mature poet for this – that we have to do with a strong poet, as it is typical of most writers that their initial work is strongly imitative.

Adopting Gnostic imagery from Valentinus, Bloom describes the strong poet's falling from the fulness (Pleroma) that was and the reestablishing of himself in its passionate workings; in other words, by wrestling with poetic tradition until he is able to counter it, but never able to escape it completely. However, the imagery also applies to Bloom the critic in his relations to the traditions of criticism and literary theory. So the effort is really the double one of pursuing critical goals different from those of traditional criticism, mainly freeing himself of any significance attached to influence, by tracing textual evidence of defence mechanisms or antitheses, and of arguing the same kind of dynamics at work in the text(s) under consideration.

For practical analytical purposes Bloom's instrument of the six revisionary ratios are discernible as tropes, that is rhetorical figures in the individual text which defend against the 'deathly dangers of literal meaning' (1975a:94).[26] Central to his argument is the proposition that the strong poem is a particularly energetic turning on its precursor poem. By violent resistance to an urge to return, the strong poem puts on display, as it were, its very anteriority. In the strong poem this struggle is visible in the imagery as the tropes equivalent to the ratios appearing one after another. For analytical – classroom – purposes, students of strong literary texts are asked to recognize certain images as belonging in groups of tropes relating to the defence mechanisms of the six ratios not, however, necessarily in the order suggested. The important thing is the dialectical working of substitution, with representations and limitations in incessant interaction in a process – the dialectic of revisionism – described, with recourse to Luria, as a 'triple rhythm of contraction, breaking apart, and mending, a rhythm continuously present in time even as it first punctuated eternity' (1975b:39); in Bloom's own map of misprision as the repeated process of limitation, substitution and representation (1975a:84), the 'governing dialectic of Post-Enlightenment or Revisionist poetry' (1975b:61).[27] This is an analytical procedure which in principle is no different from any other image-hunting in Wolfgang Clemen and Wilson Knight on Shakespeare searching for thematic clusters or in Frye on Blake searching for elements of quest imagery – But Bloom has radically different aims.

Bloom invites judgement of his theory of poetry as argument (1973:13), which is quite fair, since all theories of poetry are ultimately arguments or hypotheses, whose validity must be proved by the acceptability of the kind of insight they yield. Bloom's aim is to be able to lay bare the 'melancholy of the creative mind's desperate insistence upon priority' (1973:13), the priority of the natural order transcending the authority of the spiritual order. The struggle of priority and authority is the essence of poetry, and its realization constitutes Vico's 'Poetic Wisdom' (1973:13) or Bloom's 'dreadful necessity' (1973:13).

Bloom's quest is a darkly Romantic one, the search for a life – or better text – principle best described in terms from Gnosticism or the Kabbalah.[28] The Kabbalah, especially in the Lurianic version, is a model for creation, and Bloom finds his critical inspiration by analogy in the texts and practices of the Kabbalah, which attempts to open Scriptural meaning by incessant, even wildly speculative interpretation (1975a:4).[29] Not that Bloom himself is a mystic in the usual sense of the word. But he is the archetypal Romantic, looking always for that of which even the strongest poetry is never more than an analogue or a metaphor. Even though reading by principles that he insists on applying to poets and poetry only, Bloom is engaging in the greater project of laying bare nothing less than an existential foundation. We will do well to remember here that to Bloom there is in principle no difference between the poet and the critic, since all poetry is criticism and vice versa. Just as the strong poet achieves his peculiar strength by misrepresenting, the critic worth his salt must take upon him the task of constantly reminding readers – including poets – that they are inevitably latecomers, the inheritors of a towering past (1975a:10), with the result that the justification of criticism is the 'study of the problematics of loss' (1975a:18).

RUMINATORS AND PROPHETS

In Bloom's poetic chronology, the metaphorics of Freud's 'family romance' coincides with a metaphorics suggesting a pre-and post-lapsarian world divided at about the time of Shakespeare, only a short time before the Enlightenment. And just as Rousseau is the great scare in his namesake Allan Bloom's diatribe against the modern, Harold Bloom puts the blame particularly on Descartes's dualism, a dualism which is to be considered a modern as opposed to a Pauline dualism, defined as the 'dumbfoundering abyss between ourselves and the object' (1973:38). The concept of influence, he suggests, is a product of the Enlightenment, replacing the organic holism of 'sonship' found, for instance, in the traditional phrase the 'sons of Ben [Jonson]' (1973:26). It may be noted in passing that this Freudian understanding of 'sonship', with its implication of filial rebellion against the father, is an instance of deliberately strong – too strong? – interpretation. Quoting Kierkegaard's maxim 'He who is willing to work gives birth to his own father' (1973:26), Bloom now introduces an ethical dimension to supplement the aesthetic dimension. Ben Jonson saw influence as healthy imitation, the partaking of a public fund of poetic materials, the honest use of which is an honest craftsman's right. But with the Cartesian dualism (or extensiveness) came a kind of dishonesty, a state of suspicion consequent on the new knowledge that thought and essence are divided. Romanticism is the logical next step, with its deferral of essence to the metaphysical. To reach this, no degree of hard work can help the poet. Only the intuitive leap will come to his aid. The poet knows it, and influence is forever combined with the anxiety of attempting not to succumb to mere imitation, but to resist it by creating his own creative space. In Bloom's terminology, 'poetic influence' is always the 'anxiety' of poetic influence, paradoxically translatable as 'poetic resistance', a branch of the larger 'intellectual revisionism', deriving from the categorical shift of meaning of the concept of influence – from something positive, to be learned from, into something negative, to be suffered and consequently resisted (1973:38).[30]

This leaves us with the situation of a greater and a lesser poetic age, with the Enlightenment as the watershed (of whose Cartesian fundament Romanticism is the first manifestation).[31] Before the Enlightenment – and in some particular instances after[32] – 'influence' seems on the whole a natural and creative force. But after Descartes, 'influence' is sidetracked into something passive and inane, contributing to the prolonged death of poetry. Only where it has worked as the resistance of influence, has 'influence' been a vitalizing force, 'as misprision, as deliberate, even perverse revisionism' (1973:50). Bloom never elaborates very much on the golden age before the Cartesian fall, apart from generally appreciative forays back to Shakespeare and Jonson, and more vaguely further back to antiquity. But when the wide-angle lens is applied to take in both antiquity and modernity, Bloom does not hesitate to let even the strongest moderns dwindle to weakness when read against Homer, Isaiah, Lucretius, Dante and Shakespeare, 'who came before the Cartesian engulfment, the flooding-out of a greater mode of consciousness' (1973:72). Bloom goes along with Curtius to see the period after Goethe as one, despite the labels that modern literary historians are eager to apply to apparently epochal divisions within the period. The question is, whether these last two centuries present a radical breaking away from the postulated unified tradition from Homer to Goethe, or the essential continuity of what has gone before for twenty-five centuries. It is too early yet to be a judge of definite discontinuities or continuities in the Western literary tradition. Bloom does not hesitate, though, to suggest that the really innovating, that is tradition-breaking element in the literature to be written, may come in the shape of the new female literature to be developed out of the heightened awareness of gender on the part of female artists. The turning to a female-dominated culture will indeed be a break with a millennia-old inheritance from Homer (1975a:33).[33] This is surely the closest that Bloom comes to identifying clearly the literary tradition with male dominance, but the prophesying of a female replacement as the ultimate rebellion against the precursor makes sense in his system. However, this is a dialectical development to come. As it is, we are still, whether male or female, a 'son or daughter of Homer' (1975a:33). In his discussion of Curtius, Bloom is tempted to go along with the proposition that we had better not introduce any discontinuities in the tradition since Homer. But Bloom is obviously hesitant to go all the way with Curtius. Romanticism as a distinctly post-Enlightenment departure is different from any 'new' developments of the past by being very much a forming of a conscious relationship with the past tradition, and a rebellious relationship at that (1975a:35). This does not rule out the future development of a completely differently based literary tradition, but it certainly preserves literary tradition as we know it as a two-stage history – pre-and post-Enlightenment.

An indication of Bloom's justification of the positive vision of pre-Enlightenment poetry in relation to the anxiety of influence is reached by going via his appreciation of Vico's theories of poetic origins.[34] To Vico poetry and prophecy are synonymous. Bloom, who admits to being at one and the same time attracted to and repelled by Vico's theories, suggests a modification to the effect that the shift from primitive to more advanced societies means a rejection of such a view of poetry. Thus, cultures from the time of the Greek Orphics to the present are 'guilt cultures' (1973:60) suffering from a rising degree of awareness of Cartesian dualism. In comparison with Empedocles, who as a *hierophant* or *vatis* practised Viconian poetics, the otherwise strong deniers of anxiety like Dante, Milton and Goethe, can be seen to be affected very much by anxiety. Only when we compare them with the affirmers emerging after the Enlightenment do they appear untainted. What makes this pre-Enlightenment period – the 'great age before the Flood' (1973:122) – which extends from Homer to Shakespeare, so special is a 'matrix of generous influence' (1973:122) that overrode the anxiety brought about by cartesian dualism, exemplified by the relationship of love and emulation on the part of Dante for Virgil. Before the 'flood' there was a state of generous sharing, afterwards there was individual isolation (1973:122–3). Or put somewhat differently, and in Freudian terms, modern poetry came about as the result of a degree of imaginative sublimation unknown to previous, and happier, times.[35]

Bloom's is definitely the period of post-Enlightenment poetry,[36] and from the Enlightenment on there is a two-strand development from Romanticism, the period during which the 'pathos lengthens as the dignity diminishes' (1973:28). One strand is the weak, even pathetic succession of the generously giving and taking poets, whether that generosity be spread out to encompass strong precursors or similarly weak ones.[37] This strand is per definition uninteresting, because it reduces the world and existence into a 'grayness of uniformity' (1973:39), yet is useful by way of being examplary of the wrong kind of development. The other strand is the strong, or rather, comparatively strong line, since post-lapsarian poetry can never live up to pre-lapsarian models. This strand, however, by sheer rebellious energy and egomaniac promotion, as it were, makes itself into the best of what we have. It is the

> *history of fruitful poetic influence, which is to say the main tradition of Western poetry since the Renaissance, . . . a history of anxiety and self-serving caricature, of distortion, of perverse, wilful revisionism without which modern poetry as such could not exist* (1973:30; Bloom's italics).

Always offering precision sparingly – supposedly the strong critic's privilege – Bloom does not make it clear if these two lines are identical with the ones termed the ruminative and fierce lines, comprising Milton, Wordsworth, Keats, Stevens in the former and Spenser, Blake, Shelley, Browning, Whitman, Yeats in the latter. However, it makes sense to treat the two as two sides of the strong strand, since the differences between them do not seem to be of the kind separating the generous poets from the 'selfish' ones, but more to do with the degree to which they assert their craving for imaginative space.

Characteristic of the truly strong poets is their total self-reliance. Not only need they not compare themselves with other poets, indeed, to compare would be to admit to failure, 'is to be not elect' (1973:19). But a stage on the road towards poetic solipsism is necessarily the conscious and vehement reaction against a powerful influence. In Bloom's view, Blake in his uneasy relationship with Milton offers a textbook example of the anxiety of influence: 'To be enslaved by any any precursor's system, Blake says, is to be inhibited from creativity by an obsessive reasoning and comparing, presumably of one's own works to the precursor's' (1973:29). This makes Blake into a crucial theorist of revisionism as well as a strong poetic practitioner. Strong poets, like Blake, are placed on an island as it were, with no need or wish for any communication whatever, and are in a situation where they can 'read only themselves' (1973:19). The anxiety of influence, which is not something ancillary to the writings of the strong poets, but the very poetry itself, is the result of the inescapable awareness of never being able really to inhabit that island alone. The poet may start out as an Adam, and weakly at that, but he ends up a Satan:

> They begin as natural men, affirming that they will contract no further, and they end as thwarted desires, frustrated only that they cannot harden apocalyptically. But, in between, the greatest of them are very strong, and they progress through a natural intensification that marks Adam in his brief prime and a heroic self-realization that marks Satan in his brief and more-than-natural glory (1973:24–5).

In other words, real strength in post-Enlightenment poets is an ambiguous state of the will to complete individuality and simultaneously the realization of its impossibility.

The difference between the 'ruminators' and the 'visionary and prophetic line' in strong English poetry is a difference founded on the degree to which a strong poet accepts or tries to reject an 'actual dualism' (1973:33). The dualism in question is one of which Milton is the central instance, and to which his Satan figure in *Paradise Lost* gives expression in the 'Farewell happy fields . . .' section of the poem. It is a heroic dualism growing out of an awareness of the perfection that was in the original Edenic state and the imperfection of post-Edenic existence, resulting in an all-pervasive sense of existential loss. Another approach, in a Freudian guise, is to see the dualism as a 'severely displaced Protestantism' (1973:152). Milton's precursor was Spenser, but in rejecting Spenserian unitarism in favour of a new-found dualism he at one and the same time integrated and superseded the 'father'. Having thus founded the Romantic longing as the – ever-doomed – attempt of the mind to overcome matter, Milton both provided the thematics for a new poetry and offered himself as the precursor who had to be overruled to create the imaginative space for new and strong poets. Milton may be said to have faced the anxiety of influence and having subsequently overcome it by turning out a peer with his precursors: 'The precursors return in Milton, but only at his will, and they return to be corrected' (1975a:142). The same is true of Shakespeare, but to a lesser degree, since his precursor to subsume was only Marlowe, a dwarf in comparison with Milton's Spenser.

Although this state of having fallen from grace and realizing it suffuses all post-Enlightenment English poetry, making for heroic but necessarily pathetic attempts to reclaim cognitively a Golden Age, the poet with a will to strength can choose to accept or to reject the dualism forced upon him. The line of ruminative poets from Milton through Wordsworth to Keats and Wallace Stevens has chosen to honestly accept this inevitable state of being, making their poetic art into its expression. The other, the visionary and prophetic line, is likewise able to trace its dilemma back to Miltonic dualism, but contrary to their colleagues Spenser, Blake, Shelley, Browning, Whitman and Yeats have chosen to rebel fiercely against it.[38] However, the difference between the two lines is not one of different ontological departures, since no Romantic/modern poet can do away with Descartes and Milton. Though the visionary and prophetic poets advertise their visions and yell their prophecies, there is no escaping the fact of God over Satan, death over life, nature over authority, in other words areas beyond the control of man. If the efforts of the former line may result in abject acceptance at worst, and at best in a fair fight, then the efforts of the latter may at best be an approximation towards the ideal, and at worst a pathetic, fearful noise.

Before we go on to consider in some detail the figures making up the tradition of strong poets, it should be added that Bloom is in no way determined to offer a canon with neat and consistent sub-divisions. Two categories of poets established on the basis of the degree to which they have turned out to have been 'affirmers' or 'deniers' of anxiety cut across the categories here chosen as guidelines, as does a distinction made on a basis of national adherence and one made on the basis of the degree to which some strong poets are characterized by their outstanding efforts to 'reduce' their precursors.

Bloom suggests a difference between English and American poets along the line that English poets seem to apply most characteristically to his revisionary ratio of 'clinamen', that is, the swerve away from the precursor, whereas American poets seem to show a tendency to fill in the lacunae – the kenosis ratio – left by the precursor.[39] When Bloom focuses on the American side of literary history, the names of Emerson, Dickinson, Frost, and Crane are added to those of Whitman and Stevens. Whether these complementary poets are really strong poets or less, is a moot point. Bloom uses the term 'major' about them all (1973:132–3).

In a roll-call of 'the strongest of modern poets in English' (1973:69) comprising Yeats, Blake, Shelley, Stevens, Coleridge, Whitman, Lawrence, Browning, Dickinson and Hardy,[40] Bloom suggests an anxiety, here called 'reductiveness' since we are operating within the tessera ratio, arranging these, the strongest, in dynamic interrelationships according to their wish to down-grade the idealisms of their precursors. In this arrangement Yeats tries to reduce Blake and Shelley, Stevens all the Romantics from Coleridge to Whitman, and Lawrence Hardy and Whitman.

As it will have emerged by now, the various permutations of Bloom's count of strong poets show a tendency towards a relatively stable and exclusive selection of names. Most of them from literatures in English, but when it comes to the list of lists, the *'strongest'* post-Enlightenment poets (1973:72; Bloom's italics), the list is more international: Milton, Goethe, Hugo (1973:72).

Bloom keeps returning to this trinity, these 'sub-gods' (cf. Nietzsche), whose outstanding quality is in their power to break out of the generally foredoomed quest for poetic strength. Theirs is the poetry that Bloom designates the fourth stage, or a 'poetry of earth' (1973:79), a degree of the very strongest poetry to which no other modern poets ever attain. From the list of post-Enlightenment English poets strong enough to attract genuine interest, only Hardy, Yeats and Stevens can be said to have reached the level of the poetry of discontinuity, a poetry of the air, which is far off the goal of the poetry of the earth.

We now begin to see the contours of a canonical hierarchy ordered into two tiers. At the very top there are Milton, Goethe and Hugo, the sub-gods, who have successfully broken out of an antithetical dynamics which for most poets leads to an abject realization of subordination to the strong poets of the past. In the second tier Bloom prefers to stay within an English-language tradition – and with the exception of Dickinson in the complementary American list completely male – comprising Blake, Shelley, Browning, Whitman, Hardy, Yeats and Stevens, but with the occasional international glance to include Baudelaire and Rilke as fellow runners-up. In *The Anxiety of Influence* the status of Emerson is somewhat vague, but in *A Map of Misreading* it emerges that the American 'prose seer and poetic theorist' (1975a:6) has come to enjoy a placement almost parallel to Milton's, that is, as the precursor of whom later poets inevitably stand in awe, but who himself has succeeded earlier poets by generously taking them in.

A CANON OF STRONG POETS

Bloom's critical studies of individual poets is even more exclusive than the canon emerging from his central theoretical works, *The Anxiety of Influence*, *A Map of Misreading* and *Kabbalah and Criticism*. The work prior to *The Anxiety of Influence* – *Shelley* (1959), *Blake* (1963 and 1965) and *Yeats* (1970) – must, according to Bloom's ideas, be strong reactions to earlier criticism, and the work after, notably *Wallace Stevens: The Poems of Our Climate* (1974) a strong reaction to that in turn.

The Shelley that emerges from Bloom's 1959 monograph is a mythmaking poet, but not in the sense of one who devises his own mythological universe, such as for instance is the case of Tolkien's Middle Earth with its profusion of made-up inhabitants. Nor is it mythmaking in the sense of elaborating some already existing mythological complex, the kind of mythopoeic poetry which is situated somewhere in between conventional mythological extension and original mythopoeia and which Bloom terms the first kind of mythopoeic poetry (1959:5). In this early work on Shelley Bloom relies on Martin Buber's doctrine of the 'I – Thou' relationship, which, as it were, short-circuits any recourse to influence and poses instead the actual meeting of poetic minds. Bloom of course here gets inspiration from the argument of Shelley's 'Defence of Poetry', the major point of which is the postulate of immediate access to the level of 'intellectual beauty' with the imagination as the only intermediary. Shelley's challenge to the Platonic epistemology, which had been accepted for the purposes of Sir Philip Sidney's poetics in favour of a position with no intervening authority between the creative imagination and its object, is a stance answering well to the 'I–Thou' relationship which Bloom relies on as his theoretical basis.

The second kind of mythopoeic poetry – the primitive kind, in Bloom's view – is one that 'embodies that direct perception of a Thou in natural objects or phenomena that the Frankforts have described for us, "a confrontation of life with life" ' (1959:5). With this kind of mythopoeia we are past any reliance on mythology proper and on our way to a creative activity that has shed any reliance on former models, and 'in which the poet enters into relationship with a natural Thou, the relationship itself constituting the myth' (1959:8).

The third kind of mythopoeia is different in degree rather than in kind from the second, or primitive kind in that here we no longer have a confrontation of the poet with a natural Thou, but a creativeness transcending any model-basis whatever: 'From his concrete I–Thou relationships, the poet can dare to make his own abstractions, rather than adhere to formulated myth, traditionally developed from such meetings' (1959:8). Although Bloom later on characterizes this third kind of mythopoeia as a 'precise . . . sense' (1959:8), its difference from the first and second senses is somewhat blurred, especially since the second kind is supposed to have shed any connections with mythology, and consequently leaves little room for the declared distinction of the third.

Martin Buber's 'I–Thou' doctrine is derived to a certain extent from Levinas's ethics which combines Judaic and Greek ancestry. The leap to the Judaic ground in the later Bloom is therefore not a very long one. Bloom retains the Judaic basis and replaces Buber's 'I–Thou' confrontation with the Freud-inspired scene of instruction paradigm. But in the early Shelley study the seed for Bloom's central anxiety-of-influence project is sown. A number of important poems by Shelley, he claims, are especially expressive of the third kind of mythopoeia: 'Their myth, quite simply, *is* myth: the process of its making, and the inevitability of its defeat' (1959:8; Bloom's italics).

It will be plain by now that Buber's phenemenological-existentialist doctrine as well as any reliance on 'myth' in the established senses of the term are merely instrumental in leading up to Bloom's dynamics of poetic strength, which is at that point still subject to a probing trial-and-error procedure.[41] The plan of the Shelley study is one of a not yet fully developed anxiety-of-influence cycle. Bloom reads *Prometheus Unbound*, 'The Sensitive Plant,' and 'The Witch of

Atlas' as the culmination of the 'myth of relationship' (1959:9), with 'Epipsychidion' as the 'downward course of Shelley's myth, its awareness of its own defeat' (1959:9), and – finally – the posthumously published fragment 'The Triumph of Life' as the 'triumph of life over Shelley's myth of relationship' (1959:9).

The degree of positive intuitive response to Shelley's poetry is borne out in Bloom's 1968 preface to the 1969 Cornell paperback of *Shelley's Mythmaking*, in which Bloom affirms the study as a 'tribute . . . to the poet I find least dispensable among those I read' (1959:vii). Obviously Shelley was not originally selected as a textual basis on which to apply a theory; the theory to grasp Shelley grew out of a preoccupation with the poet. Bloom admits in his preface to the experimental nature of his study, to it as an attempt to devise an approach that makes sense of Bloom's impression of the Romantic poet's essential effort – 'Shelley's internalized quest to reach the limits of desire' (1959:vii). The point that Bloom sought to prove was that Shelley could be construed to have first formulated his own Romantic vision (in *Prometheus Unbound*) and then to have abandoned it in favour of a response achieved at the cost of sacrificing that vision in favour of one negating and transcending it at the same time (in 'The Triumph of Life'). There is in this hesitant preface a suggestion that Bloom's attraction to Romanticism is due to the complete break with any kind of previously practised moderation in trying out imaginative space which made the Romantic 'project' unique – the limits of desire.

Although Bloom frequently refers to Wordsworth and his 'crisis' poems, there is no doubt that the more consistently revolutionary of the Romantic poets have the greatest appeal. In Bloom's perspective Shelley must be central. In his life as in his poetry he became the exile and the model of the poet whose poetry was an anxious effort to deny the natural priority of death. Whereas Wordsworth compromised in his life and letters with his early crisis poetry, Coleridge never really arrived at the point of strength, Byron – despite his exile – was at heart an imitator of eighteenth-century standards, Shelley stood up against authority. In this perspective it is hardly surprising that William Blake is another Romantic poet to receive Bloom's acceptance.

Four years after the publication of the Shelley study, Bloom's Blake study *Blake's Apocalypse: A Study in Poetic Argument* came out (Bloom 1963), followed after another two years by his commentary to Blake's poetry and prose in the anthology edited by David

V. Erdman (Erdman 1965). Both study and commentary are more conventional, however, than the reader might have expected from the iconoclastic promises of the Shelley volume.

Blake's Apocalypse follows the chronology of Blake's work, with the emphasis on Blake's epic poems *The Four Zoas, Milton* and *Jerusalem*. The overall less daring approach to Blake is visible not only in the conventional reliance on the chronology, but also in the preface which, in contradistinction to the bold *in medias res* opening of the earlier study, makes a point – again rather conventionally – of acknowledging debts to both philologists and the formalists/New Critics and myth critics who later on (in 1973, 1975a and 1975b) came in for severe criticism.

If there is a programme for the Blake study, it is to the effect that the object is the demonstration of the beauty of Blake's poetry, an object which, according to Bloom, is frequently forgotten in the effort to make the poetry the vehicle of 'spiritual or intellectual history' (1963:9). The beauty is the effect of a 'masterful design', which is 'carried through into the minute articulations of each poem' (1963:9). It is important to note that Bloom's interest is in the verbal texture of the poetry, even down to the heretical omission of any consideration of the engravings, which are asserted to be immaterial to the power of the poetry.

Bloom's eclectic and impressionistic approach to Blake's poetry is a painstaking and well-documented guided tour towards the goal of a universal humanist apocalypse: 'The identification of all forms as human is one with hearing the beloved creation of those forms as the name of Jerusalem, for the liberty of all things is to be human' (1963:433). This is Bloom's suggested solution to the problem of a too simplified interpretation in terms of revolution and reaction in the early 'A Song of Liberty' about which it may be said that this conflict is also one of a 'clash of creative forces' (1963:98), the nature of which is probed by Blake in his later writings until the apocalyptic insight of *Jerusalem*.

Whereas Bloom's reading of Blake is very similar to the kind of reading offered by Frye, whose influence is duly noted in the preface, it is possible to trace the outline suggested in the Shelley study, especially with the benefit of hindsight obtained from the theoretical writings: Blake the ephebe struggling against his forerunners, especially Milton, rebelling against and absorbing them at the same time, coming out on the other side, scarred but in possession of a hard-won poetic victory.

Bloom's great study of Yeats follows on the studies of Shelley and Blake, the relation of Yeats to whom is made quite clear in the very first lines of the preface: 'Yeats was a poet very much in the line of vision; his ancestors in English poetic tradition were primarily Blake and Shelley, and his achievement will at last be judged against theirs' (1970:v). This study is remarkable not only for the very fine readings of a 'difficult' poet but also for the way Bloom now is able to formulate what was latent in the earlier studies with regard to critical vision or method (cf. 1970 'Introduction,' pp. 3–22) and ready to begin thinking in canonical terms.

Bloom's twentieth-century triumvirate of strong poets writing in English, Yeats, Hardy and Wallace Stevens, comparable with the strongest of the previous century, is here declared with an almost polemical gibe at the widely acknowledged Parnassus of the modern century. Bloom predicts with equanimity the likely diminishing reputations of Eliot, Pound, Williams, Frost, Graves, and Auden, the first two of whom may turn out to be the 'Cowley and Cleveland of this age' (1970:v). Bearing in mind the preference on the part of Eliot for such 'obscure outsiders' as Cowley, Bloom might be construed to imply a canon plot devised by not great, perhaps only capable, poets.

Bloom's theory of poetic influence was fully elaborated in the mid-1970s. Kindled by Romantic poetry and Kabbalistic lore, a canon of poets writing in English was coming into its own, with an English and an American legacy. In the three theoretical works from the mid-1970s the distinction between an English and an American tradition, emerging out of the shared Romantic ground, is one of lesser and greater emphasis on the vehemence with which the anxiety of influence can be shown to have lodged itself in the texts. In *Wallace Stevens: The Poems of Our Climate* from 1977 the distinction implied earlier seems to be recognized as the state of the canonical, and the basis for the distinction is one of degree of reaction: 'Emerson and the Americans after him differed from British Wordsworthians in the extremism with which they defended against the Wordsworthian stance' (1977:2). The Wordsworthian stance is one that results in crisis-poems recording rebellion against influence, and is easily recognizable in the work of both Emerson and Whitman, but conspicuously lacking in Wallace Stevens. On the one hand, then, Bloom is left with a poet whom he wants to celebrate,[42] on the other there is not much evidence in the work of this poet of the violent responses to crisis visible so clearly elsewhere in the Romantic tradition yielding Bloom's canon of strong poetry. Bloom escapes through the horns of this dilemma by devising a supplement to the revisionary ratios, called 'poetic crossing'.

'Poetic crossing' as a 'process of disjunction, a leaping of the gap between one kind of figurative thinking and another' (1977:2), and in analytical terms to be located in the 'breaks between one mode of figurative thinking and a mode sharply antithetical to that one' (1977;16–17), can be accommodated within the map of misprision, and can indeed be seen as a troping of its relational ratios. The three crossings – the crossing of Election from ironic to synecdochal thinking, of Solipsism from metonymic to hyperbolic thinking, and of Identification from metaphoric to transumptive thinking – are parallel to the Romantic dialectic of ethos, logos and pathos, which is developed into the peculiarly American dialectic of 'Fate, Freedom, and Power' (1977:2–3). The development from the Romantic to the American dialectic, from Wordsworth to Emerson,[43] is designated a 'modulation' by Bloom. The term is telling in its musical etymology of transposing from one key to another, without changing the tune, but certainly lending to it a different mood. Bloom gives yet another twist to the screw in his transformation of these three, evidently suiting Emerson, into the parallel 'Necessity, Solitude, and Surprise' (1977:5). It is this parallel triad that gives to American strong poetry a specific flavour, distancing it from its transatlantic sister tradition. In Bloom's words,

> such a triad is a version of the three governing deities of American Orphism, the natural religion of our poetry, where Necessity takes the place of the goddess Ananke or the Muse, while Solitude stands for Dionysus or Bacchus, the god meaning-through-*sparagmos*, and Surprise substitutes for Eros, the ultimate form of *pathos* or representational power (1977:5; Bloom's italics).

Given these much-troped premises, Bloom is able to conclude that '*surprise* is the American poetic stance, in the peculiar sense of surprise as the poet's Will-to-Power over anteriority and over the interpretation of his own poem' (1977:6; Bloom's italics). Perhaps nowhere in Bloom's poetics do we get such a clear statement about the peculiar quality of poetic strength and its suitable applicability to a certain poetic tradition.

American poetry in the strong Romantic tradition, from Emerson via Whitman and Dickinson to Stevens, is one that hinges on fate, freedom and power. Bloom says about Emerson that he 'wanted Freedom, reconciled himself to Fate, but loved only Power, from first to last, and I believe this to be true also of the central line of American poets coming after him' (1977:8). Taken out of its poetics context and into a more spacious one, there is certainly a wedding of Nietzsche here to the values of the melting-pot and manifest-destiny nation. With his celebration of Stevens, Bloom has attained the goal of lodging in a poet generally recognized as modernist a strong Romantic element. There is nothing more anti-thetical than the diametrical opposite, and thus Bloom's reading of Stevens turns into the strongest possible reading of Stevens. The relish of pronouncing on 'one of *Harmonium's* most insouciant and apparently anti-Romantic poems' as the 'American Romantic stance of Stevens where his critics are least inclined to place it' (1977:25) is obvious.

With *The Western Canon* (1994) Bloom centres on what has pre-viously been left rather vaguely as the culmination from which all later writers derive the inferiority complexes energizing them for their agonistic battles royal, Shakespeare. The great names pre-vious to the English playwright exist, *Commedia*-like, in involuntary limbo. But, Bloom's argument goes, we need to see Shakespeare in a perspective of Kantian-Copernican revolution.

When Bloom pronounces Shakespeare to be the Western canon, it is because he 'changes cognition by changing the representation of cognition' (1994:283). In that way all writing previous to Shakes-peare is consequently seen in a Shakespearian light. As God was created by the Yahwist in Genesis (cf.1990 and 1994:474–5), West-ern man has been created in the shape of the Renaissance Globe Theatre producer. This view gives Bloom ammunition to fight his despised opponents in the so-called School of Resentment. His favourite example is Freud's readings of Shakespeare and Freud-derived 'psycho-analytical criticism', Bloom's point being that Freud has already been shaped by Shakespeare.

In *The Western Canon* Bloom discusses at length 26 writers, culled from Western literature, a few of them, however, not creative wri-ters in the traditional sense of the term. Taking over the Renaiss-ance Italian philosopher Giambattista Vico's cyclical view of history, Bloom divides literary history into the theocratic, the aristocratic, the democratic, and the chaotic ages. The more than three hundred titles collected in these four periods are Bloom's ultimate bid for a comprehensive Western literary canon.

Whereas *The Western Canon* hardly offers any new developments from the original ideas put forward in *The Anxiety of Influence* from 1973, and repeated throughout his prodigious *oeuvre*, Bloom is finally – and triumphantly – able to put his finger on the *terminus a quo* and the *terminus ad quem* of all literature.

Since 1973 Bloom had been talking about the belatedness of modern, that is post-Enlightenment authors, but apart from offering suggestions about the culminatory greatness of figures like Homer and Dante, and the relative mediocrity of everybody coming after, it has been difficult to define a Parnassus. However, in *The Western Canon*, Shakespeare is made to stand out as the great literary name of all times: Shakespeare being the epitome and the archetype of all literature, that is the literature worth preserving and reading still, contains the canon and makes it available at the same time. Those who came before him became absorbed in his work, and those coming after have never been able to escape his influence. Shakespeare is the greatest mind-developer of all times, and any belated author will have to relate to him – or despair of his task.

Shakespeare belongs in what Bloom decides to call the 'aristocratic age', borrowing the notion, with some changes, of successive cultural cycles from Vico. Of course, the idea of a great past from which the present is an increasingly fading imitation, is well known from literary criticism since the Renaissance. It was Vico who was behind Peacock in his facetious attack on literature back in 1820, to the bait of which Shelley rose the year after in his 'A Defence of Poetry', and which can actually be shown to lurk beneath the surface of much of Bloom's thought. After the aristocratic age came the 'democratic age', the nineteenth century that we associate first and foremost with realism in fiction and poetry. And our own century is the 'chaotic age', from which we may hope yet again to enter into a truly aristocratic age.

Bloom argues for the essentially private nature of literature on a basis of aesthetics. Contemporary criticism, he suggests, is a matter of getting away from truly literary concerns. Marxist criticism reads literature as a symptom of society at any given time, gender criticism documents matters to do with the function of gender and sex, and psychoanalytical criticism makes literature a symptom of the mind at work with its energy patterns. But according to Bloom it is completely wrong to read literature in these extra-literary ways. Literature does not give us examples of the goings-on of the libido, since the libido is nothing but the discovery of Shakespeare in *Hamlet*. Freud misunderstood the situation when he formed his hypothesis of the Oedipal desire by pointing to Shakespeare. We shall simply have to look at things the other way round: Freud is determined by Shakespeare in the first place, so he does not throw light on *Hamlet*, but *Hamlet* throws light on Freud. And consequently Freud becomes one of the 26 authors singled out for particular attention as the great canonical league in Bloom's accumulating book.

Bloom insists that he is concerned with the aesthetics of literature in contrast to all those belonging to various branches of what he derogatively terms the School of Resentment (contemporary critics hate literature and try to get away from it at all costs, is the implication). Aesthetics is where literature acts out its peculiar nature, which is that of an ongoing struggle to keep in power. Looking closely into the implications of Bloom's aesthetics, however, his object of concern turns out to be the literary character, brilliantly conceived by Shakespeare at its most all-roundedly human in Falstaff.

That the character is at the very centre of Bloom's interest ought to surprise no one. Bloom's dogma of agonistics is of course something unthinkable if not in terms of humans wrestling for power and dominance. His criticism has always focused on authors in their agony of liberating themselves from dominating influences, the end-all of which is Shakespeare. His critical debating has always been directed very much at other colleagues in his own struggle for critical space, and there is next to no interest in what could be called the formal or structural characteristics of literature.

What is the use, then, of getting to know outstanding figures from the canon, or put more generally, what is the use of literature, and consequently of being on the receptive side as readers of books and audiences of drama (Bloom will have nothing to do with other 'textual' media)? The answer is as brief as it is depressing: literature always reminds us of time and death, and is the central way humans may attempt to set up lies to avert attention from the inescapable demands of existence. Contemplating his own survival, the author has to put up his defence in terms of the agon or struggle with his predecessor, and this is the loneliest possible situation, just as the reader in meeting with the text has his own inevitable fate before his eyes. But in the realization of the fleeting of time and the fact of death, literature offers consolation by being essentially a struggle for dominance and survival, as close to a negation of the facts of life that we may ever hope to have. There is no getting away from this. Whatever the critics may be doing in the various classrooms in the School of Resentment, they are evading the issue, sidetracking existential concerns away from the main course.

And Bloom's narrow canon? *The Western Canon* deals at length and in detail with the following: Shakespeare (the greatest author ever), Dante, Chaucer, Cervantes, Montaigne, Molière, Milton, Dr Johnson (the greatest critic ever), Goethe, Wordsworth, Austen, Whitman, Dickinson, Dickens, George Eliot, Tolstoy, Ibsen, Freud, Proust, Joyce, Woolf, Kafka, Borges, Neruda, Pessoa, and Beckett. But in addition to this handful of strong and agonistically successful authors – all of them incarnations of Shakespeare in one form or another – Bloom winds up his book with an extensive 31-page list of authors and works of canonical stature, in which he hopes that 'literate survivors will find some authors and books . . . that they have not yet encountered and will garner the rewards that only canonical literature offers' (p. 528).

Bloom's comparatively short list of strong poets is not very different from the average essentialist canon that may be boiled down from so many conventional literary histories. But the foundation on which Bloom's list builds is certainly different from that of conventional literary history. Bloom's antithetical criticism builds on a critical rationale quite different from any – with the possible exception of Paul de Man's, Jacques Derrida's and Geoffrey Hartman's – commonly practised criticism. Although Bloom's procedure is characterized by great – and often esoteric – knowledge and analytical sharpsightedness, the standard requirement of scholarly work to be verifiable and reproducible seems not to apply in his case. Apart from the habit of not providing chapter and verse for his numerous quotations – at best flattery of the reader, at worst arrogance – central methodological operations remain obscure. Such an important thing as to determine exactly the deviation of the clinamen of the poem under consideration in order to find the precursor poem seems to be a matter of some intuitive effort.[44] Another central issue is the phenomenon of misprision, the extent of which is likewise left to the critic's highly personal measuring tools. But then criticism is inextricably tied up with poetic creation, since deliberate misinterpretation,[45] in contrast to interpretation which is supposed to clarify, is critical work on a par with the poem, both swerving from their precursor texts: 'Criticism is the *art* of knowing the hidden roads that go from poem to poem' (1973:96; my italics).

Any attempt to accommodate Bloom's criticism neatly as a kind of criticism just aiming at pointing out where poets have evaded influence is to misconstrue it categorically. Bloom's favourite kabbalistic metaphorics rules this out as banal in the extreme.

An appreciation of Bloom's 'system', and with that his canon within this framework, depends on the sympathetic reader, who is willing to shift his ground from traditionally scholarly handlings of texts to that of art with its reliance on felt rather than demonstrated truths.

A GOSPEL OF GLOOM?

In a conventional critical framework, Bloom's 'system' is just another effort at establishing an eclectic poetics, with heavy objection to tradition and formalist studies, inspired more than Bloom cares to admit by various poststructuralist schools and generally couched in esoteric learning, the very nature of which defies conventional handling in terms of traditional Western scholarship. In that perspective Bloom's approach to the concept of literary tradition seems at one and the same time strangely warped with its post-Enlightenment focusing on a Romantic–modernist strain and the net outcome that reads deceptively like the defence of a fundamentalist canon. A negative view of Bloom's canon-making efforts would perhaps also claim Bloom's ultimate goal to be the exaltation of the American tradition from Emerson and Whitman as a particularly forcefully logocentric line of poets (cf. 1975a:176), a line of demiurges (1975b:64) with a particularly high standing.

In his own perspective, however, we have to do with a highly coherent poetics; not only joining practical-criticism activities with the setting up of a poetic tradition based on tropes of defence, but also assuming that there is no such thing as a dividing line between the creation and the criticism of literature. The poem exists in its being received by a reading consciousness, which can be said to be the last stage in a long process of taking in and at the same time reacting violently against a text recognized as potentially influential to the degree of swallowing up whatever comes after. The crucial stage in the process that brings a poem into being is consequently its reading or interpretation, an activity no less poetic than what went into creating its object, since criticism, to be successful, must create its own space, and can do so only by misprision. The history of literature is a history made up of strong texts mediated by poets and critics equal in stature to their task.

The canon of literature is the accumulation of texts which have demonstrated their power as efforts to lie against time, but canonization is also in itself a way of troping against the past with a view to safeguarding the future – ill-advisedly since this construction will in time be overturned, but it is all we have. The troping of canonization is the 'most extreme version of what Nietzsche called Interpretation, or the exercise of Will-to-Power *over* texts' (1975b:100). The canon comes into being with the efforts of successive strong poets, and with time the ephebe has not only a looming precursor to struggle against, but an ever-more discouraging tradition, in which strength seems accumulating in exponential fashion. The canon, then, exists both as something to be lied against and as an attempt to be part of that lie. In that second perspective Bloom can formulate the 'thesis that canonization is the final or transumptive form of literary revisionism' (1975b:100). But no sooner is it recognized as such than it becomes the target of attack.

No more than the poem does the canon exist outside of its reading or interpretation. It can never be made to stand still, as it were. It presents a formidable barrier to any ephebe's creative energies, yet is part of his armoury to fight it. Bloom's canon is a list of certified strong strugglers, who must not be seen as safely arrived, now deserving a civil list pension, but as exemplary of the kind and degree of power involved in clearing existential space. The literary tradition, if it is worth anything at all, cannot be made to stand still, as, in Bloom's words about Eliot's relating to tradition, it is a 'hedge against the daemonic' (1975b:97). The strong tradition is necessarily one of individual works rebelling against stasis, and so contains the daemonic as an integral force. Hence tradition can be said to be a 'daemonic form' (1975b:98) itself. This daemonic aspect of tradition is analogical to the rhetorical tropes of hyperbole and litotes in poetic texts, manifest as images of high and low (cf. the map of misprision in 1975a:84), thus explaining Bloom's characterization of tradition as an 'image of the heights by being driven down to the depths, or of the depths by being raised to the heights' (1975b:98). Such an antithetical or resistant state of affairs does not yield itself to containment within a traditional epistemology of reference. Tradition is always in motion, a dynamics of negation, always shedding itself of permanence. The dialectical logic of this argument is analogic to the logic of the anxiety of influence applying to the individual text:

> 'Influence' exposes and de-idealizes 'tradition,' not by appearing as a cunning distortion of 'tradition,' but by showing us that all 'tradition' is indistinguishable from making mistakes about anteriority. The more 'tradition' is exalted, the more egregious the mistakes become (1975b:103).

Against this background Bloom is justified in claiming that '[t]radition is itself then without a referential aspect, like the Romantic imagination or like God' (1975b:98). The very act of making a text into a classic is, if the text is recognized as a strong text, to betray its essence of wilful distortion of the precursor. No wonder then that the 'choosing and classicizing of a text itself results in the most powerful kinds of misreading' (1975b:98) exposed to the attention of the ephebe as the potentially strong poet, who consequently perforce 'caricatures tradition' (1975b:103) and is in turn 'necessarily mis-read by the tradition that he fosters' (1975b:103). But this still leaves an impression of a distant and de-individualized tradition seen as unapproachable, like a missile in free space forever travelling in a curve away from sight. It is only fair to Bloom to remind the reader here of the ontology of the poem in Bloom's 'system' as only realized in the act of reading, which is also the moment when the reader really comes to know literary history. In the moment of perception the reader, who is indistinguishable from the critic, appreciates the ephebe, who can only be seen as such in relation to his precursor. In this experiential triad of reader, ephebe and precursor, tradition comes into being as something that happens, as an event of misprision of reading just as the relationship between ephebe and precursor was an event of misprision – 'To interpret is to revise is to defend against influence' (1975b:64). Tradition comes into this as the influence to be defended against, hence tradition exists, though potentially destructively, at the moment of reading.

In his ironic and overbearing attitude to the contemporary scene – 'surrounded by living classics, in recently dead poets of strong ambition and hysterical intensity, and in hyperactive novelist non-novelists, who are I suppose the proper seers for their armies of student non-students' (1975a:28) – Bloom seems to join the ranks of the canon fundamentalists. Even though this may be the conclusion of his canonical considerations, his premises, as we have seen, are certainly different from those of the other three critics studied in the present volume. Bloom's preoccupation with the time from Milton to Stevens is a celebration of a literary tradition as a 'tradition' just as differently conceived as 'influence' is from influence. Like so many fundamentalists, Bloom declines to pronounce on the value of his contemporaries, since the passing of considerable time is needed for tradition to 'justify its own selectivities' (1975a:28).[46] Tradition is supposed to transcend the merely timely if it is to be of any critical use, otherwise it becomes just another convention. This makes of tradition something different from an institution, whether seen as Eliot's constantly expanding bookshelf, Leavis's shrine of citizen virtues or Frye's transformation of the quest myth.[47] It is the openness, the inclusiveness, in principle the sense of bland comradeship of tradition as viewed conventionally, which makes it so forbidding to a supporter of a primal-scene approach to existence. For Bloom existential values do not just cumulate automatically and in harmonious succession; they have to be wrenched in mortal battle with those dearest to you. Essentially with the same kind of positive inclusiveness as Eliot, Bloom situates Frye's then very much acclaimed search for continuities in the sixties intellectual climate as the logical response to an ethos. This, in the perspective of the seventies, when Bloom's seminal poetics manifestos were written, has changed into a climate characterized by the 'interplay of repetition and discontinuity' (1975a:30), for which the proper response is one of a revisionary dialectic. Bloom's assessment of the intellectual dominants of the two decades – the first being a need of continuities, the second an opposite need of discontinuities – carries the mark of seigneurial sweep usual for Bloom whenever the hard facts of cultural history are called for.[48] Even though Frye was popular in many quarters throughout the sixties – and the seventies, for that matter – the Canadian literary cosmopolitan was hardly the only influential voice to make an impression at Yale and elsewhere. Structuralism, with a great variety of poststructuralist departures hard on its heels, was taking dominion everywhere, with the consequence that to most critics and theorists the seventies became the period of critical confusion, if viewed negatively, or of critical synthesis, if viewed positively. If continuities were needed in critical response to the sixties, it is indeed hard to see why they were not needed in the immediately following decade, when a reassuring critical framework seemed even

more necessary to contain a virtual Pandora's box of critical initiat-
ives. Unless this position is to be seen as a special application of
the revisionary dialectic on general critical history, there is a lack
of consistency, a mere change in the degree of critical pluralism –
from the sixties to the seventies – which requires a changed response in terms of kind of meta-critical activity.

Essential to an estimate of Bloom's work is the appreciation of his
idea of anxiety of influence and the practice of misprision as the
inevitable fate of post-Enlightenment literature, a state of affairs
forming the basic existential condition of Romantic and later
poetry. Although it may appear that Bloom is eager to market
misprision as *the* creative principle of modern literature, it is indicative of a fall from a better state, that is, a pre-Enlightenment
tradition for which rebellion was unnecessary since poetic succes-
sors were in a position to accommodate their precursors. The principle of critical revisionism has been forced upon us with the
introduction of Cartesian dualism, and, generally speaking, literature has been in decline ever since. But the obverse side of the
revisionist coin is the tendency for all resistance to pronounce itself
in messianic terms. Whatever is startlingly different from what went
before quickly assumes pride of place. This explains the eagerness
of poets and critics since the Enlightenment to see redemptive
differences in wave after wave of new work. Energy is mistaken for
literary value. A Mailer or a Lowell are ardently canonized and new
categorization principles of literary history, such as ethnic or gender grouping are hailed as truer than those of the past. This is all
part of the spirit of revisionism, an inevitable effect of a creative
dynamics relying upon rebellion and eagerness for replacements.
But until we are able to place in the right perspective our contemporary literature as continuous with or discontinuous from the
Homeric tradition, we shall not be able to pronounce anything of
lasting value. And that is not for us, but for increasingly encum-
bered future generations, to do.

Bloom tends to be dismissed as one of the major eccentrics of
contemporary literary criticism. Admittedly, his unpreparedness to
consider critical positions other than his own, the general arrogance in his writings, which completely lack any traditional note and
reference apparatus, and the esoterism especially in his early work
(for which he draws heavily on Kabbalah and Gnosticism) make
him formidably forbidding. But that we have to do with a man
deeply absorbed in and equally deeply in love with literature is

beyond the merest shadow of doubt. Bloom's refusal to comply
with the conventions of the academic treatise is a deliberate move
to demonstrate his internalization of literature: if literature has a
meaning and a function, it must be part of the mental make-up of
author and reader alike. If you cannot quote from memory – and
we do not need to bother about any total recall – literature has not
sufficiently imprinted itself, for only the strongest literature merits
a place in the mind.

7

Literary History, Criticism and Canon

[T]o transform the canon and the surveys in response to changing constituencies has less to do with rewriting the story than with reinterpreting it (Fox-Genovese 1986:136).

[A]ttempts to revise or reconstitute literary canons rest upon prior – though often tacit – interpretive acts of rendering a canonical historical reading of the crisis that in part authorizes literary canons (West 1987:193).

Depending on perspective, the trajectory of twentieth-century canon-formative criticism in English is bound to look widely different to different observers. From one angle there seems to be a succession of defenders of relatively narrow codices of texts, in which the titles selected for inclusion may vary, but not the underlying principle of fastidiousness. From another there seems to be a growing inclusiveness of titles, even to the point where there is no longer any sense in applying any notion of literary canon whatsoever. What unites the spokespersons of either effort, however, is the centrality of the canon discussion for the general agenda of literary criticism.

The reason for the foregrounding of issues to do with the canonical in contemporary criticism may be, as suggested by Guillory (1993, cf. Chapter 2), a symptom of a grand-scale legitimization shift in literary criticism, or it may be the reflection of a process in many Western societies towards a greater awareness of identities on levels lower than that of the nation-state. The one does not, however, exclude the other as the explanation of the present state of affairs, but they probably interact as mutually reinforcing motivating elements.

The growing professionalization of literary criticism, which has meant the growth of 'theory' as a meta-and cross- disciplinary area, has come about also as the response to a critical interest in literatures only marginally related to, or completely outside the conventional canon. The most obvious case in point is the effort with which feminist and gender criticism has worked to draw attention to canon-related issues regarding their areas. Not only have alternative, anti-or counter-canons found their way into the critical debate, but since the ruling canon has been considered repressive in the very discourse traditionally applied, new critical discourses have been constructed, contributing highly to the current mandarin status of 'theory'. This is a development which can be seen to have taken place in other expanding critical fields as well, for instance to a very great extent in the criticism applied to post-colonial literatures, for which likewise a completely new critical discourse is in the process of being forged.

CANON AND INFLUENCE

The recruitment of students for higher education has grown radically in most Western countries since the First World War, and at an accelerated pace since the Second. The shift of power from a hereditary or money aristocracy to a meritocracy has resulted in the professionalization of college and university education. A college or university degree is the ticket to a well-paid job, employment security and social status. But in contrast to the time when higher education was restricted to such an aristocracy, for whom the BA meant general cultural polishing and not the qualification for a job, the situation over the past fifty years has been for the university degree to confer social utility by force of that degree. To the new vastly expanding numbers of graduates wanting job qualifications at the highest level, two things are required from the degree programme: immediate usefulness of given disciplines, and the offering of disciplines with the kind of rigour and ready applicability that makes them into suitable exam material. It is the concern for the march of the mass society with its tendency to the putting on of collective blinkers which motivated T. S. Eliot's advice to rally an elite so as to ensure the preservation of the cultural values which, in the final analysis of Eliot's cultural preferences, are typically those of a privileged class. Leavis puts up a defence of much more concrete values against what he sees as the same kind of threat. Even with the rivalry between early twentieth-century Oxford and

Cambridge English, the more radically minded institution's English programme and methodology was the manifestation of a wish to stay within the text, as it were, and protect its aesthetic dimension against any onslaught from any kind of potential utility purpose, apart from the vaguest possible ethical considerations. And even though Allan Bloom and Harold Bloom differ regarding immediate premises for their respective crusades for the Great Books, it is ultimately the fear of any instrumental use of literature that unites them in their shrill warnings against any dilution or differentiation of the canon. The former fears the reduction of literature to, at best, a nether rung on the undergraduate's career ladder, the latter fears its reduction to an easily documentable by-product of sociological phenomena under examination in the disciplines that Bloom collectively nominates the School of Resentment (1994). With a concern reminiscent of that of Matthew Arnold a century-and-a-half previously, the agonist of the Book and the School of the Ages faces a situation of total existential, including cultural responsibility:

> The teacher of literature now in America, far more than the teacher of history or philosophy or religion, is condemned to teach the presentness of the past, because history, philosophy and religion have withdrawn as agents from the Scene of Instruction, leaving the bewildered teacher of literature alone at the altar, terrifiedly wondering whether he is to be sacrifice or priest (Bloom 1975a:39).

Siding in principle with both Blooms, Frye offers a less desperate voice in his challenge of *Bildung* fundamentalists, such as the Bennett of *The Book of Virtues* (1993):

> books appear from time to time telling us that the educational establishment in our society has betrayed our cultural heritage and allowed young people to grow up barbarously ignorant of its traditions. Such books are often warmly received, with everyone apparently convinced that something should be done. Nothing is done, mainly because the only implicit recommendation for action is to prod the educational bureaucracy. I think this starts at the wrong end, besides introducing assumptions in the philosophy of education that may be mistaken and are in any case unnecessary. Surely only a constant awareness of the widest

possible audience for scholarship in the humanities can start the educational breakthrough that everyone seems agreed is needed (Frye 1990:xix–xx).

All in all, then, there are numerous reasons why the canon, and issues raised by the concept of canon, have loomed large over the past decades. But it would be wrong to approach literary history as a monolithic structure only recently having started to show cracks. In English literary history it is possible, for all practical purposes, to trace the canon debate back to the Middle Ages, when Chaucer in *The Canterbury Tales* implicitly questioned inherited ecclesiastical and classical authority. When we approach English literary history – indeed all literary histories – in terms of textual interrelationships, we always see the contours of a canonical dynamic, for which the notion of 'influence' has conventionally been used; as we can when it has actually been employed to indicate a more complex relationship.

The idea of influence lies behind the concept of literary canon as a kind of sounding board. Without influence, there is no tradition, since the sense of a literary tradition is created from an impression of a succession of texts according to a principle of coherence. The predilection of literary history for 'period' and '-ism' is the result of attributing to one or several generations of authors the sharing of ideas and writing conventions handed down in time or across space – in geographical exchange from one author to another. The idea of influence also connects period with period, both in the case of successive periods and in the case of periods at a distance from each other.

Influence as a category of textual investigation has been institutionalized since the mid-nineteenth century when, together with the biographical method, academic criticism came into its own in response to the general intellectual climate of positivism. The rationale of influence studies depends on a view of literature as an organic growth, in which forms and genres live their 'lives' – mature, breed, degenerate and die. Influence treated in this man-ner presupposes proximity of textual phenomena and linearity of development. It also presupposes the presence of a strong stock to ensure the power of development. The coming into being of literary canons thus owes much to the application of influence as the 'scientific' rationale of literary studies.

Influence has since been central to traditional literary history as practised in the academy. Indeed, departments, degree programmes, and journals have been formed on the assumption of authors influencing one another across national boundaries, so that 'comparative literature' is the approach validated. Successfully succumbing to the test of influence – and Bloom's 'anti-influence' is indeed a way of relating to it – is very often what places a given work in a canon. Literary historians are familiar with the problem of what to do with those who do not 'fit' into their categories and periods, and who are frequently given their separate outsider chapter in general accounts. An example: in most surveys of English modernist fiction the twenties novels by Aldous Huxley do not appear with the work of Joyce, Woolf and Lawrence. Some would no doubt put this down to a question of literary quality. However, Huxley's work shares neither the narrative modes characteristic of Joyce and Woolf, nor Lawrence's diagnosis of the diseases of industrial society and his longing for a compensatory letting loose of the libido. The standard treatment of the early Huxley is to give him a personal niche, with its own line of influence from Norman Douglas and back to Peacock's satiric novels of manners. Given an ancestry of comparable authors, Huxley is home free but in a tradition apart from the main one.

The neat order of literature set up by positivist approaches did not survive the general scepticism of the early twentieth century. With the cultural atmosphere shifting from nineteenth-century optimism to a new pervasive feeling of bewilderment, literature and criticism increasingly abandoned totalizing, historical sweeps and began looking around for role models disregarding any principles of proximity and linearity.[1] Modernism as a literary movement estifies to this reorientation, with Eliot as one of its central figures.

Eliot retained the concept of influence, but abandoned any recourse to neat lines of development. He looked for an era of intellectual integrity and stability and found it in seventeenth-century English lyrical poetry, with the result that, due to his own wide influence, the canon suddenly came in for an overhaul. Seventeenth-century lyrical poetry had been an ancillary rather than a main stream before Eliot (and Grierson). Now it came in as a dangerous rival to a broadly accepted canon which had posited Milton as the all-important seventeenth-century figure.

Not only did Eliot shift the weight of the literary past, even recast the chronology of the past, as it were, but he also problematized the concept of influence in such a way as to – partly – anticipate Harold

Bloom, and at any rate to indicate that 'influence' is not a simple and tradition-conserving phenomenon:

> The poet, certainly, in a mature age, may still obtain stimulus from the hope of doing something that his predecessors have not done; he may even be in revolt against them, as a promising adolescent may revolt against the beliefs, the habits and the manners of his parents; but, in retrospect, we can see that he is also the continuer of their traditions, that he preserves essential family characteristics, and that his difference of behaviour is the difference in the circumstances of another age (Eliot 1944b: 119).

The revolt in question is admittedly a modest palace revolution, in so far as neither institution nor succession are endangered by the disturbance. But then we should not be misled by Bloom's more vehement language concerning such uprisings. Bloom focuses on the agony of the struggle, whereas Eliot is eager to arrive at the point from which he can survey the whole situation in the perspective of past action. In both cases there is, however, confidence in the persistence of a tradition, strong and therefore spacious enough to contain an internal dynamic of strong reaction. When Eliot uses the concept of influence, it is under the assumption of such an entropic dynamic, which sets the process of influence apart from mere imitation, since the 'difference between influence and imitation is that influence can fecundate, whereas imitation – especially unconscious imitation – can only sterilize' (Eliot 1961:18).[2] The distance to Bloom is shortened further in Eliot's barely concealed advice to the budding writer to use writers in one's own place and language of the (immediate) past as 'something definite to rebel against' (Eliot 1953:56). It is indeed possible to see Bloom anticipated to an even closer degree when Eliot makes a distinction in his 1942 essay 'The Classics and the Man of Letters' between the secondary writers, whose function is to preserve the continuity of literature, and the great writers who can take their nourishment from the sense of continuity. The great writers have to be seen in the context of the continuity furnished by the ephemeral secondary writers. In this perspective

> we can see that, among the great, even some of the most formal and correct have been also innovators and even rebels, and that

even some of the most revolutionary have carried on the work of those from whose influence they rebelled (Eliot 1942:147).

If Eliot anticipates sympathetically central issues in Harold Bloom, there are also elements in Bloom's doctrines which carry on Eliot's – and, for that matter, Leavis's – basic tenets. Like Eliot, Bloom believes in an aristocracy of learning – literary learning, that is. Dismissing cultural criticism as 'another dismal social science' (1994:17), he pronounces literary criticism an art, which *qua* art 'always was and always will be an elitist phenomenon' (1994:17). Sharing the highly individualist stance with art, the method of literary criticism, relying likewise on the self, is 'therefore a branch of wisdom literature' (1994:184). Although never bothering to set up an ideal sociology like the one suggested by Eliot in his general cultural criticism, Bloom nonetheless, like Eliot, sees the need to 'teach more selectively, searching for the few who have the capacity to become highly individual readers and writers' (1994:17).

Despite the circumstance that Eliot's use of 'influence' to some extent can be said to have elements in common with Bloom's application of the concept, and despite the inclination in both critics for an elitist programme, the differences between them are, however, more telling than their similarities. First and foremost Eliot's eventual subordination of any cultural manifestation to the common denominator of the religious is intolerable to Bloom. The ethics of Bloom's poetics is always a question of aesthetics. His praise of Dr Johnson rests precisely on this principle:

Unlike T. S. Eliot, he [Dr Johnson] does not make aesthetic judgments on religious grounds. Johnson was very unhappy with both Milton's politics and Milton's spirituality, yet the power and originality of *Paradise Lost* persuaded him, despite their ideological differences (1994:185).

But the dissimilarity between the two is perhaps at its most distinct in the way they see the literary tradition. Whereas Eliot – cf. 'Tradition and the Individual Talent' – thinks in terms of an order of works, constantly modified by the arrival of new, that is significantly new, titles, Bloom, in consequense of his agonistic premises, applies a perspective of individual works: 'I always return with fresh wonder to this unrealized truth about the Western Canon:

works are appropriated by it for their singularity, not because they
fit smoothly into an existing order' (1994: 147). To Bloom the tradition – the canon – is a question of a succession of individual works
related to each other in terms of strong negative reaction, whereas
in Eliot we have to do with an ever-expanding and spacious literary
tradition, for which the addition of new works means that we have
'enlarged our conception of the past' (Eliot 1953:57). Eliot's concept
of the literary tradition is perforce cumulative, which in quantitative terms implies a relativist aesthetics.[3] Eliot wisely does not
pronounce on the qualitative consequences of this cumulative dynamic, which would of course imply a doctrine of constant amelior-
ation. But nonetheless it is the logic of this stance, which comes out
quite clearly in his essay on Matthew Arnold from 1933: 'each new
master of criticism performs a useful service merely by the fact that
his errors are of a different kind from the last; and the longer the
sequence of critics we have, the greater amount of correction is
possible' (1933b: 109).[4] In this Platonic dynamic culture is bound to
improve, not, as in Frye's system, because the imagination offers
the possibility of going one better than reality, but in the quite
rational way of trial and error.

Leavis underwrote Eliot's new effort, but with the difference that
he found his safe haven in a slightly later period. Also Leavis
contributed to the introduction of another reactive measure against
the idea of organic growth behind positivist criticism, the focus on
the individual text as fully justifying critical analysis in its own
right, a critical stance in agreement with what was happening
elsewhere, in Czech and Russian formalism, and in US Agrarian
New Criticism. But the three strands in Leavis's criticism – the
longing for a society of integrated values, as in the neo-classical
period, the morality aspect, and the need for the close scrutiny of
texts – united in a kind of criticism directed at existential goals at
one at the same time more and less general than Eliot's. More
general in the sense that Leavis does not arrive at an absolute
existential framework like that contained in Eliot's *The Idea of a
Christian Society*, but refuses to be circumscribed by any tradition.
Less general in the sense that Leavis makes it clear that the present
is definitely inferior to his chosen ideal period of the past. Eliot
seems to address this nostalgia aspect of Leavis's criticism in his
thoughts on the ideal Christian society outlined in 1939: 'bearing in
mind that it can neither be medieval in form, nor be modelled on
the seventeenth century or any previous age' (1939:25), and further-

more: 'I am not advocating any complete reversion to any earlier state of things, real or idealised' (1939:31).

It is exactly when it comes to the nature and function of influence that Frye differs markedly from both Eliot and Bloom. Whether cumulative and expanding or reactive and exclusive, both Eliot and Bloom give high priority to the author as the focus of the literary tradition in terms of influence. As long as Frye stays tuned on the same wavelength, he agrees in principle with the conventional view that influence understood as imitation is at best uninteresting: 'Poets who can at will produce verse on approved moral, religious or patriotic themes seldom make a deep impression on the history of literature' (Frye 1990:52). But this is not really what it is all about. A writer may indeed nurse anxieties, but such are the products of his 'ambiguous relation to the ideology around him' (Frye 1990:48). When it comes to productive influence on a writer's work, the 'real literary descent is not through personalities, but through conventions and genres' (Frye 1990:48).

When in 1949 Wellek and Warren codified many of the efforts of modernist literary criticism in their *Theory of Literature*, the early-twentieth-century reactions to the growth metaphor in literature had really had its time. Wellek and Warren try to compromise between views of literature seen either as isolated works (Eliot, Leavis, New Criticism) or as placed in a long line of influential relations.[5] Instead a literary work should be approached in the perspective of its total life, as the 'result of a process of accretion, i.e. the history of its criticism by its many readers in many ages' (Wellek and Warren 1949:42). For this particular approach they adopt the term 'perspectivism' which implies a merging of literary history in the work-contemporary sense, literary criticism, and literary theory. This is another, and more systematic way of putting Eliot's view on the literary tradition as expressed thirty years previously in his 'Tradition and the Individual Talent', serving central purposes of the Continental-European formalist schools and the US Agrarian-derived aesthetics known by the late 1940s as the New Criticism.[6] It was also a view anticipating the mytho-structuralism of Northrop Frye, justifying his a-historical poetics, and, though harder to see, likewise a view of literary history underpinning Bloom's dogma of a love-hate anxiety of influence, operating with precursors quite capable of having their temporal orientation reversed.

Wellek and Warren proceed on what has now become almost a truism to all those concerned with representations of the past, from diplomatic to art history, and for which the justification is the assumption that '[t]here are simply no data in . . . history which are completely neutral "facts" ' (Wellek and Warren 1949:40). Literary history, like other kinds of history, is a continuous readjustment of data from the past in ways which are considered necessary by a later age, thus characterizing that age more than the past reviewed. If this were not so, there would be no need to write new histories.

All literary histories are indeed selections from a vaster number of texts than those actually included. Although the history of literary histories hardly supports any allegation of an intentional male-white-hegemony conspiracy – if there has indeed been a conspiracy, it appears to have been by default – the tendency through the last two centuries during which the writing of literary history established itself as an expanding business has been to retain that which was already there, but then to change the critical perspective. This is a circumstance often overlooked by those in favour of the conspiracy theory: few literary historians have bothered to see if there are any other streams apart from what appears to be the stream boldly called the main one, tacitly assuming that any other streams will be small in comparison.

CLASSIC AND ROMANTIC: A CANONICAL DYNAMICS

Bernard Bergonzi has suggested (1986) that with Harold Bloom the wheel of literary history has turned over once more, so that now the focus is once again, as in nineteenth-century post-Romanticism, on the Romantics. It is true that in Bloom's frame of reference Blake and Shelley are foregrounded to a degree of prominence unprecedented in major criticism of the twentieth century, but this prominence is hardly interesting, if it is the focusing of one critic only. However, interest in Romantic poets and poetry seems to have been growing, and not just in the era of Bloom – beginning in the late fifties with his book on Shelley (1959) – but also with Frye's study of Blake (1947), generalized into the *Anatomy* ten years later. Symptomatically the critical interest of the so-called school of (Yale) deconstruction has had for one of its favourite study objects the Romantic period, notably in the critical work of Paul de Man and G. Hartman.

This renewed interest in Romanticism and in the writers of the period does not necessarily indicate that the post-Second World

War period is one that is best described as (post-post-) Romantic. In the first place Frye and Bloom, though extremely influential, do not necessarily stand as the highest common denominators of the period. In the second place, the intellectual climate dominating the last half century has been one of cultural pluralism: movements, tendencies, schools and -isms existing alongside each other rather than in succession, as we prefer to approach the periods of literary and cultural history.[7]

Certainly both Frye and Bloom show Romantic predilections, both in their chosen fields of literature underpinning their critical arguments, and in their critical projects, which are of a totalizing nature, as well as displaying a metaphysical dimension.

Frye makes a point of situating his work in contrast to the contemporary shift of critical consciousness and inclining towards the readerly perspective. He wants to retain critical interest in the 'distinctive social function of literature, and ... the basis of the poet's authority, if he has any' (Frye 1990: xxi). This unwillingness to move with the trend of the time marks his kind of criticism, he somewhat wryly suggests, as 'old-hat Romanticism' (Frye 1990:xxi). But there is more to it than merely this *ad hoc* contrast. The very climate of deconstruction and reader-response criticism, with the critical – indeed even sometimes the creative – perspective shifted to the reader, is individualized to a degree to which we may be justified in calling such tendencies the heir of Romanticism, and Frye's effort to place the text in the positivist-inspired arena of comparative criticism as the rational-istic response. However, this is only true with regard to Frye's methodology. In his aim to provide an exhaustive poetics in accord with an ethics of similar ambitions we certainly recognize the kind of intellectual activity characterizing Romanticism. Also, for more practical purposes the period of Romanticism is the pivot of Frye's criticism, since the 'fact that mythology is the narrative source of literature gradually emerged during the Romantic period' (1990:49).

Bloom likewise resorts to a somewhat wry and defensive adoption of the Romantic stance in his attempt to ward off the onslaughts of what he sees as new schools of literary criticism traitorous to a true aesthetics:

Resenters of the aesthetic value of literature are not going to go away, and they will raise up institutional resenters after them. As an aged institutional Romantic, I still decline the Eliotic nostalgia for Theocratic ideology, but I see no reason for arguing with anyone about literary preferences (Bloom 1994:518).

The insistence on going it alone, refusing to argue – argument being the rationalistic stance *par excellence* – marks the Romantic attitude, if anything does.

The aetiology of Bloom's mature work is very much similar to that of Frye's; both begin with mythologically oriented studies of the two most visionary of the Romantic poets – Blake and Shelley respectively. The kind of cyclical thinking represented by Vico – and Shelley in the identical line – has been of major importance for the evolution of critical theory. In his introduction to the second part of his biblical study, Frye acknowledges a partial debt for *The Great Code*, which 'owed a good deal to Vico, the first modern thinker to understand that all major verbal structures have descended historically from poetic and mythological ones' (1990: xii). And the whole structure, transposed according to need, of Bloom's *The Western Canon* is explicitly Viconian.[8]

To unite Frye and Bloom as latter-day Romantics is indeed possible, but this is not, however, how the picture looks from all angles. In 1975 Bloom pronounced a severe verdict on Frye, when he derisively suggested that

> Northrop Frye, who increasingly looks like the Proclus or Iamblichus of our day, has Platonized the dialectics of tradition, its relation to fresh creation, into what he calls the Myth of Concern, which turns out to be a Low Church version of T.S. Eliot's Anglo-Catholic myth of Tradition and the Individual Talent . . . Freedom, for Frye as for Eliot, is the change, however slight, that any genuine single consciousness brings about in the order of literature by joining the simultaneity of that order (Bloom 1975:39).

There certainly seems to be a line in twentieth-century criticism which begins with Eliot and ends with Frye, a line which puts the individual writer in second place to his or her work. Eliot offered a theory of the impersonality of poetry, seconded in theory and practice by the various schools of the New Criticism, and, after them, to be continued by the various schools of structuralist and poststructuralist theory.[9] Also, to Frye, the individual creator of a text is of less significance than the text itself – and its interaction with other texts:

We are so possessed by the modern notion that all the qualities we admire in literature come from the individuality of an author that it is hard to realize that this relentless smashing of individuality [in the Bible] could produce greater vividness and originality rather than less (Frye 1982a: 204).

With Bloom, however, this line is broken. In his 'parallel' to Frye's biblical studies in *The Book of J*, the point is to identify a likely candidate responsible for the first book of the Hebrew Bible, to challenge the prevailing theological view of redaction or shared authorship. In this perspective Bloom stands out single-handedly as a rather lonely – and Romantic – critic.

In his eager promotion of a new age of neoclassicism, Hulme was less concerned with the historical period than with the implications of neoclassicism as a convenient tag for an existential outlook for which there has been a particularly British tradition, first and foremost in a preference for empirical and sceptical philosophy, but also in a pragmatic attitude in politics, some would say ever since Magna Carta. In contrast to this rationalistic tradition Romanticism appears at best vague, at worst detrimental to human decency and always carries the flavour of imported goods, *in casu* from German idealistic philosophy.

Although it could not fairly be said of Eliot that the kind of texts implicitly canonized in his critical work belong in any distinctly classic or neoclassic tradition, his whole approach to literature is that of the gentleman amateur, an image which he strove consciously to emulate in his own life. Furthermore, the texts he gives priority to may seem individually very different, ranging from Dante to Kipling, but together they appear unified as the collection of rarities, in the tradition of a chest of curiosities in the house of a Horace Walpole. Leavis never tries to hide his preference for the values he believes expressed in the lyrical poetry of the mid-eighteenth century, and both in his enunciation of explicit values and in his seigneurial approach the amateur ideal is readily seen. Both Eliot and Leavis handle their chosen texts with a kind of care which is at one and the same time the expression of utter fondness and an often astoundingly studied lack of professionalism. Not that this lack of professionalism is for want of ability to apply the proper instruments. It has to do with a specific cultural heritage.

It seems inevitable that any deliberate approximation to the ways of life and ideas of any earlier period will contain not only the points of interest focused on by contemporaries but also their own attitudes of observation. In this way the Heisenberg uncertainty principle applies also to cultural-historical periods. When, for instance, neoclassic man is busy observing the Hellenic and Roman pasts, he is engaging in an attitude transcending the object of observation, so that to later periods that attitude becomes part of the view of the periods further back. We are very much aware of that when we read Gibbon on the decline and fall of the Roman Empire. What to Gibbon was a past deplorably dead and gone, is to the modern observer not only the past dead and gone, but also a particular taking in of that past dead and gone. To historians – literary, cultural, political or economic – this may seem a trivial argument since the justification of re-writing history rests just as much on the present always being the filter of the past as on the appearance of new empirical materials, but it is important for this different context.

To use the words classic and neoclassic in connection with Eliot and Leavis is possible, then, in recognition of their shared general amateur attitude, manifest in their preference for texts appealing directly to the reader's longing for an ethos making more sense than the one they discern in their own time. With Eliot and Leavis, one always has the impression that literature is an indulgence, like the collection of china or stamps: neither necessary nor useful, essentially a luxury.

If the classic is both a liking for the Hellenic and the Roman *and* a stance implying the well-informed amateur collector of fragments and curiosities with the diachronic-linear as the 'archetype' and realism as existential orientation, the Romantic can be said to be an attraction to medieval times accompanied with a longing for wholes and all-inclusiveness, with the synchronic-cyclical as 'archetype' and idealism as the analogical existential orientation.

Frye and Bloom are Romantic in this systematic rather than periodic definition of the concept just as Eliot and Leavis can be said to be classic or neoclassic. Both base their work on Romantic writers, Frye starting with Blake, Bloom with Shelley, but going on to Blake in due course. Methodically both favour the cyclical mode, with argumentation spreading out from a centre, as it were.[10] There are other striking parallels between the two, not necessarily with the origin in specifically Romantic concerns, but nevertheless attributable to a concern for existence as something whole. I am here thinking of their shared interest in verbal etymology, constant recourse to matters biblical, and a shared focus on Wallace Stevens as *the* modern poet.

Like Leavis in relation to classicism, Bloom is the one most conspicuously related to the Romantic, both as period and as idea. But Frye, especially in his preoccupation with romance, makes the cyclical into the very basis of our approach to existence.

To agree with Bergonzi about the emergence of a new Romantic era is tempting, as are all invitations to categorize phenomena in neat and recognizable categories. But to the extent that labels such as classic and Romantic are applicable in the contemporary conceptual climate, they should be thought of in terms of simultaneity rather than history. In such a perspective, in which the diachronic yields to the synchronic, it makes sense to orientate any critical discourse according to inclination to one or the other, on a principle not unlike that according to which David Lodge, following Jakobson, orientates the literary text in terms of metaphor or metonymy (Lodge 1977). Critics inclining towards the classic tend, when it comes to the canonical, to argue in favour of set standards, acceptance of inherited values and partial views of history, whereas critics of the Romantic inclination tend to suggest individualized 'systems', to create value taxonomies from scratch, and devise holistic 'histories'. In such a dichotomy, Eliot and Leavis have classic leanings, whereas Frye and Bloom incline towards the Romantic.

CANON AND THE POSTMODERNIST CLIMATE

Whereas canonical awareness may be argued to be central to premodernist and modernist literature alike, the climate of postmodernism – here conceived of as a breaking away from modernism rather than a radical continuation of it – is, in its very nature of extreme plurality, relativity and simultaneity, alien to any such awareness.

The concept of a literary canon owes its existence partly to a wish to maintain a set of commonly accepted values seen to be reflected in a list of selected literary works, partly to conventions and traditions in literary studies. On both fronts, however, postmodernist philosophical and critical work and theories have pointed to weaknesses in established dogma and suggested alternatives likewise damaging to the accepted values of the past.

Following Lyotard, the canon may be argued to be just another meta-narrative, serving generally heuristic purposes of a bourgeois culture in need of justification. At a time when Western societies have a hard time questioning the very foundations on which they achieved power and influence, it is only logical that the formal props in that foundation – including the literary canon – are approached with a keen eye for cracks and alternative construction principles. If the very concept of such a thing as a set of common values – 'Western civilization' – is questioned from a political perspective (minority rights movements) and from a philosophical perspective (values seen as potentially collapsible discourses when deconstructed) a major landslide begins, leaving the landscape permanently changed once the new balance has been found. When the central list of the canon is diversified into so many 'peripheral' new 'centres', each serving purposes of a non-consensus nature, the stage is ready for approaches to literature in new terms of radical relativity and extreme pluralism. The US debate discussed in Chapter 2 is symptomatic of this change: on the political side, there is a rising demand for the recognition of the many ethnic groups making up the population of the nation, going right against the grain of the official melting-pot ideology. On the philosophical/theoretical/critical side there is a growing interest in stances of approach that imply the undermining or negation of unity as the characteristic of literary texts and the value systems of which they have usually been taken to be the verbal manifestation. This political-theoretical challenge to a world view based on unity has been enhanced by and is in turn enhancing what is going on in the field of information technology.

It can be argued that canon-defenders, canon-attackers and canon-innovators alike all are late for a train which left the station a long time ago. In an age when the electronic media have consolidated themselves not just as incredibly fast vehicles of communication, but also – and rather more significantly – have established completely new agendas for interhuman relationships in areas to do with material as well as immaterial life conditions, 'old standards' like the literary canon, indeed literature as usually defined, have come in for radical re-examination.

The borderlines between genres have for a long time been the subject of problematization. Metafiction has played around with conventions and reader expectations to such an extent that any novelties from this quarter seem unlikely. However, advanced information technology has given literature, defined as fiction and poetry published in book format, a role in digitalized, interactive and multiple computerized media, which is not as a form of communication any different from any other piece of information. In cyberspace it makes very little sense to maintain a special status for literature, especially when the book is rendered in principle obsolete. Literature will probably continue as a certain form of enunciation, and as enjoying a certain function among its recipients. But it will be obvious that the literary text in the future will have no privileged status as authoritative *text*.

In a culture with multiple centres and with an increasingly pervasive sense of values as relative to standards set by such centres, the recognition of a central literary canon will become increasingly meaningless as one of the rallying points of Western civilization. Electronic information retrieval systems will have facilitated the identification of what are now enjoying the secondary status of literary sub-cultures. Interactive learning systems will have facilitated the use of textual material not on the accredited, and hence easily obtainable syllabus; once installed in a database, there will be no such thing as 'out of print', since texts will be constantly available on-line. With this electronic landslide, and with a civilization apparently less and less interested in standards unifying large segments of it along traditional political-geographical lines, the survival of the concept of a literary canon will probably be restricted to clearly demarcated political-geographical areas of much smaller extension than we have been used to, or relating to a segmentation along lines that cut across such areas, for instance in the form of ethnic, gender or class canons, of which we have seen the beginning since the early seventies.

This inevitable reorientation of the canonical is bound also to affect the way we approach the canonical in literary and critical history. In the postmodernist context we can look back on the 'battle of the books' of the latter half of the twentieth century as an anachronistic struggle between factions who still believed that it is possible to claim a victory for either a conservative-fundamentalist canon supposed to support ideals of *Bildung*, or who thought that alternative canons ought to replace central ones. The truth of the matter is rather that those in the one camp will have to tolerate the existence of those in the other, and that peaceful coexistence is the best solution to a situation when absolute victory is not only impossible, but really beside the point.

It follows from this that a critical appreciation of canonical issues in literary criticism applies the wrong perspective by mustering this, that or the other critic in favour or against any one canon. It makes much better sense, as has been the procedure of this study, to examine a given body of criticism in terms of its intrinsic objectives. If the issue of the canonical plays a role for a critic, it should of course be included in any appreciation of the critic's work. If it is of crucial significance, as it is in the criticism of Eliot, Leavis, Frye and Bloom, no appreciation would be possible without making it into a major field of meta-critical investigation. But to use the four critics as proof of the existence of any one traditional and generally accepted canon would be, in this perspective, to hamper severely their potential for future productive criticism.

CANON AND VALORIZATION

With the hundreds of thousands of literary titles published over the centuries, the singling out of any limited number for closer scrutiny by its very nature remains an issue of valorization, aesthetic in the first place perhaps, but with a very fine line indeed separating the aesthetic from the ethical. Such valorization may be passive or tacit to the extent that a given canon is taken over and made the object of scholarly and critical work. Much academic criticism, although probably far less than believed by the canonical iconoclasts, has been of this kind for the past hundred years. But it may also be an active or quite conscious valorization to the extent that a critic decides to part from from the well-travelled path in search of other regions, or with a view to fencing in even greater tracts.

An issue of valorization, any suggestion to do with the canon, concerning its continuity or its discontinuity, is a rhetorical manoeuvre, bearing on interests for which the literary work is merely instrumental, very often with extra-aesthetic objectives in view. Censorship and indexing are infamous but widespread measures to ensure lack of challenge to the established. To burn books at the stake, or, in reaction to severe censorship, to cherish literature illicitly, as the outcasts in Ray Bradbury's *Fahrenheit 491* do by learning whole books by heart, are symbolic activities, in which literature is made to stand for freedom of the mind rather than as the expression of love for the Metaphysical conceit or the Tolstoyan syntactic cadence.

The smaller the number of observations bearing on a given area, the graver the risks of misrepresentation. This is a truism of statistics, and of course also applies to any critical study attempting to lay down 'rules' from a given number of 'facts'. To set up rules of genre, the knowledge of a sufficient number of texts is required to distinguish between the necessary and the contingent. To distinguish between differences in the intellectual climate of a given period also requires sufficient quantities of the kinds of sources which for one reason or another can be considered of central indicatory importance. To suggest, then, that Eliot, Leavis, Frye and Bloom together constitute the twentieth-century critical achievement would be open to severe criticism, if we go by strictly statistical standards. But the point of this study having been to suggest that the four critics between them have absorbed and given shape to features we think of as typical of this century, it hardly amounts to misrepresentation. The selection of the four has indeed been an act of valorization in so far as they have been made to mark the most significant rallying points within a tradition of literary criticism determined to see literature as a strong factor for the formation of the individual as well as society. This is exactly where the kind of canon criticism espoused by critics of the kind and calibre of Eliot, Leavis, Frye and Bloom parts ways from that of critics bent on opening up the canon. Much work, and sound work too, has gone into the exploration of writers for various reasons neglected and forgotten about. To the extent that such work has been directed at setting up literary lineages to support feelings of lacking senses of identity, as in the fields of gender and ethnic studies, the aim coincides in principle with that of the Western-canon supporters. There ought to be no quarrel between them, although they may see themselves to be in opposition to another. Where there seems to be an opportunity for a legitimate quarrel, however, is between those on the one hand who attempt, by reconsidering the status of known texts or by appraising that of newly discovered ones, to use literature for what may perhaps be best described by a term long ago gone out of use, moral improvement, and those on the other hand seeing literature either as the predetermined product of any given society or as a mass of indeterminable textual phenomena subject to a kind of criticism likewise in constant flux, the kind of criticism that Bloom calls the School of Resentment, but which, in this perspective, should perhaps be renamed the School of Indifference.

Anything to do with the canonical in criticism hinges on existential values. No canon is brought into existence because of thematic, structural or otherwise aesthetic characteristics of a given number of writings. Indeed, canonical considerations rarely even respect whatever traditional demarcations there may be between literary and non-literary texts.[11] Nor is genre synonymous with canon. No one would suggest that the genre of the drama constitutes a canon of drama, unless canon is used deliberately in this sense. The concept of canon comes into play when a selection is made from all literature available. We do not put works or authors together in a canon because a number or them share an interest in, for instance, social criticism or sexual morality. As soon as we begin to talk about canon, we distance ourselves from whatever the individual work is about or what may be a major concern on the part of a writer. Suddenly literature, including various texts not usually thought of as such, emerges as something different from other kinds of human activity, most distinctly different from purely utilitarian activities but very closely related to the other arts. The reason for this distinction is a functional rather than a material one. Literature, along with the other arts, is supposed to do something for you, that something being the effect of something specifically literary, something which is aesthetic in origin but ethical on consumption.

In the cases of the four critics the existential support lent by literature is different. It seems impossible and not really desirable to decide if the difference depends on certain literary preferences in the first place, developed individually and perhaps to some extent unconsciously into extra-literary cognitive and ethical complexes, or on certain attitudes prior to reading being confirmed in specific kinds of literature. What can be decided, however, is that literature is approached in a broad, existential manner. The self-styled elegiac critic Bloom may seem somewhat desperate in his pronouncement on canonical literature as essentially a power-struggle of strong lies serving to oppose the knowledge of time and death, thus making us able to survive individually. But this approach to the existential function of literature is paradigmatic of any canonical concern, transposed into Eliot's united sensibility, Leavis's Arcadia, or Frye's imagination-based meeting of civilized minds.

Literature thought of as a specific entity, capable of triggering certain kinds of behaviour, dates back to Plato and Aristotle, with frequent subsequent confirmations. Shelley pointed out, after a period of frustrated didactic manoeuvres in his early work, that there can be expected to be no immediate stimulus-effect pattern from literary work to behaviour, but that literature operates in a much subtler way by keeping the mind optimally tuned to handle all kinds of problems. It is this Shelleyan twist, derived to a great extent from Sir Philip Sidney and designed to overcome his unpleasant Platonic dilemma, which is the more or less accepted position today among many critics and educators. Literature, or simply 'books', are considered beneficial. To read literature is said to open the mind, to make for tolerance and understanding, in brief, to further the humanity in human beings, the humanity being understood exactly as that particular characteristic – inherited or acquired – which is commensurable with literature.

Canon supporters share a belief in this 'humanizing' effect of reading, which is enhanced when the reading matter is literature and whatever texts enjoy similar status. This supposition underlies the canon-defending position of the four critics discussed in this study, however much their views of specific texts and writers may differ, or, when similar, however much the premises for the same views may differ.

Eliot, Leavis, Frye and Bloom share the view that literature has a unique status when it comes to broad education into full maturity. They differ, however, in their approach to the instrumentality of literature for this end. When those eager to 'open up' the canon attack what they see as the curators of an outmoded critical tradition, they tend to forget that the allegedly monolithic nature of the canon, considered at less distance, is made up of a great variety of minerals, with a lot of cracks, and – despite an impression of impenetrable solidity observed at great distance – is subject to constant erosion and reformation.

Notes

2 Canons in the Making

1. Cf. 'There is a certain complicity between the formation and reproduction of the discipline of English (the dominant form of literary studies) and the notion of modernism itself. It is no coincidence that Eliot's *The Waste Land*, Joyce's *Ulysses*, Pound's first *Cantos* and I. A. Richards's *Principles of Literary Criticism* all appeared within a few years of each other in the early 1920s. . . . – indeed, *Principles of Literary Criticism* ends openly with a defence of Eliot' (Connor 1989:105).

2. Cf. A. N. Wilson in his biography of Lewis: 'Supremely, however, this generous desire to show us the best in an author is manifested in his long chapter about Spenser, and there he marks himself out not as a kindly eccentric, but as a pioneer of modern taste. Thanks very largely to Lewis, Spenser is now once more regarded as one of the greatest English poets, having sunk into almost total obscurity before *The Allegory of Love* was written' (1990:145).

3. '[T]he relationship between teaching and the canon cannot be underestimated. . . . the canon and the academy mutually reinforce one another, even while undergoing change' (Rabb 1988:5).

4. Considering information provided on the back cover: 'Allan Massie provides a splendidly lucid and enjoyable survey of contemporary British fiction. Defining his subject as those novels written in English and first published in the United Kingdom . . .' (Massie 1990), a conspicuous lacuna, however, is the exclusion of John Fowles.

5. A curious case, however, is the British Council exhibition 'Contemporary British Novelists' from 1990 and its accompanying pamphlet. A fairly comprehensive survey, the exhibition – and the pamphlet – comes in two varieties: one with and one without Mr Rushdie. No doubt motivated by assessment of national sensibilities following on the events concerning the publication of *The Satanic Verses* (1988), the two-version exhibition is one of the more depressing attempts at official canon censorship in modern times.

6. Cf. also the recurring famous persons' personal book choices invariably published in major newspapers and magazines before the Christmas and summer vacations.

7. The two-heat dynamic of the Booker Prize is a central case in point. If there is such a thing as short-term canonical fame, it is produced by the adoption of marketing procedures usually associated with spectator sports and gambling. This does not imply that the titles entered for the such prizes as the Booker are poor. On the contrary, most of them are, by any standard, surprisingly good and not seldom demanding on their readers, but the life-spans of winners and

runners-up alike are very much subject to the general fast-oblivion laws of the media which marketed them in the first place. Also of short-term duration is the fame of the books donated in full public view by the British Book Trust to the British royal family for summer-holiday reading.

8. A comparison of the *Norton Anthology* (one vol., ed. Baym 1989) and the Random House *The American Tradition* (one vol., ed. Perkins 1985) with the *Heath Anthology* (Lauter 1990) in the identically named sections 'American Poetry since 1945' reveals that the Heath anthology indeed includes more female poets than Norton and Random; percentage of female poets: Heath 46 (19 out of 41), Norton 29 (11 out of 37), Random 16 (3 out of 18), but still less than half the poets listed are female.

9. No need here to go into the earlier history of the canon debate, since the field is excellently covered already, see for instance Gorak 1991 (chs 1 and 2) or Scholes 1986.

10. E.g. 'for more than twenty years after Curtius the topic was left unguarded by scholars. . . . It took a political awakening to bring the problem of canons to the attention of a new generation of literary scholars. From the start this renewed interest has taken the shape of an angry, damning critique of canon formation from frankly Marxist, feminist, and Third World perspectives. Its outbreak can be dated from the early seventies' (Myers 1989:612–13).

11. Cf. 'The pronounced tendency of our own time has been toward a new inclusiveness, a taking into the canon of philosophers and theorists of culture, previously neglected women writers, unrecognized minority writers, practitioners of folk poetry and other forms of expression once held to be sub-literary' (Alter 1988:574–5).

12. 'The works and authors I have in mind include, but are not limited to, the following: from classical antiquity – Homer, Sophocles, Thucydides, Plato, Aristotle, and Vergil; from medieval, Renaissance, and seventeenth-century Europe – Dante, Chaucer, Machiavelli, Montaigne, Shakespeare, Hobbes, Milton, and Locke; from eighteenth – through twentieth-century Europe – Swift, Rousseau, Austen, Wordsworth, Tocqueville, Dickens, Marx, George Eliot, Dostoyevsky, Tolstoy, Nietzsche, Mann, and T. S. Eliot; from American literature and historical documents – the Declaration of Independence, the Federalist Papers, the Constitution, the Lincoln–Douglas Debates, Lincoln's Gettysburg Address and Second Inaugural Address, Martin Luther King, Jr.'s "Letter from the Birmingham Jail" and "I have a dream . . ." speech, and such authors as Hawthorne, Melville, Twain, and Faulkner. Finally, I must mention the Bible, which is the basis for so much subsequent history, literature, and philosophy' (Bennett 1984:11). Bennett is interested in the text as the medium of values considered worthy of preservation, irrespective of conventional generic boundaries. It would be beside the point to enter here on a discussion of generic distinctions, but of course there are significant differences in the ways that fiction and non-fiction relate to and express values.

13.   Bennett followed up on his report in several books intended to show
       the alleged paucity of American spiritual life, all of them with telling
       titles, like e.g. *The De-Valuing of America: The Fight for Our Culture and
       Our Children* (1992). Into his modern-style conduct book *The Book of
       Virtues: A Treasury of Great Moral Stories* (1993) he culled texts and
       text excerpts for the 'time-honoured task of the moral education of
       the young' (1993:11) under the headings of Self-Discipline, Compas-
       sion, Responsibility, Friendship, Work, Courage, Perseverance, Hon-
       esty, Loyalty and Faith.

14.   'Let me give some concrete examples of the kinds of core information
       I mean. American readers are assumed to have a general knowledge
       of the following people (I give just the beginning of a list): John
       Adams, Susan B. Anthony, Benedict Arnold, Daniel Boone, John
       Brown, Aaron Burr, John C. Calhoun, Henry Clay, James Fenimore
       Cooper, Lord Cornwallis, Davy Crockett, Emily Dickinson, Stephen
       A. Douglas, Frederick Douglass, Jonathan Edwards, Ralph Waldo
       Emerson, Benjamin Franklin, Robert Fulton, Ulysses S. Grant, Alex-
       ander Hamilton, and Nathaniel Hawthorne. Most of us know rather
       little about these people, but that little is of crucial importance,
       because it enables writers and speakers to assume a starting point
       from which they can treat in detail what they wish to focus on'
       (Hirsch 1987:29).

15.   First column of the list: '1066; 1492; 1776; 1861–1865; 1914–1918;
       1939–1945; abbreviation (written English); abolitionism; abominable
       snowman; abortion; Abraham and Isaac; Absence makes the heart
       grow fonder; absenteeism; absolute monarchy; absolute zero; ab-
       stract expressionism; academic freedom; a cappella; accelerator; par-
       ticle; accounting; AC/DC (alternating current/direct current);
       Achilles; Achilles' heel; acid; acid rain; acquittal; acronym; acropho-
       bia; Acropolis; Actions speak louder than words' (Hirsch 1987:152).

16.   A collection of Bloom's essays previous to and contemporary with
       his best-selling book appeared in 1990 under the telling title *Giants
       and Dwarfs: Essays 1960–1990.*

17.   Other titles to support the Bennett–Bloom position as modern-style
       intellectual conduct books are e.g. Barzun 1991, Kernan 1990. Luns-
       ford *et al.* 1990 offers an attempt to approach the concept of cultural
       literacy from a variety of angles.

18.   Cf. Lauter's assurance that 'Every week I revive to hope and struggle
       reading and teaching Toni Morrison and Frances E. W. Harper,
       Rolando Hinojosa and Tillie Olsen, Charles W. Chessnutt and Louise
       Erdrich, Henry David Thoreau and Alice Walker. I find my students,
       like students a quarter century ago, eager for the challenge of re-
       building a democratic, varied, and equitable society – not in Lithua-
       nia but here, in the United States. They read Thomas Paine and
       Thomas Jefferson and David Walker and William Lloyd Garrison
       and Angelina Grimké and Harriet Beecher Stowe and Herman Mel-
       ville and Frederick Douglass; they think of the long struggle for
       freedom; and they cannot help but wonder whether the unique
       opening now before us will be foreclosed by dull, arrogant, vision-

less men of affairs, who have no language but that of war and no object but that of control' (1991:xiii).

19. There is a parallel here to E. D. Hirsch's notion of 'cultural literacy' the point of which is exactly that those who possess it have power, and that power is not a function of what concretely constitutes the items making up the lists of cultural literacy, but the ability to navigate in it at ease.

20. 'The moment of theory is determined, then, by a certain defunctioning of the literary curriculum, a crisis in the market value of its cultural capital occasioned by the emergence of a professional-managerial class which no longer requires the (primarily literary) cultural capital of the old bourgeoisie. This crisis calls forth a redefinition of literature itself, a redefinition which incorporates as a new aspect of literary study the "technical" quality of the knowledge valued by the professional-managerial class' (Guillory 1993:xii).

21. It could be added here that the argument in the final chapter of Jan Gorak's *The Making of the Modern Canon: Genesis and Crisis of a Literary Idea* (1991) in favour of 'cultural studies' as a dominant new canon complements Guillory's selection of 'theory'.

22. On the nexus between UK cultural studies and canon cf. the last chapter in Gorak 1991.

23. These problems are familiar to those who have worked in the field of, e.g. generic fiction or gender-determined criticism, for which the otherwise simple task of generating of a body of texts presents a great variety of difficulties, some of them as banal as getting hold of titles long out of print.

24. By recourse e.g. to the de-stabilizing critical discourses of a Lacan, a Foucault or an Edward Said.

25. Cf. also 'the evolution of a literary system and the concomitant stabilizing effect of the canonization of authors within it are at least as much the work of . . . rewriters as of the writers themselves' (Lefevere 1986:6).

26. '[T]he unveiling of the canon as an institutional construction has had so demystifying an effect upon the ideology of tradition as to bring about a legitimation crisis with far-ranging consequences' (Guillory 1987:483).

27. 'Though the critic's text is apparently addressed to the solution of theoretical problems – to finding adequate and coherent descriptions of the poet's creative act or the reader's poetic experience or the poem itself from the poet's act or stimulating the reader's, together with the function of all these acts in society – though the critic's text may appear to be addressed to these problems, it may actually be meant to create a taste which can sanction transformations in the kinds of poems that are written and read, to prepare poets to write them and audiences to read them. In such critical works we can glimpse the dream of literary empire' (Krieger 1986:196).

3 Eliot: The Constant Modification of Tradition

1. I am thinking here particularly of Hulme's 'Classicism and Romanticism' (1924) and Pound's *ABC of Reading* (1934).
2. Cf. *The Mirror and the Lamp* (1953).
3. At a late point in his life Eliot made it clear that he considered himself a poet-critic's poet-critic, and really despised attempts to criticize poetry by critics without first-hand experience of the creative act (cf. Eliot 1961:25).
4. Eliot's celebrated view of tradition as a dynamic process of ongoing modification is perhaps generated from his work on the philosophy of F. H. Bradley in his dissertation completed in 1916, three years before the publication of 'Tradition and the Individual Talent' (1919), and in which we find the formulation relating to the phenomenology of the object or thing: 'the thing is thoroughly relative, . . . it exists only in a context of experience, of experience with which it is continuous' (1916:165).
5. In criticism, Eliot reacted against the school of Arnold, as he saw it continued in the writings of Walter Pater, Arthur Symons, Addington Symonds, Leslie Stephen, F. W. H. Myers, and George Saintsbury (1933c:123)
6. Eliot acknowledges a debt to Hulme as well as to Babbitt and Charles Maurras in his considerations on classicism and Romanticism, cf. 1961:17.
7. Eliot reacted strongly against the position of one observer of his critical contributions, allegedly working on the assumption that Eliot had, at the outset of his career as a literary critic 'sketched out the design for a massive critical structure, and spent the rest of my life filling in the details' (1961:14). It is obvious to readers of Eliot's criticism that such a Fryean enterprise was never the intention. But just as we may choose to approach a literary text from the angle advantageous to whatever purpose we have in mind, we may choose to disregard Eliot's own protestations and see in his critical work if not a massive critical structure then at least the organic coherence produced by a personality.
8. In criticism there was, Eliot suggests, an eclipse between Jonson and Dr Johnson, to the effect that at best the Augustan critical effort is mediocre (1932:58–62). Since the Augustan age criticism has been beset by either a degree of formalism that excludes from the poetry what it has to say, or by dominant attention to this aspect so that poetic essence is lost in the process (1932:64–5). This bifurcation of critical focus is coinstantaneous with the dissociation of sensibility, with Johnson – late and in isolation – the last critic to express himself in an atmosphere of unified sensibility, in a 'civilisation which, being settled, has no need, while it lasts, to enquire into the function of its parts' (1932:65).
9. It is symptomatic that Eliot sees a grave risk in possible consequences of Erastianism in the form of 'varieties or irresponsible and irreflective enthusiasm' (1939:51), a situation obtaining in England in the

period in question. Cf. also his statement 'It is not enthusiasm, but dogma, that differentiates a Christian from a pagan society' (1939:59).

10. This explains Eliot's simple and straightforward view of interpretation as the effort to explicate the historical facts relevant to the text in question (cf. 1919a:45–6 and 1923:75). Interpretation is thus different from critical work, which, with echoes of Matthew Arnold, means the comparison with other texts as standards (cf. 1919a:45–6). The essence of any new – and great – poem is something that 'must remain unaccountable however complete might be our knowledge of the poet' (1956:112). And the meaning of any poem is not 'exhausted by any explanation, for the meaning is what the poem means to different sensitive readers' (1956:113).

11. Eliot seems to be using the term 'major' as interchangeable with 'great' and 'important'. Only stylistic considerations seem to justify alternations.

12. In his characteristically cautious fashion Eliot argues as an example that although long poems like Thomson's *Seasons* or Cowper's *Task* do not live up immediately to our expectations from Spenser, Milton, Wordsworth, Byron or Keats, thus to be categorized as minor long poems, they nonetheless cannot be discarded simply as minor poems because we often come upon them only as extracts – and furthermore as anthology pieces. Eliot bases his defence of them as different from minor poetry on their supposedly added-value potential.

13. Eliot lists the three main reasons for reading as follows: 'the acquisition of wisdom, the enjoyment of art, and the pleasure of entertainment' (1948:86).

14. Cf. Eliot's prefatory remarks to *The Idea of a Christian Society* in which the interrelationship between the two components is indicated in the suggestion that his findings regarding the organisation of values and direction of religious thought 'must inevitably proceed to a criticism of political and economic systems' (1939:6). And political philosophy derives its authority from ethics, which in turn depends on the 'truth of religion' (1939:63).

15. 'In so far as in any age there is common agreement on ethical and theological matters, so far can literary criticism be substantive. In ages like our own, in which there is no such common agreement, it is the more necessary for Christian readers to scrutinize their reading, especially of works of imagination, with explicit ethical and theological standards' (1934:93).

16. I am not here arguing that religion in Eliot was a chrysalis waiting to unfold, but that the drift of Eliot's early thoughts on poetics was tuned in such a way as to facilitate the later adoption of a deliberately religious stance, also prepared for and supported by the acceptance of the authority of a literary tradition, a canon.

17. Eliot finds Arnold's use of 'culture' too narrow, since it lacks in social background (1939:22). Also, he finds fault with an attitude to poetry which substitutes it for something else. If one finds that religion has outplayed its function, there is nothing that can take its place: 'noth-

ing in this world or the next is a substitute for anything else; and if you find that you must do without something, such as religious faith or philosophic belief, then you must just do without it' (1933b:113).

18. Eliot is quite aware of the inevitability of education being always accommodated to suit specific ends, cf. 'Every definition of the purpose of education, therefore, implies some concealed, or rather implicit philosophy or theology' (1950:75).

19. Eliot uses 'culture' and 'civilisation' synonymously, except in the cases when a difference is clearly indicated by context, the distinction being left to the reader (1939:13).

20. Cf. 'Culture can never be wholly conscious – there is always more to it than we are conscious of; and it cannot be planned because it is also the unconscious background of all our planning' (1948:94).

21. The nature of the local is particularly evident in poetry, whose function is restricted to the area in which its language is still active, since '[p]oetry is the constant reminder of all the things that can only be said in one language, and are untranslatable' (1943:23).

22. The local exists on, as it were, the manifest level, with the universal existing on the unconscious level, cf. 1953:54.

23. Eliot's defence of poetic rhythm against the onslaught of free verse based on the view that 'freedom is only truly freedom when it appears against the background of an artificial limitation' (1917:187) is emblematic of his general position.

24. '[C]omposed of both clergy and laity, of the more conscious, more spiritually and intellectually developed of both' (1939:42). But it would exist within a framework of the possibility of formalized religious observation, including the existence of religious orders (1939:60).

25. Eliot's analysis, here as elsewhere, is marked by a certain vagueness when it comes to verifiable documentation and strict methodology. His identification of the dominant social class of the past with the cultural elite is thus introduced by the very personal 'I think that in the past . . .' (1948:42).

26. It must be noted that Eliot sees the danger of the levelling, if not downright deterioration of cultural values, as something that traverses social classes. A mob comes into being when men and women become 'detached from tradition, alienated from religion, and susceptible to mass suggestion' (1939:21). On the other hand, Eliot shows an implicit concern for the extent to which the mass of a population in a Christian society can be entrusted to practise a conscious form of Christianity. So it is better for the mass to be able to live their lives in unconscious compliance with Christianity (1939:30). Democracy in its present varieties is not strong enough to withstand negative forces, but a pliable instrument potentially in their control. God is the only forceful enough protector against a Hitler or a Stalin (1939:63).

27. Religious scepticism is also a symptom of the '*intellectual* respect' (1939:8; Eliot's italics) with which Christianity ought to be treated.

28. This is a fact not enunciated by Eliot, but implied as a consequence of his suggestions.
29. It is obvious that the two senses – hence the lack of need to distinguish – of 'Catholic' suits Eliot well for this line of argument which places him on the horns of a dilemma.
30. Cf. also 'I believe that the Catholic Church, with its inheritance from Israel and from Greece, is still, as it always has been, the great repository of wisdom' (1933d:117).
31. Cf. 'I mean by a "lower middle class society" one in which the standard man legislated and catered for, the man whose passions must be manipulated, whose prejudices must be humoured, whose tastes must be gratified, will be the lower middle class man. He is the most numerous, the one most necessary to flatter. I am not implying that this is either a good or a bad thing: that depends upon what lower middle class Man does to himself, and what is done to him' (1939:78).
32. In concrete terms Eliot in his 1953 address to Washington University, St Louis, Missouri, mentions as the essentials of a good school education: 'Latin and Greek, together with Greek and Roman history, English and American History, elementary mathematics, French and German' (1953:45).
33. E. g. 'for we all agree about the "cultural breakdown" ' (1948:105) and 'the culture of Europe has deteriorated visibly within the memory of many who are by no means the oldest among us' (1948:108). One of the more curious examples to support his view Eliot finds in the alleged decline of British cooking standards in the interwar years (1948:27).
34. In his 1950 essay on education Eliot reveals his concern about the march of what has come to be known as visual media culture, a state of affairs bringing about what Eliot calls 'secondary illiteracy' (1950:94).
35. E.g. Eliot's reminder that his idea of an ideal society can 'neither be medieval in form, nor be modelled on the seventeenth century or any previous age' (1939:25), or 'I am not advocating any complete reversion to any earlier state of things, real or idealised' (1939:31). Cf. Blake Morrison: 'In the mid-1950s, several critics dubbed the Movement poets "Augustans" or "New Augustans", and, in relation to this idealizing of the eighteenth-century audience, the description seems apposite. The wistful longing to re-create Augustan conditions seems to have been in large part due to the Movement's exposure to the teaching of the Leavises' (Morrison 1980:113).

4 Leavis: Elitist in Pursuit of Common Values

1. The previous sentence reads: 'In dealing with individual poets the critic, whether explicitly or not, is dealing with tradition, for they live in it. And it is in them that tradition lives' (1936:10–11).
2. Cf. 'The Romantic conceptions of genius and inspiration developed (the French revolution and its ideological background must, of

course, be taken into account) in reaction against the Augustan in-
sistence on the social and the rational' (1936:95). Here, of course,
Leavis is in complete accordance with the Imagist foundation of
Anglo-American modernism.

3. Leavis is less general and more precise in an earlier passage:
    'strength appears here as critical intelligence, something intimately
    related to the sureness of touch and grasp. . . . The relation between
    the firmness of the art and the firm grasp on the outer world appears
    most plainly in the ode *To Autumn*. . . . The ripeness with which
    Keats is concerned is the physical ripeness of autumn, and his genius
    manifests itself in the sensuous richness with which he renders this
    in poetry, without the least touch of artistic over-ripeness' (1936:
    244–5).

4. Cf. 'The Romantic poets have among themselves no attachments of
    the kind that link the poets in the line from Donne and Ben Jonson to
    Pope and the line from Pope to Crabbe. If the character of the period
    [Romantic period] is to be rendered, the full separate treatment of the
    individuals is necessary' (1936:13).

5. There seems to be no interest in drama anywhere in his critical work.
    Despite his admiration for the early Augustan age, there is no criti-
    cism on Restoration drama in Leavis's work.

6. Cf. Eliot: 'There is however one contemporary figure about whom
    my mind will, I fear, always waver between dislike, exasperation,
    boredom and admiration. That is D. H. Lawrence' (Eliot 1961:24).

7. Cf. also: 'As a matter of fact, when we examine the formal perfection
    of *Emma*, we find that it can be appreciated only in terms of the moral
    preoccupations that characterize the novelist's peculiar interest in
    life' (1948:17–18).

8. Cf. with reference to Wells: 'there is an elementary distinction to be
    made between the discussion of problems and ideas, and what we
    find in the great novelists' (1948:16).

9. Cf. e.g. Marxist criticism in general and Georg Lukács in particular.

10. 'The aim is to keep as close as possible to the concrete, and to deal
    with general considerations in terms related as immediately as
    possible to practice – or to particular proposals conceived as practi-
    cal' (1943:21).

5 Frye: The Grand Vision of a Liberal-Arts Education

1. Cf. Frye's remark in his respondent essay to the 1966 English In-
    stitute volume: 'I do not think of the *Anatomy* as primarily syste-
    matic: I think of it as rather schematic. The reason why it is schematic
    is that poetic thinking is schematic' (Krieger 1966:136). In his essay in
    the same volume Hartman uses 'system' about Frye's poetics, but
    Krieger concedes the superiority of Frye's less rigorous designation
    (Krieger 1966:5).

2. The shared critical concerns of the *Anatomy* and the two Bible studies
    is borne out by Frye's characterization of *Words with Power* as 'some-
    thing of a successor also to the much earlier *Anatomy of Criticism*

(1957). In fact, it is to a considerable extent a summing up and restatement of my critical views' (1990:xii). Frye's speculations on 'romance' are further elaborated in *The Secular Scripture: A Study of the Structure of Romance* (1976).

3. Cf. Murray Krieger's characterization of the *Anatomy*: 'His followers and his ensuing works produce in the main simplifications and extensions of – even footnotes to – the *Anatomy*, the Word propagated and translated, thinned in order to be spread' (Krieger 1966:2). Written in 1966, this may also be said to have been the case afterwards.

4. This work neatly sums up what can be gathered from such other works of Frye's speculating on the relations between literature and society, in *The Educated Imagination* (1963), *The Well-Tempered Critic* (1963), *The Stubborn Structure: Essays on Criticism and Society* (1970), *The Modern Century* (1967; although its starting point is the Canadian context), *Spiritus Mundi: Essays on Literature, Myth, and Society* (1976), *Creation and Recreation* (1980), *Northrop Frye on Culture and Literature: A Collection of Review Essays* (1978, ed. R. D. Denham), and *On Education* (1988).

5. A general exegesis in sympathy with Frye's system, with a bibliography up to 1987, is available in Hamilton 1990.

6. *A Natural Perspective* (1965), *Fools of Time* (1967), *The Myth of Deliverance* (1983), and the collection of brief studies edited by Robert Sandler, *Northrop Frye on Shakespeare* (1986).

7. *The Return of Eden: Five Essays on Milton's Epics* (1965).

8. *A Study of English Romanticism* (1968).

9. *The Bush Garden: Essays on the Canadian Imagination* (1971), including the conclusion to a *Literary History of Canada*, *Divisions on a Ground: Essays on Canadian Culture* (1982).

10. *T. S. Eliot* (1963).

11. Frye points out that his use of 'archetype' in the sense of stable structural units is the established usage in literary criticism, different from Jung's, which he considers the more idiosyncratic usage (1982:48). 'Desire' in Frye's vocabulary is used in the most inclusive sense of the term.

12. Another, and more detailed definition, runs: 'Anagogically, the symbol is a monad, all symbols being united in a single infinite and eternal verbal symbol which is, as *dianoia*, the Logos, and, as *mythos*, total creative act. It is this conception which Joyce expresses, in terms of subject-matter, as "epiphany," and Hopkins, in terms of form, as "inscape" ' (1957:121).

13. Although not really related to Jung's archetypes, since exclusively literary in origin, it is this kind of statement which has linked Frye with that particular branch of psychology, but cf. Frye: 'because I found the term "archetype" an essential one, I am still often called a Jungian critic, and classified with Miss Maud Bodkin, whose book I have read with interest, but whom, on the evidence of that book, I resemble about as closely as I resemble the late Sarah Bernardt' (1971a:16). A decisive difference from Jung is, indeed, in Frye's insistence on the origin of the structures of myth as responses to

specific existential situations: 'Such structural principles are certainly conditioned by social and historical factors and do not transcend them, but they retain a continuity of form that points to an
identity of the literary organism distinct from all its adaptations to its
social environment' (1990:xiii). It is in this sense that a quasi-Jungian
statement like this one should be understood: 'mythological thinking
cannot be superseded, because it forms the framework and context
for all thinking' (1990:xvi).

14. Cf. Frye's suggestion about the contrast between explicit and poetic
meaning, the latter of which by its very nature allows for a certain
degree of indeterminacy: 'Grasping real meaning of poetry gives us
an orbit or circumference of meaning, within which there is still
some latitude for varieties of interpretation and emphasis, both in
commentary and, with a play, in performance' (1971a:70).

15. In his analysis of Frye's conclusion Robert Lecker cleverly suggests
that Frye's discourse transforms the history of Canadian literature
into a successful quest pattern: 'After all, the conclusion affirms that
for Frye, history making will in some way enact a dream of self-cre-
ation in literary time, a dream that replaces closure with conception
and history writing with fables of identity' (1993:285).

16. Frye's predilection for the Aristotelian stance is obvious, as it must be
for a critic extolling literature as the potentially most valuable form
of human 'action'.

17. Cf.: 'Traditionally, the Bible's narrative has been regarded as "literally" historical and its meaning as "literally" doctrinal or didactic:
the present book takes myth and metaphor to be the true literal
bases' (1982a:64).

18. '[L]iterature represents the *language* of human concern. Literature is
not itself a myth of concern, but it displays the imaginative possibilities of concern, the total range of verbal fictions and models and
images and metaphors out of which all myths of concern are constructed' (1971a:98).

19. Cf. 'When a myth of concern has everything its own way, it becomes
the most squalid of tyrannies, with no moral principles except those
of its own tactics, and a hatred of all human life that escapes from its
particular obsessions. When a myth of freedom has everything its
own way, it becomes a lazy and selfish parasite on a power-struc-
ture' (1971a:55).

20. In sociological terms, the manifestation of the myth of freedom is
'guarded' by a 'critical, and usually an educated, minority'
(1971a:45). Hence the crucial role of universities to Frye.

21. Frye argues that the joy experienced in the creation or experience of
literature is a product of the disinterestedness of the myths that go
into literature; by being forms of human creativity, 'they communi-
cate the joy . . . that belongs to pure creation' (1971a:169). More specifically, the pleasure we experience from 'listening to poetry or
music is the fulfilling of a *general* expectation, of a sort that is possible
only in highly conventionalized art' (1971a:40). Frye adduces the
example of the whodunit: we do not want to know from the begin-

ning who committed the crime, but we like to know that the genre implies its detection.

22. Cf. 'From the universities in particular, the concern of the educated minority, which is centered on the myth of freedom, leaks out to society as a whole' (1971a:135).

23. 'The educational contract is the process by which the arts and sciences, with their methods of logic, experiment, amassing of evidence and imaginative presentation, actually operate as a source of spiritual authority in society. What they create is a free authority, something coherent enough to help form a community, but not an authority in the sense of being able to apply external compulsion' (1971a:163).

6 Bloom: Swerving into Ever-Renewed Strength

1. The best very short accounts given by Bloom himself of his poetics are found in 1975b:88–9 and 1977:393–4. A longer, but still condensed version is offered as the first chapter of *Poetry and Repression* (1976:1–27) and in the more roaming introductory chapters of *Agon: Towards a Theory of Revisionism* (1982:3–90). A good and brief introduction to the key concepts and their relations in Bloom's poetics is John Hollander's in his edition of essays and chapters by Bloom: *Poetics of Influence: Harold Bloom* (1988:xi–xlvi).

2. Following this kind of logic through, it makes sense that Bloom, despite acknowledging Johnson and Coleridge (and the critic W. J. Bate) as among the 'great affirmers' of the anxiety of influence, and Nietzsche and Emerson as among the 'great deniers', has learnt more from the latter than from the former (1973:50). Somewhat further on in his 'tessera' chapter, Bloom extends the list of affirmers to include Ruskin, and the list of deniers to include Goethe, Mann, Thoreau, Blake, Lawrence, Pascal, Rousseau and Hugo (1973:56).

3. Cf. '[T]he kind of ideas that poems are' (1975b:55).

4. Bloom suggests that 'meaning in belated texts is always wandering meaning' (1975b:82).

5. Bloom's careless attitude to definitions is very much in evidence in his discussion about the ontology of the poem, cf., e.g.: 'the verbal image (however you want to define an image)' (1975b:65).

6. Falstaff is very much at the centre of interest in *The Western Canon*, where that character is related – agonistically – to Chaucer's Wife of Bath (115). Bloom goes so far as to suggest a parallel of character, in which he professes his interest over plot (112), to 'virtual reality' (105).

7. Cf. '[T]he deepest or most vital instances of influence are almost never phenomena of the poetic surface' (1975b:66).

8. The three works from 1973 and 1975 are a trinity of Bloomian poetics, with the first sketching the theory of anxiety of influence in terms of six revisionary ratios, while the latter two elaborate on the Freudian and the Kabbalistic aspects respectively. The first coherent articula-

tion of the theory is in Bloom 1970:3–22 (the introduction to the Yeats study). Bloom has returned to theoretical issues of his poetics from time to time since 1975, notably in *Agon: Towards a Theory of Revisionism* (1982), and in *Ruin the Sacred Truths* (1989), but here repeating rather than developing his views.

9.   Cf. 'There is no anxiety of representation for a strong poet, . . . because that anxiety was met and overcome already for the strong ephebe by the precursor (and for the Kabbalists by God)' (1975b:82).

10.   Bloom recognizes the existence of ideas and images taken over by succeeding generations of poets, and also the justified work of criticism to trace such influences, as they belong to discursiveness and to history (1973:71).

11.   Bloom suggests a relation of Kabbalah to Freudian theory in the proposition that '[a]s a psychology of belatedness, Kabbalah manifests many prefigurations of Freudian doctrine' (1975a:43).

12.   Inspired by Cordovero, whereas the triad of dialectic revisionism is derived from Luria.

13.   As the aim in the present study is not an exegesis of Bloom's theory in general, but the pursuit of its significance for canon formation, there is no need to go further into details about or to problematize these six revisionary ratios. For an exemplification of the interaction of these for the reading of any strong crisis poem – the master text for Bloom – cf. 1975a:95–104 and the reading of Browning's 'Childe Roland' poem 1975a:105–22. For an application of the six behinah of the sefirot in general cf. 1975b:66–71. In the later – post-1977 – theory, this is supplemented by the troping into the analytical device of 'poetic crossings'.

14.   The parallel of Bloom's theory of poetic misprision to Kabbalistic usage is well worth noting: 'In its degeneracy, Kabbalah has sought vainly for a magical power over nature, but in its glory it sought, and found, a power of the mind over the universe of death' (1975b:47), and further on: 'Let us say (following Vico) that all religion is apotropaic litany against the dangers of nature, and so all poetry an apotropaic litany, warding off, defending against death' (1975b:52). Also Bloom links psychic defence closely to the fear of dying, cf. 1975b:84.

15.   In addition to the great amount of indirect evidence for the prominence of Shelley's poetics in Bloom's critical works, the debt is duly acknowledged from time to time, e.g.: 'In Shelley's *A Defence of Poetry*, which Yeats rightly considered the most profound discourse upon poetry in the language' (1973: 39).

16.   Bloom does not even feel sure about the exact nature of Romanticism. The impression from the first chapters of *The Anxiety of Influence* of Romanticism as strong prophecy is later on problematized as perhaps only an 'intensity of repression' (1973: 111–12).

17.   Shakespeare already here – before *The Western Canon* – presents a special case in Bloom's view, since he is the only English poet to have absorbed his source of influence, Marlowe. Also, Shakespeare belongs to a time when the anxiety of influence was not 'central to

poetic consciousness' (1973: 11), and since his form was dramatic rather than lyric, the 'shadow cast by the precursors' (1973: 1) was less dominant.

18. Bloom suggests a very neat transformation in terms almost of Kantian *Anschauungsformen*: 'Kabbalah is a doctrine of Exile, a theory of influence made to explain Exile. Exile, in a purely literary context, wanders from the category of space to that of time, and so Exile becomes Belatedness' (1975b: 83).

19. In the mid-1970s situation of his 1975a, he has nothing but scorn for the academic profession of letters on the Continent, characterized as an 'anthropology half-Marxist, half-Buddhist' or in Britain, denounced as a 'middle-class amateurism displacing an aristocratic amateurism' (1975a: 30).

20. Bloom's rejection of criticism on mimetic grounds is implied in his very approach, but also stated in so many words, e.g. 'Poems rise not so much in response to a present time, as even Rilke thought, but in response to other poems' (1973: 99).

21. Cf. such slogan-like expressions as 'Discontinuity is freedom' (1973: 39). Also telling in this respect is Bloom's fondness for radically etymological considerations, e.g. the attention to the word 'revision' as made up of parts meaning 'to see again' (1975a: 4). It is certainly true that Bloom escapes classification in any one critical school or movement. Only a critic as unclassifiable as Bloom can afford an unambiguously structuralist credo like: 'there are *no* texts, but only relationships *between texts*' (1975a: 3; Bloom's italics). Bloom relies to a certain extent on the efforts of deconstruction, and of Derrida in particular, to pave the way for his own suggestions. (Also the shevirat of the Lurianic dialectic applies to a text in much the same way as the deconstructionist search for the contradictory element in a given text, cf. 1975b:85.) But Derrida, daring as he may appear, is not radical enough for Bloom, cf. 1975a:48–9, since he attributes primacy to writing over the oral tradition implied by the primacy of the Scene of Instruction, synonymous with the six-phased revisionary ratios (1975b: 63). Bloom's dislike of on the one hand deconstructionists like Derrida, de Man and Hillis Miller and on the other the archetypal critics in the school of Frye is that the two de-spiritualize and over-spiritualize respectively (1975a: 79). Bloom sees himself as a restorer and redresser rather than a deconstructor or de-idealizer of meaning (1975a: 175). But that he is walking on a tightrope with regard to a possible affiliation with the deconstructionists is obvious, and he comments somewhat obliquely with an observation on the conventions of the 'Gematria', the 'explanation of words according to their numerical values or the equivalents, by set rules' (1975b: 45) as a 'kind of parody of the sometimes sublime Kabbalistic exaltation of language, and of the arts of interpretation' (1975b: 46).

22. Cf. Brooks and Warren, *Understanding Poetry* (1938) and *Understanding Fiction* (1943) and Brooks and Heilman, *Understanding Drama* (1948), which held sway in practical criticism for the

next generations, at many places of learning well beyond the introduction of structuralism and various poststructuralist new ortho-
doxies.

23. In his 1959 study of Shelley, Bloom's opposition to the comparative-
literature approach is made quite plain in a statement the point of
which is to defy one of the most open-and-shut cases of influence:
'As to the influence of Plato upon Shelley's poetry, whatever it may
have been, we will not know how to talk about it, as critics, until we
understand more about the process of poetic influence than we do
today' (1959: viii).

24. In the revisionary-ratio perspective of 'apophrades' – the return from
the dead – the particularly Bloomian sense of influence is taken to its
logical limit, as when Bloom cannot escape reading the ephebe Ashbery into the poetry of Ashbery's precursor Stevens (1973: 144). Or
the case of Stevens's 'The Rock' sequence, forcing us to read differently Wordsworth, Shelley, Blake, Keats, Emerson and Whitman
(1973: 147). Or the case of Shelley in 'The Witch of Atlas' having read
too deeply in Yeats (1973: 153).

25. Thus Joyce Carol Oates is made the ephebe of Dreiser (1975a: 164).

26. Bloom's definition runs: 'a trope is *a willing error*, a turn from literal
meaning in which a word or phrase is used in an improper sense,
wandering from its rightful place' (1975a: 93; Bloom's italics).

27. In 1977 Bloom supplements the Kabbalistic triad by the analogical
concepts of 'ethos, logos, and pathos' which are found more suitable
for the purpose of analyzing Wordsworth's poetry.

28. Bloom's attempt at dramatizing his Gnostic concepts in *The Flight to
Lucifer: A Gnostic Fantasy* (1979) comes across, however, as a somewhat too didactic and unconvincing science-fiction adventure.

29. Bloom relies for his Kabbalistic analogues exclusively on Isaac Luria,
as rendered by Gershom Scholem in his book *Kabbalah* (1975a: 5).
Scholem, according to Bloom, enjoys a status in relation to Kabbalah
comparable to that of Milton to earlier poets (1975b: 18). Bloom,
following Scholem, offers a capsule history and commentary on
Kabbalah in 1975b: 15–47, and here and elsewhere frequently points
out that Kabbalah translates into 'tradition' in the sense of 'reception'.

30. Quite in accordance with his fondness for semantic games, Bloom
turns the 'negative aspect of poetic influence' into *'influenza* in the
realm of literature, as the influx of a epidemic of anxiety' (1973: 38;
Bloom's italics).

31. The exact date of the literary Fall is somewhat uncertain in Bloom's
vague historical outline. His post-Enlightenment borderline is fairly
imprecise, but Bloom suggests that we consider the romantic crisis
poetry in the manner of Wordsworth's 'Intimations' ode as the
watershed from the late to the belated eras, cf. 1975b: 90.

32. Milton, Goethe and Nietzsche are, according to Bloom, 'absorbed
precursors with a gusto evidently precluding anxiety' (1973: 50).

33. Bloom finds that only 'Shakespeare and Spenser alike appear to
leave some room for the female in all creativity' (1975a: 78).

34. To be noted here are of course the striking parallels between Vico and Shelley.

35. At this point in his argument, Bloom makes Wordsworth the inventor of modern poetry, by an 'enormous curtailment' (1973: 125).

36. A typical passage evidencing Bloom's period interest runs like this: 'the true history of modern poetry would be the accurate recording of these revisionary swerves' (1973: 44).

37. 'Where generosity is involved, the poets influenced are minor or weaker; the more generosity, and the more mutual it is, the poorer the poets involved' (1973: 30). And compare Bloom's comment on Norman Mailer: 'any reader of *Advertisements for Myself* may enjoy the frantic dances of Norman Mailer as he strives to evade his own anxiety that is, after all, Hemingway all the way' (1973: 28).

38. Even though Bloom counts Spenser in this line, and calls him 'mild' (1973: 33), being pre-Milton, this poet obviously presents a case different from the others.

39. Bloom suggests that the reason why there is this difference between English and American poets in terms of ratio emphasis is to be found in the strong individualistic stance of poets like Emerson and Whitman. As a result we find a much more pronouncedly rebellious attitude among American poets, with much more radical misprisions. Cf. also 1975a: 52–3 and 193.

40. With even this radically short canon Bloom seems to hesitate from time to time. Having pronounced Hardy and Stevens the only strong poets of the twentieth century, he categorizes Yeats with Lawrence and Frost as merely great poets, unable to keep up strength, but nonetheless existing on a level higher than major poetic innovators like Pound and Williams, who 'may never touch strength at all' (1975a: 9).

41. Cf. 'The use of Buber in this study is of course heuristic' (1959: vii).

42. Bloom's attraction to Stevens is presumably very much a matter of congenial spirits, cf. the poem quoted 1977: 16.

43. Bloom pronounces Emerson a 'kind of American Wordsworth' (1977: 11).

44. It is quite to the point that Bloom rallies the two famously strong subjective critics Walter Pater and Paul Valéry as providers of epigraphs for his two important sections of 1975b.

45. Misinterpretation does not stop with the poem in relation to the precursor poem, but is at work even in the poem itself as the misinterpretation of what the poem might have been (1973: 120).

46. Bloom does, however, report that on being asked which contemporary poets to read, he would suggest Robert Penn Warren, Elizabeth Bishop, A. R. Ammons, John Ashbery, and Geoffrey Hill. This roll-call of four American and one British poets shows an inclination towards a decidedly modernist tradition.

47. Bloom considers Eliot and Frye of the same kind, with Frye being the 'Low-Church version of T. S. Eliot's Anglo-Catholic myth of Tradition and the Individual Talent' (1975a: 30).

48.   Bloom is very much against any view of the readerly 'we' as someone less than an entity that to him transcends sex, race and social class. The touchstone for the humanity in question is the need to depend on a scene of instruction (1975a: 38).

7 Literary History, Criticism and Canon

1.   At the time when modernism won through, however, academic or university criticism had already become so entrenched that 'comparative literature', that is, literary criticism executed according to a positivist-inspired concept of influence, became more or less synonymous with literary criticism. Although challenged by a succession of competing schools of criticism, comparative literature is still a powerful element in academic criticism.

2.   A true disciple is under the influence of his master to the extent that he is 'impressed by what his master has to say, and *consequently* by his way of saying it; an imitator – I might say, a borrower – is impressed chiefly by the way the master said it' (Eliot 1953: 54). This might be true of the relationship of Leavis to Eliot.

3.   Cf. '[E]ach generation, looking at masterpieces of the past in a different perspective, is affected in its attitude by a greater number of influences than those which bore on the generation previous' (1956: 104).

4.   Cf. also Eliot's dictum on the end of criticism, which is the double one of the 'elucidation of the work of art and the correction of taste' (1923: 69). Frye sees in the function of criticism rather the perspective under which literature is consumed in contrast to the productive aspect of its creation: 'In literature the creative structure is normally produced by an individual; criticism represents the forming of a social consensus around it' (1990: 28).

5.   Wellek and Warren argued specifically against *Geistesgeschichte*, the branch of positivist-inspired criticism then particularly popular in Germany that attempted to place a work in a wider context of its contemporary intellectual climate.

6.   In 1956 Eliot recognized the notion of 'The New Criticism' to describe a variety of different critical approaches, all of them differing in significant ways to the criticism of the immediate past, cf. 1956: 103.

7.   It is indeed a question whether the telescoped perspective we have of the intellectual climates of the past does not thwart the reality of the past. What we see as successive dominance may very well have appeared to contemporary observers as a situation of plurality. Wordsworth's and Coleridge's reaction against neoclassicism did not stop the principle of restraint in verse, but made it the supplement of a metaphysically more ambitious line, which in turn was not stopped by modernism, but given supplementary status in turn.

8.   The liking on the part of both critics for the etymological analysis of words to get down to the rock bottom, as it were, of essential concepts, may be construed in support of a rationalistic as well as of a

romantic inclination, but in a general context of romantic leanings, the etymological urge is symptomatic of a wish to create concepts from their very bases. (Cf. e.g. Bloom 1975a: 42 and Frye 1990: 126).

9. Placed somewhat 'awkwardly' in the neat succession of the line from New Criticism via structuralism to post-structuralism, Frye nonetheless shares quite a few similarities with structuralism in its French provenance, cf. his tacit agreement with Claude Lévi-Strauss's recommended study of myth as considering the search for an *ur*-myth a blind alley, instead suggesting it 'simpler to assume that the real sense of profundity is derived from the opposite process – that is, the accumulation and constant recreation of Grail stories through the centuries to our own day' (Frye 1990: 55)

10. In the case of Frye there is immediate proof of this in the very arrangement of his major works, cf. especially *Anatomy of Criticism* and *The Great Code*. And cf. a typical pronouncement by Frye on 'phases' in the Bible: 'Each phase is not an improvement on its predecessor but a wider perspective on it' (1982a: 106).

11. Cf. e.g. both A. Bloom and W. J. Bennett.

References

(Year in parenthesis immediately after name indicates original publication year. Titles from same year by same author distinguished by appended letter. Publication data of edition consulted after title.)

Abrams, M. H. (1953). *The Mirror and the Lamp: Romantic Theory and the Critical Tradition*. London: Oxford University Press, 1971.

Allnut, G., D'Aguiar, F., Edwards, K., Mottram, E., (1988). *the new british poetry*. (sic!) London: Paladin.

Alter, R. (1988). 'The difference of Literature.' *Poetics Today*, v. 9 (3), 573–91.

Barzun, J. (1991). *Begin Here: The Forgotten Conditions of Teaching and Learning*. Chicago: University of Chicago Press.

Baym, N. *et al.* (eds) (1989). *The Norton Anthology of English Literature*. (3rd edn shorter). New York: W. W. Norton & Company.

Bennett, W. J. (1984). *To Reclaim a Legacy: A Report on the Humanities in Higher Education*. Washington: National Endowment for the Humanities.

Bennett, W. J. (1992). *The De-Valuing of America: The Fight for Our Culture and Our Children*. New York: Summit Books.

Bennett, W. J. (1993). *The Book of Virtues: A Treasury of Great Moral Stories*. New York: Simon & Schuster.

Bergonzi, B. (1986). *The Myth of Modernism and Twentieth Century Literature*. Brighton: The Harvester Press.

Bloom, A. (1987). *The Closing of the American Mind: How Higher Education Has Failed Democracy and Impoverished the Souls of Today's Students*. New York: Simon & Schuster.

Bloom, A. (1990). *Giants and Dwarfs: Essays 1960–90*. New York: Simon and Schuster.

Bloom, H. (1959). *Shelley's Mythmaking*. Ithaca, NY: Cornell University Press, 1969.

Bloom, H. (1963). *Blake's Apocalypse: A Study in Poetic Argument*. London: Victor Gollancz.

Bloom, H. (1970). *Yeats*. New York: Oxford University Press.

Bloom, H. (1973). *The Anxiety of Influence: A Theory of Poetry*. New York: Oxford University Press.

Bloom, H. (1975a). *A Map of Misreading*. New York: Oxford University Press.

Bloom, H. (1975b). *Kabbalah and Criticism*. New York: The Seabury Press.

Bloom, H. (1976). *Poetry and Repression: Revisionism from Blake to Stevens*. New Haven: Yale University Press.

Bloom, H. (1977). *Wallace Stevens: The Poems of Our Climate*. Ithaca and London: Cornell University Press.

Bloom, H. (1979). *The Flight to Lucifer: A Gnostic Fantasy*. New York: Farrar Straus & Giroux.

Bloom, H. (1982). *Agon: Towards a Theory of Revisionism*. New York: Oxford University Press.

Bloom, H. (1989). *Ruin the Sacred Truths*. Cambridge, Mass.: Harvard University Press.

Bloom, H. (1990). *The Book of J*. London: Faber & Faber, 1991.

Bloom, H. (1994). *The Western Canon: The Books and the School of Ages*. New York: Harcourt Brace.

Bradley, A. C. (1904). *Shakespearean Tragedy: Lectures on Hamlet, Othello, King Lear, Macbeth*. London: Macmillan, 1965.

Brooks, C. and R. P. Warren. (1938). *Understanding Poetry*. New York: Holt, Rinehart and Winston, 1960.

Brooks, C. and R. P. Warren. (1943). *Understanding Fiction*. New York: Appleton, Century, Crofts, 1959.

Brooks, C. and R. B. Heilman. (1948). *Understanding Drama*. New York: H. Holt.

Buell, L. (1987). 'Literary History Without Sexism? Feminist Studies and Canonical Reconception.' *American Literature*, v. 59, pp. 102–14.

Burgess, A. (1984). *Ninety-Nine Novels: The Best in English since 1939*. London: Allison and Busby.

Butler, M. (1987). 'Revising the Canon.' *The Times Literary Supplement*, 4–10 Dec. 1349 and 1359–60.

Connor, S. (1989). *Postmodernist Culture: An Introduction to Theories of the Contemporary*. Oxford: Basil Blackwell.

Curtius, E. R. (1948). *European Literature and the Latin Middle Ages*. New York: Harper and Row, 1953.

Delany, S. (1971). *Counter-Tradition: A Reader in the Literature of Dissent and Alternatives*. (With a Foreword by Louis Kampf.) New York: Basic Books.

Denham, R. D. (ed.) (1978). *Northrop Frye on Culture and Literature: A Collection of Review Essays*. Chicago and London: The University of Chicago Press.

Eliot, T. S. (1916). *Knowledge and Experience in the Philosophy of F. H. Bradley*. London: Faber & Faber, 1964.

Eliot, T. S. (1917). 'Reflections on Vers Libre' In *To Criticize the Critic and Other Writings*. London: Faber & Faber 1965, 183–9.

Eliot, T. S. (1919a). 'Hamlet.' In *Selected Prose of T. S. Eliot*. London: Faber & Faber, 1975, 45–9.

Eliot, T. S. (1919b). 'Tradition and the Individual Talent.' In *Selected Prose of T. S. Eliot*. London: Faber & Faber, 1975, 37–44.

Eliot, T. S. (1921). 'The Metaphysical Poets.' In *Selected Prose of T. S. Eliot*. London: Faber & Faber, 1975, 59–67.

Eliot, T. S. (1923). 'The Function of Criticism.' In *Selected Prose of T. S. Eliot*. London: Faber & Faber, 1975, 68–78.

Eliot, T. S. (1932). 'The Age of Dryden.' In *The Use of Poetry and the Use of Criticism: Studies in the Relation of Criticism to Poetry in England*. London: Faber & Faber, 1964, 53–65.

Eliot, T. S. (1933a). 'Shelley and Keats.' In *The Use of Poetry and the Use of Criticism: Studies in the Relation of Criticism to Poetry in England*. London: Faber & Faber, 1964, 87–102.

Eliot, T. S. (1933b). 'Matthew Arnold.' In *The Use of Poetry and the Use of Criticism: Studies in the Relation of Criticism to Poetry in England*. London: Faber & Faber, 1964, 103–19.

Eliot, T. S. (1933c). 'The Modern Mind.' In *The Use of Poetry and the Use of Criticism: Studies in the Relation of Criticism to Poetry in England*. London: Faber & Faber, 1964, 121–42.

Eliot, T. S. (1933d). 'Catholicism and International Order.' In *Essays Ancient and Modern*. London: Faber & Faber, 1936, 113–35.

Eliot, T. S. (1933e). 'Modern Education and the Classics.' In *Essays Ancient and Modern*. London: Faber & Faber, 1936, 161–74.

Eliot, T. S. (1934). 'Religion and Literature.' In *Essays Ancient and Modern*. London: Faber & Faber, 1936, 93–112.

Eliot, T. S. (1936). 'Francis Herbert Bradley.' In *Essays Ancient and Modern*. London: Faber & Faber, 1936, 45–61.

Eliot, T. S. (1939). *The Idea of a Christian Society*. London: Faber & Faber, 1962.

Eliot, T. S. (1941). 'Rudyard Kipling.' In *On Poetry and Poets*. London: Faber & Faber, 1957, 228–51.

Eliot, T. S. (1942). 'The Classics and the Man of Letters.' In *To Criticize the Critic and Other Writings*. London: Faber & Faber, 1965, 145–61.

Eliot, T. S. (1943). 'The Social Function of Poetry.' In *On Poetry and Poets*. London: Faber & Faber, 1957, 15–25.

Eliot, T. S. (1944a). 'What is Minor Poetry?' In *On Poetry and Poets*. London: Faber & Faber, 1957, 39–52.

Eliot, T. S. (1944b). 'What is a Classic?' In *Selected Prose of T. S. Eliot*. London: Faber & Faber, 1975, 115–31.

Eliot, T. S. (1948). *Notes towards the Definition of Culture*. London. Faber & Faber, 1963.

Eliot, T. S. (1950). 'The Aims of Education.' In *To Criticize the Critic and Other Writings*. London: Faber & Faber, 1965, 61–124.

Eliot, T. S. (1953). 'American Literature and Language.' In *To Criticize the Critic and Other Writings*. London: Faber & Faber, 1965, 43–60.

Eliot, T. S. (1956). 'The Frontiers of Criticism' In *On Poetry and Poets*. London: Faber & Faber, 1957, 103–18.

Eliot, T. S. (1961). 'To Criticize the Critic.' In *To Criticize the Critic and Other Writings*. London: Faber & Faber, 1965, 11–26.

Elliott, E. *et al.* (eds) (1988). *Columbia Literary History of the United States*. New York: Columbia University Press.

Erdman, D. V. (ed.) (1965). *The Poetry and Prose of William Blake*. New York: Doubleday. (Commentary by Harold Bloom.)

Evans, I. (1940). *A Short History of English Literature*. Harmondsworth: Penguin, 1963.

Farrow, N., Last, B., Pratt, V. (1990). *An English Library*. London: Book Trust in Association with Gower.

Fiedler, L. and Houston A. Baker, Jr. (1981). *English Literature: Opening up the Canon. (Selected Papers from the English Institute, 1979)*. Baltimore: The Johns Hopkins University Press.

Fox-Genovese, E. (1986). 'The Claims of a Common Culture: Gender, Race, Class and the Canon.' *Salmagundi*, 72 (Fall), 131–43.

Frye, N. (1947). *Fearful Symmetry: A Study of William Blake*. Princeton: Princeton University Press.

Frye, N. (1957). *Anatomy of Criticism: Four Essays*. Princeton, NJ: Princeton University Press, 1971.

Frye, N. (1963a). *Fables of Identity: Studies in Poetic Mythology*. New York: Harcourt, Brace and World.

Frye, N. (1963b). *The Educated Imagination*. Toronto: Canadian Broadcasting Corporation.

Frye, N. (1963c). *T. S. Eliot*. Edinburgh: Oliver and Boyd.

Frye, N. (1963d). *The Well-Tempered Critic*. Bloomington: Indiana University Press.

Frye, N. (1965a). *The Return of Eden: Five Essays on Milton's Epics*. Toronto: University of Toronto Press.

Frye, N. (1965b). *A Natural Perspective: The Development of Shakespearean Comedy and Romance*. New York and London: Columbia University Press.

Frye, N. (1965c). 'Conclusion to *A Literary History of Canada*.' In Frye 1971b, pp. 213–51.

Frye, N. (1967a). *The Modern Century*. Toronto: Oxford University Press.

Frye, N. (1967b). *Fools of Time: Studies in Shakespearean Tragedy*. Toronto: Toronto University Press.

Frye, N. (1968). *A Study of English Romanticism*. Toronto.

Frye, N. (1970). *The Stubborn Structure: Essays on Criticism and Society*. Ithaca: Cornell University Press.

Frye, N. (1971a). *The Critical Path: An Essay on the Social Context of Literary Criticism*. Bloomington and London: Indiana University Press.

Frye, N. (1971b). *The Bush Garden: Essays on the Canadian Imagination*. House of Anansi Press.

Frye, N. (1976a). *The Secular Scripture: A Study of the Structure of Romance*. Cambridge, Mass.: Harvard University Press.

Frye, N. (1976b). *Spiritus Mundi: Essays on Literature, Myth, and Society*. Bloomington and London: Indiana University Press.

Frye, N. (1980). *Creation and Recreation*. Toronto: Toronto University Press.

Frye, N. (1982a). *The Great Code: The Bible and Literature*. New York and London: Harcourt Brace Jovanovich.

Frye, N. (1982b). *Divisions on a Ground: Essays on Canadian Literature*. Ed. James Polk. Toronto: Anansi.

Frye, N. (1983). *The Myth of Deliverance: Reflections on Shakespeare's Problem Comedies*. Toronto: The Harvester Press.

Frye, N. (1986). *Northrop Frye on Shakespeare*. Ed. Robert Sandler. Markham, Ont.: Fitzhenry and Whiteside.

Frye, N. (1988). *On Education*. Markham, Ont.: Fitzhenry and Whiteside.

Frye, N. (1990). *Words With Power: Being a Second Study of The Bible and Literature*. New York and London: Harcourt Brace Jovanovich.

Gorak, J. (1991). *The Making of the Modern Canon: Genesis and Crisis of a Literary Idea*. London: Athlone.

Grierson, H. J. C. (1921). *Metaphysical Lyrics and Poems of the Seventeenth Century*. Oxford: Oxford University Press, 1995.

Guillory, J. (1987). 'Canonical and Non-Canonical: A Critique of the Current Debate'. *Journal of English Literary History (ELH)*, v. 54 (3), (Fall), 483–527.

Guillory, J. (1993). *Cultural Capital: The Problem of Literary Canon*. Chicago: University of Chicago Press.

Hamilton, A. C. (1990). *Northrop Frye: Anatomy of his Criticism*. Toronto: University of Toronto Press.

Harris, C. B. (1988). 'Canonical Variations and the English Curriculum.' *ADE Bulletin*, v. 90, (Fall), 7–12.

Hirsch, E. D. (1983). 'Cultural Literacy.' *The American Scholar*, 52, (1982/83), 159–69.

Hirsch, E. D. (1987). *Cultural Literacy*. Boston: Houghton Mifflin.

Hollander, J. (ed.) (1988). *Poetics of Influence: Harold Bloom*. New Haven: Henry Schwab.

Hulme, T. E. (1924). *Speculations. Essays on Humanism and the Philosophy of Art*. (Ed. Herbert Read.) London: Routledge & Kegan Paul, 1960.

Kampf, L., Lauter, P. (1972). *The Politics of Literature: Dissenting Essays on the Teaching of English*. New York: Vintage Books.

Kenner, H. (1988). ' "Tradition" Revisited.' *Renascense: Essays on Value in Literature*, v. 40 (3), (Spring), 171–5.

Kermode, F. (1988). 'Canons'. *Dutch Quarterly Review of Anglo-American Letters*, v. 18, (4), 258–70.

Kernan, A. (1990). *The Death of Literature*. New Haven: Yale University Press.

Krieger, M. (ed.) (1966). *Northrop Frye in Modern Criticism: Selected Papers from the English Institute*. New York and London: Columbia University Press.

Krieger, M. (1986). 'Literary Invention and the Impulse to Theoretical Change: "Or Whether Revolution be the Same".' *New Literary History*, v. 18 (1), (Autumn), 191–208.

Larkin, P. (ed.) (1973). *The Oxford Book of Twentieth Century English Verse*. Oxford: The Clarendon Press.

Lauter, P. (ed.) (1983). *Reconstructing American Literature: Courses, Syllabi, Issues*. New York: The Feminist Press.

Lauter, P. *et al.* (ed.) (1990). *The Heath Anthology of English Literature*. Lexington, Mass.: D. C. Heath.

Lauter, P. (1991). *Canons and Contexts*. New York: Oxford University Press.

Leavis, F. R. (1930). *Mass Civilisation and Minority Culture*. Norwood, Pa.: Norwood Editions, 1976.

Leavis, F. R. (1932). *New Bearings in English Poetry*. Harmondsworth: Penguin, 1972.

Leavis, F. R. (1936). *Revaluation*. Harmondsworth: Penguin, 1972.

Leavis, F. R. (1943). *Education and the University*. London: Chatto and Windus, 1948.

Leavis, F. R. (1948). *The Great Tradition*. Harmondsworth: Penguin, 1972.

Leavis, F. R. (1952). *The Common Pursuit*. London: Chatto and Windus, 1965.

Leavis, F. R. (1962). *Two Cultures? The Significance of C. P. Snow*. London: Chatto and Windus.

Leavis, F. R. (1967). *English Literature in Our Time and the University*. London: Chatto and Windus, 1969.

Leavis, F. R. (1969). *Lectures in America*. London: Chatto and Windus.

Leavis, F. R. (1975). *The Living Principle: 'English' as a Discipline of Thought*. London: Chatto and Windus.

Lecker, R. (1993). ' "A Quest for the Peaceable Kingdom:" The Narrative in Northrop Frye's Conclusion to the Literary History of Canada.' *PMLA*, v. 108, (2), (March), 283–93.

Lefevere, A. (1986). 'Power and the canon, or: How to rewrite an author into a classic.' *Journal of Literary Studies/Tydskrif vir Literatuurwetenskap*, v. 2, (2), pp. 1–14.

Lunsford, A. A. *et al.* (1990). *The Right to Literacy*. New York: MLA.

Lewis, C. S. (1936). *The Allegory of Love*. London: Oxford University Press, 1973.

Lodge, D. (1977). *The Modes of Modern Writing: Metaphor, Metonymy, and the Typology of Modern Literature*. London: Edward Arnold (1979).

Massie, A. (1990). *The Novel Today: A Critical Guide to the British Novel 1970–1989*. London: Longman.

Morrison, B. (1980). *The Movement: English Poetry and Fiction of the 1950s*. Oxford: Oxford University Press.

Morse, J. M. (1986). 'Some Variations On – and From – Scholes' Theme.' *Salmagundi*, v. 72, (Fall), 148–63.

Motion, A. (1993). *Philip Larkin: A Writer's Life*. London: Faber & Faber.

Myers, D. G. (1989). 'The Bogey of the Canon'. *The Sewanee Review*, v. 97, (1), (Winter), 611–21.

Palgrave, F. T. (1861). *Palgrave's Golden Treasury*. London: J. M. Dent & Sons. (ed. E. Hutton), 1906.

Perkins, G. *et al.* (ed.) (1985). *The American Tradition in Literature*. (6th edn shorter.) New York: Random House.

Pound, E. (1934). *ABC of Reading*. London: Faber and Faber, 1963.

Rabb, M. A. (1988). 'Making and Rethinking the Canon: General Introduction and the Case of Milennium Hall.' *Modern Language Studies*, v. 18, (1), (Winter), 3–16.

Rodden, J. (1988). 'Literary Studies and the Repression of Reputation'. *Philosophy and Literature*, v. 12, (2), (Oct.), 261–71.

Scholes, R. (1986). 'Aiming a Canon at the Curriculum'. *Salmagundi*, v. 72, (Fall), 101–17.

Shelley, P. B. (1821). 'A Defence of Poetry.' In D. J. Enright and Ernest de Chickera (eds) *English Critical Texts*, pp. 225–55. London: Oxford University Press, 1962.

Spiller, R. E. *et al.* (eds.) (1948). *Literary History of the United States*. New York: Macmillan Publishing Co.

Stewart, J. I. M. (1963). *The Oxford History of English Literature* . (Vol. 12: Eight Modern Writers.) London: Oxford University Press, 1966.

Stewart, J. I. M. (1987). *Myself and Michael Innes: A Memoir*. London: Victor Gollancz.

Tillyard, E. M. W. (1943). *The Elizabethan World Picture*. London: Chatto & Windus.

Todorov, T. (1993). 'Letter from Paris: The Consecration of Art.' *Salmagundi*, 100 (Fall), 26–35.

Wellek, R. and Warren, A. (1949). *Theory of Literature*. Harmondsworth: Penguin, 1963.

West, C. (1987). 'Minority Discourse and the Pitfalls of Canon Formation'.
   The Yale Journal of Criticism, v. 1, (1), (Fall), 193–201.
Wilson, A. N. (1990). *C. S. Lewis: A Biography*. London.

Index